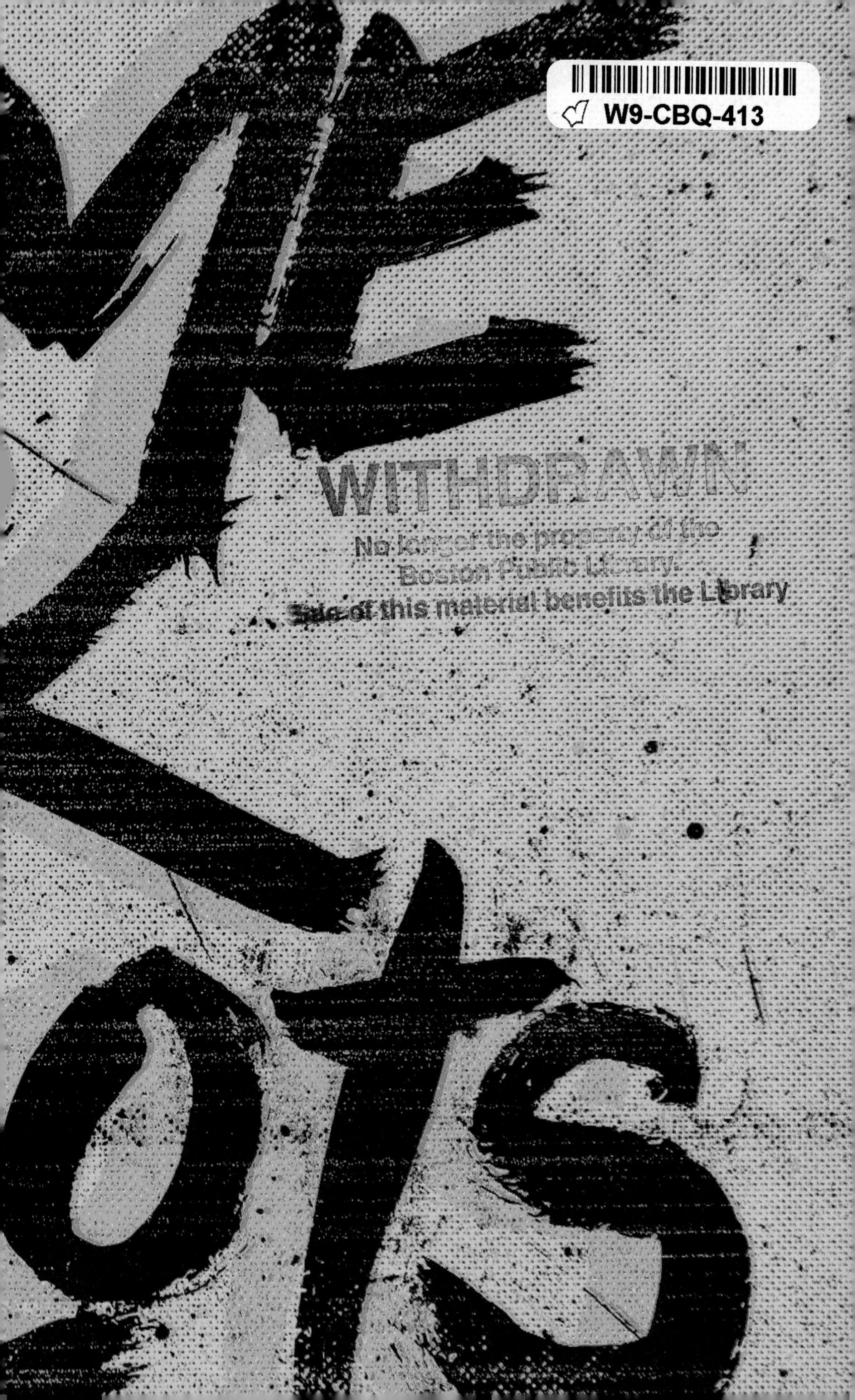

TONIGHT!

Dan Watters, Writer
and Caspar Wijngaard, Artist

With:

Aditya Bidikar: Letterer
Tom Muller: Designer
Erika Schnatz: Production Artist

PRESENT:

IMAGE COMICS, INC.
Todd McFarlane: President
Jim Valentino: Vice President
Marc Silvestri: Chief Executive Officer
Erik Larsen: Chief Financial Officer
Robert Kirkman: Chief Operating Officer

Eric Stephenson: Publisher / Chief Creative Officer
Nicole Lapalme: Controller
Leanna Caunter: Accounting Analyst
Sue Korpela: Accounting & HR Manager
Marla Eizik: Talent Liaison
Jeff Boison: Director of Sales & Publishing Planning
Dirk Wood: Director of International Sales & Licensing
Alex Cox: Director of Direct Market Sales
Chloe Ramos: Book Market & Library Sales Manager
Emilio Bautista: Digital Sales Coordinator
Jon Schlaffman: Specialty Sales Coordinator
Kat Salazar: Director of PR & Marketing
Drew Fitzgerald: Marketing Content Associate
Heather Doornink: Production Director
Drew Gill: Art Director
Hilary DiLoreto: Print Manager
Tricia Ramos: Traffic Manager
Melissa Gifford: Content Manager
Erika Schnatz: Senior Production Artist
Ryan Brewer: Production Artist
Deanna Phelps: Production Artist

Tara Ferguson: White Noise marketing

HOME SICK PILOTS

Home Sick Pilots
created by
Dan Watters and Caspar Wijngaard

Originally published as HOME SICK PILOTS #1–5

HOME SICK PILOTS, VOL. 1: TEENAGE HAUNTS. Second printing. December 2021. Published by Image Comics, Inc. Office of publication: PO BOX 14457, Portland, OR 97293. Copyright © 2021 Dan Watters & Caspar Wijngaard. All rights reserved. Contains material originally published in single magazine form as HOME SICK PILOTS #1-5. HOME SICK PILOTS, and the likenesses of all characters herein or hereon are trademarks of Dan Watters & Caspar Wijngaard, unless expressly indicated. "Image" and the Image Comics logos are registered trademarks of Image Comics, Inc. No part of this publication may be reproduced or transmitted in any form or by any means (except for short excerpts for journalistic or review purposes), without the express written permission of Dan Watters & Caspar Wijngaard or Image Comics, Inc. All names, characters, events, and places herein are entirely fictional. Any resemblance to actual persons (living or dead), events, or places, without satiric intent, is coincidental. Printed in the USA. All inquiries: licensing@imagecomics.com.

IMAGECOMICS.COM

ISBN: 978-1-5343-1892-2

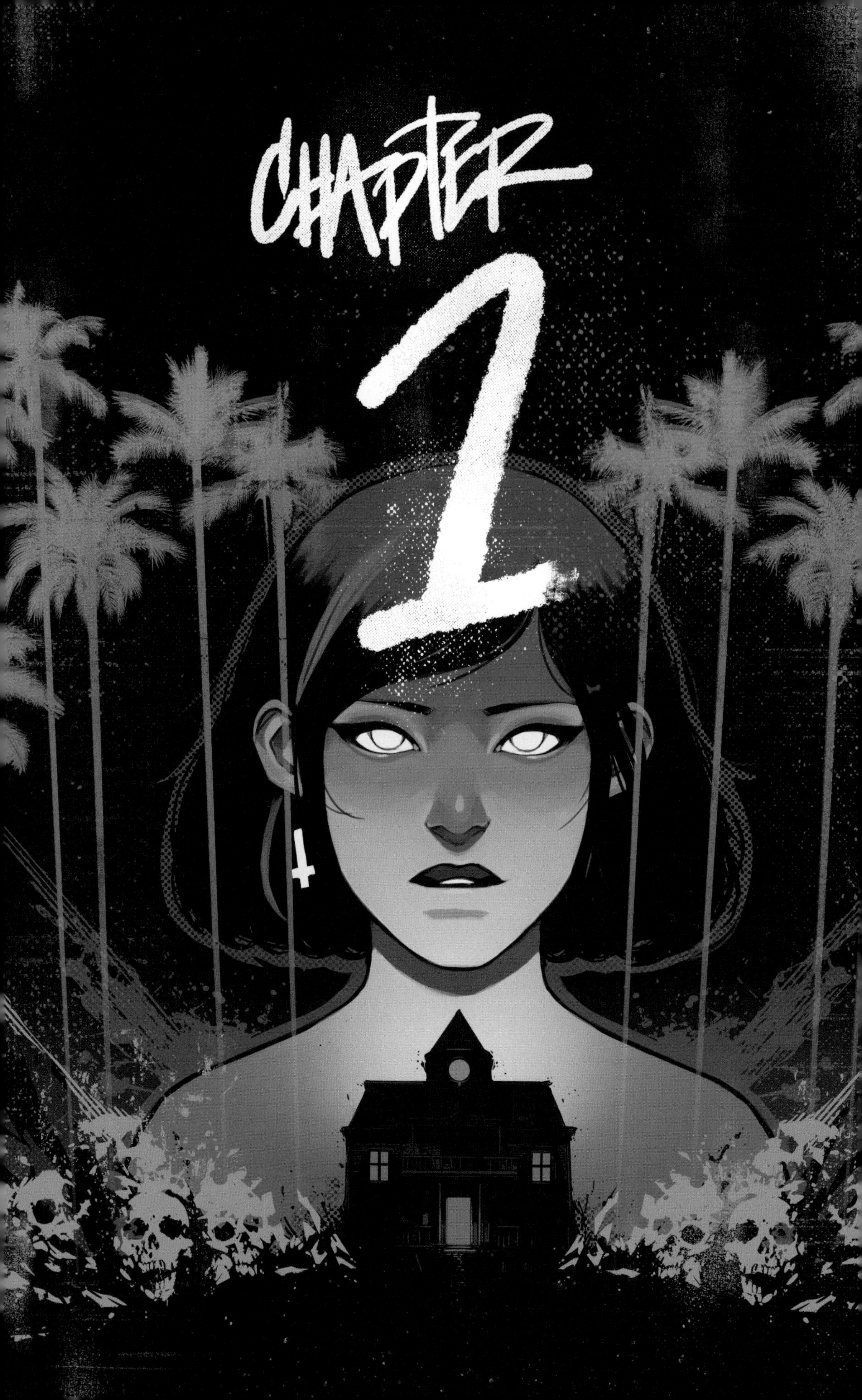
CHAPTER
1

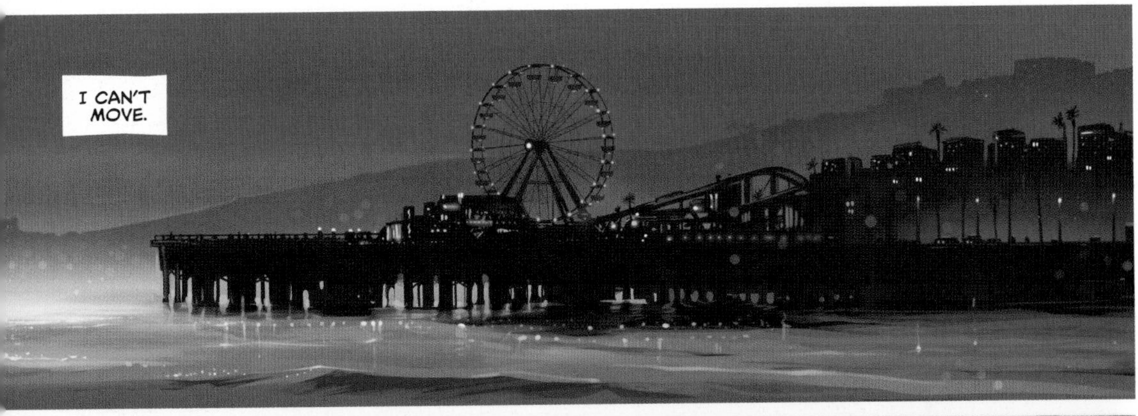
I CAN'T MOVE.

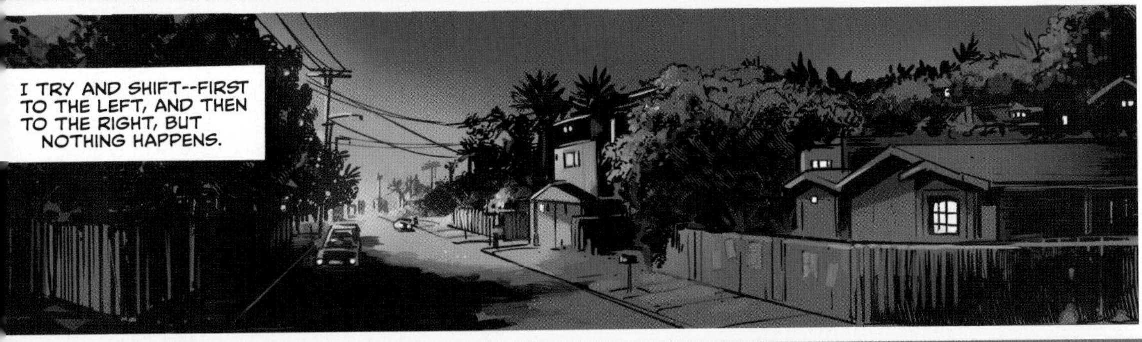
I TRY AND SHIFT--FIRST TO THE LEFT, AND THEN TO THE RIGHT, BUT NOTHING HAPPENS.

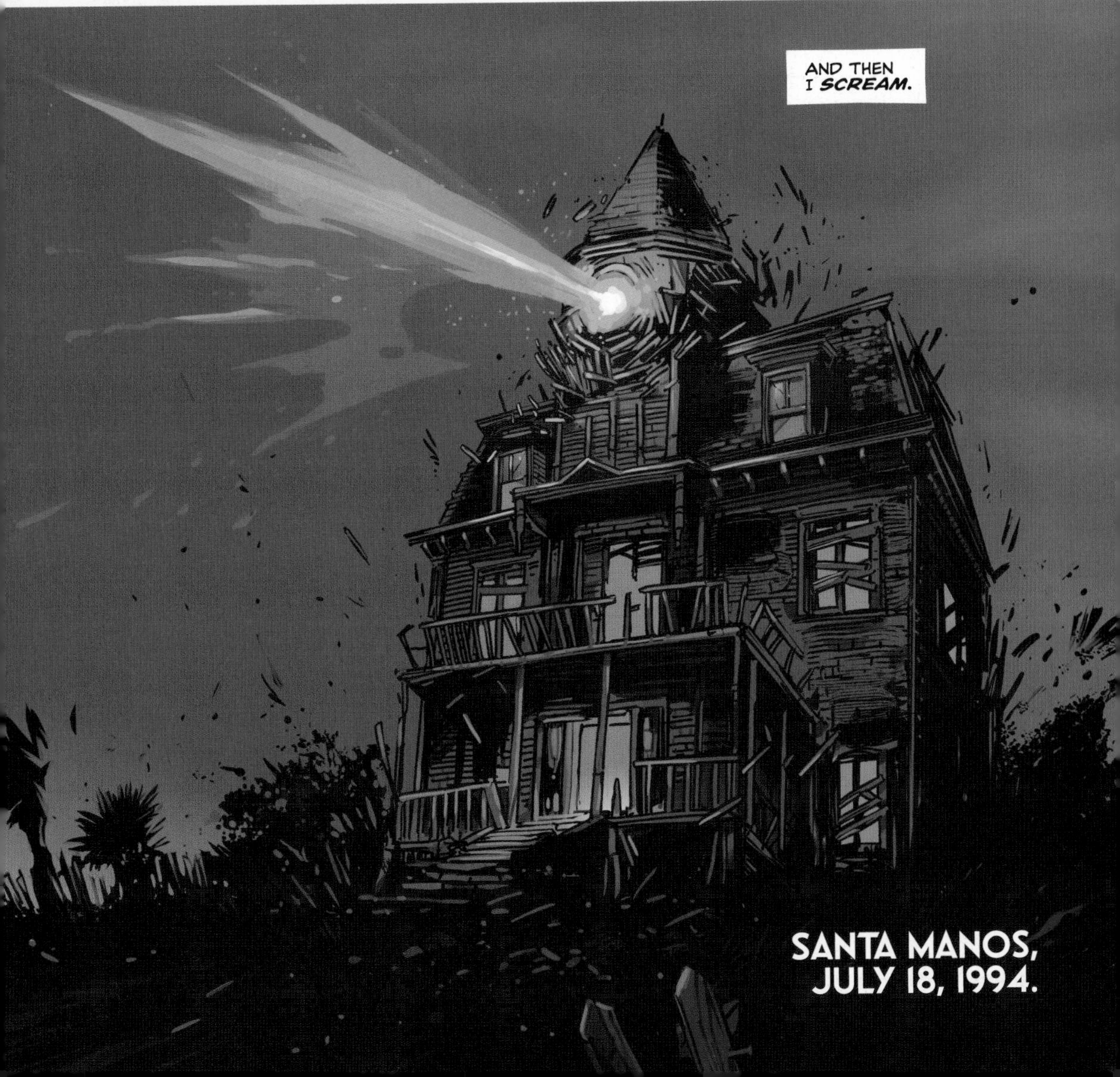
AND THEN I *SCREAM.*
SANTA MANOS, JULY 18, 1994.

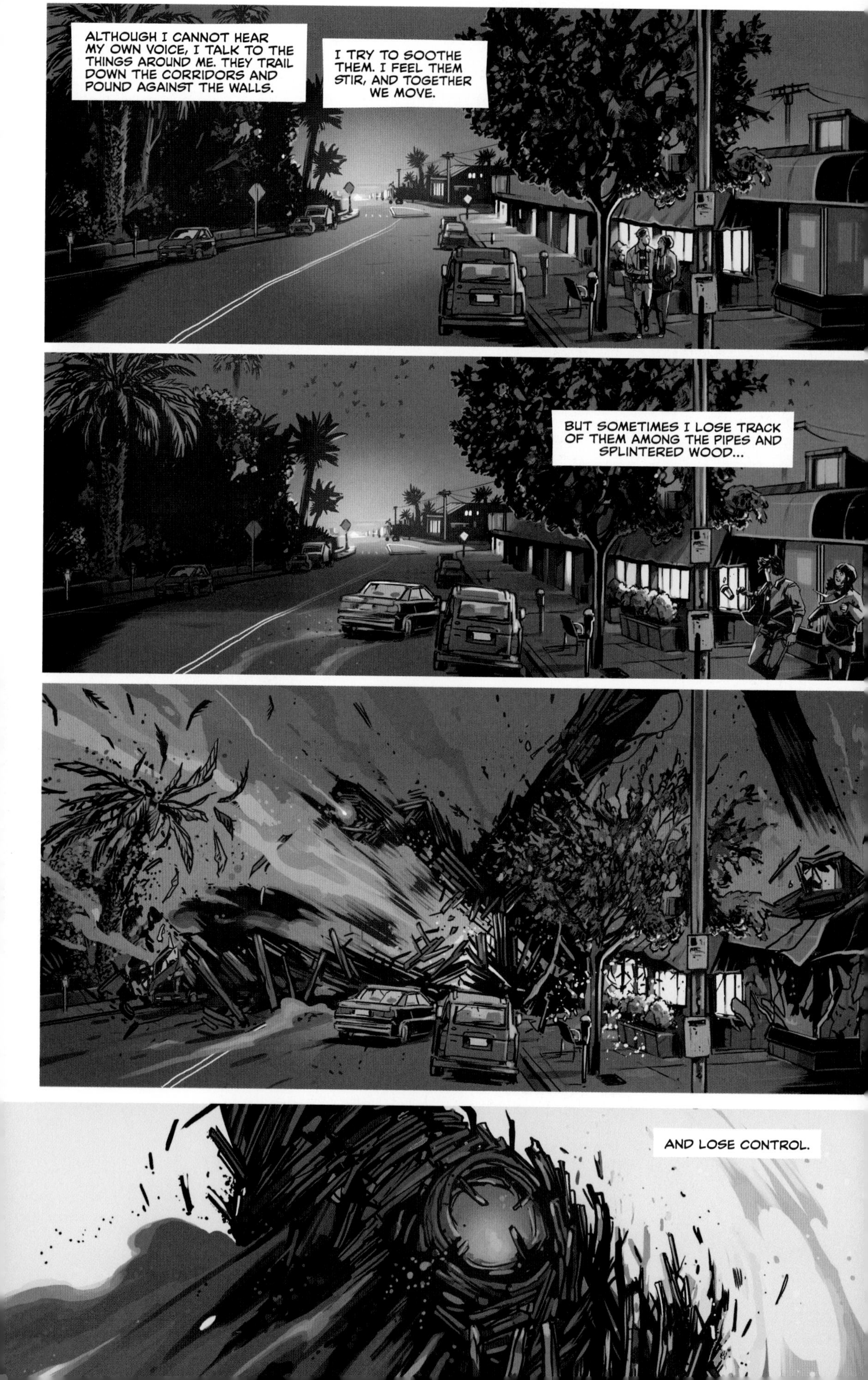
ALTHOUGH I CANNOT HEAR MY OWN VOICE, I TALK TO THE THINGS AROUND ME. THEY TRAIL DOWN THE CORRIDORS AND POUND AGAINST THE WALLS.
I TRY TO SOOTHE THEM. I FEEL THEM STIR, AND TOGETHER WE MOVE.
BUT SOMETIMES I LOSE TRACK OF THEM AMONG THE PIPES AND SPLINTERED WOOD...
AND LOSE CONTROL.

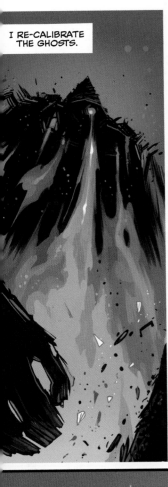

I RE-CALIBRATE THE GHOSTS.

WE BALANCE TOGETHER.

I WHISPER THEM ASSURANCES.

I WISH THAT WE'D NEVER GONE TO SEE THE NUCLEAR BASTARDS THAT NIGHT.

THE NUCLEAR. FUCKING. BASTARDS.

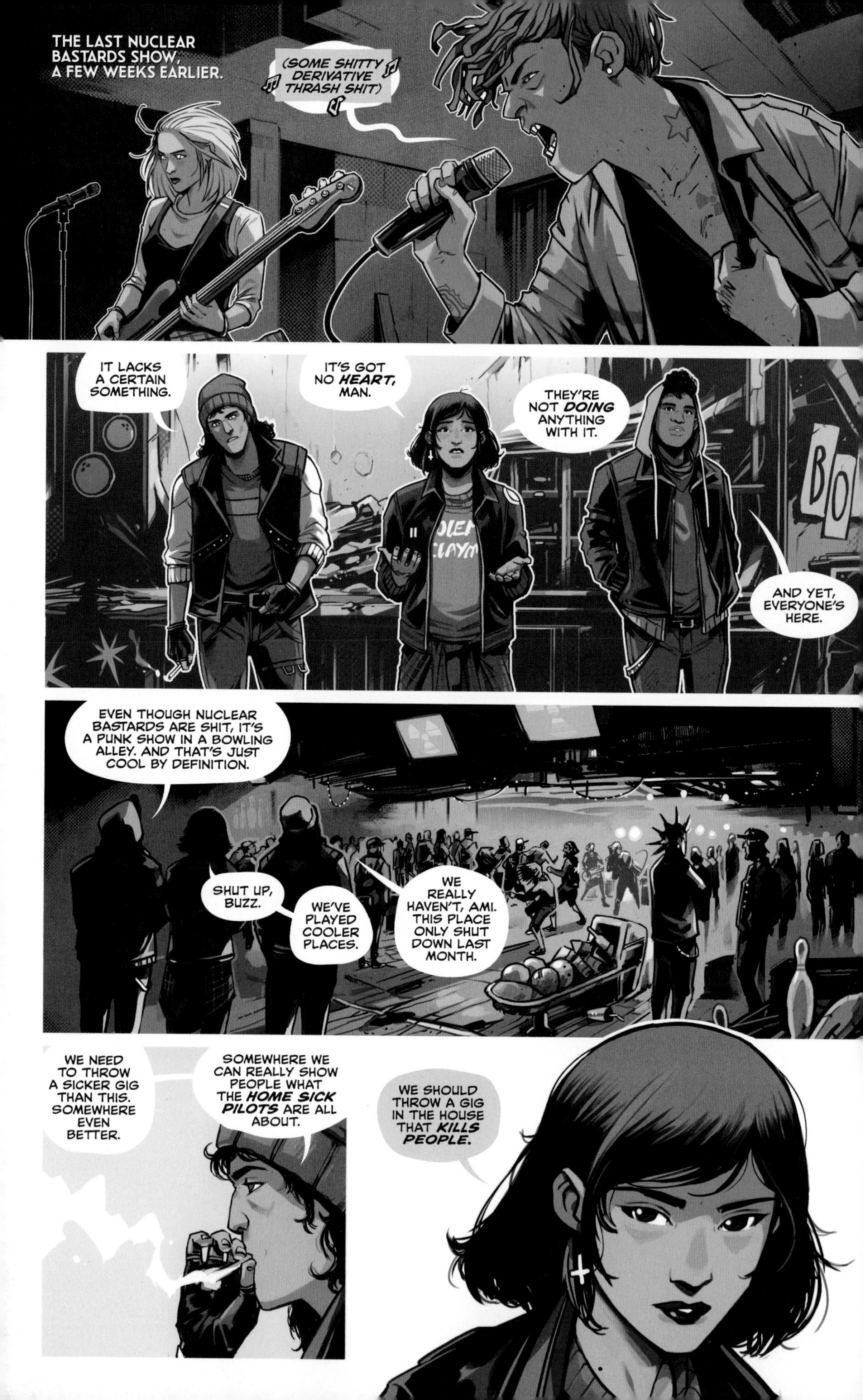
THE LAST NUCLEAR BASTARDS SHOW, A FEW WEEKS EARLIER.
(SOME SHITTY DERIVATIVE THRASH SHIT)
IT LACKS A CERTAIN SOMETHING.
IT'S GOT NO HEART, MAN.
THEY'RE NOT DOING ANYTHING WITH IT.
AND YET, EVERYONE'S HERE.
EVEN THOUGH NUCLEAR BASTARDS ARE SHIT, IT'S A PUNK SHOW IN A BOWLING ALLEY. AND THAT'S JUST COOL BY DEFINITION.
SHUT UP, BUZZ.
WE'VE PLAYED COOLER PLACES.
WE REALLY HAVEN'T, AMI. THIS PLACE ONLY SHUT DOWN LAST MONTH.
WE NEED TO THROW A SICKER GIG THAN THIS. SOMEWHERE EVEN BETTER.
SOMEWHERE WE CAN REALLY SHOW PEOPLE WHAT THE HOME SICK PILOTS ARE ALL ABOUT.
WE SHOULD THROW A GIG IN THE HOUSE THAT KILLS PEOPLE.

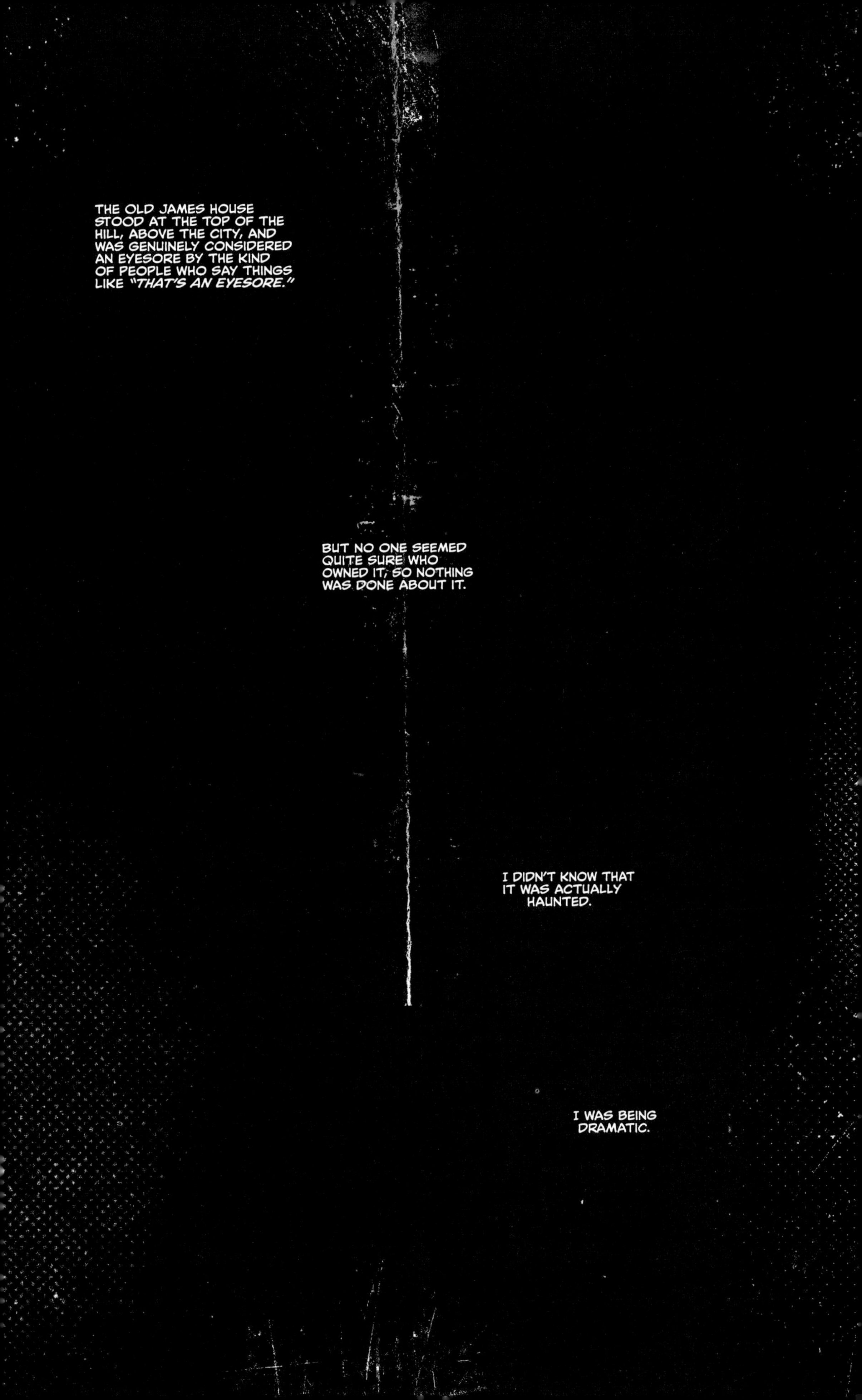
THE OLD JAMES HOUSE STOOD AT THE TOP OF THE HILL, ABOVE THE CITY, AND WAS GENUINELY CONSIDERED AN EYESORE BY THE KIND OF PEOPLE WHO SAY THINGS LIKE *"THAT'S AN EYESORE."*
BUT NO ONE SEEMED QUITE SURE WHO OWNED IT, SO NOTHING WAS DONE ABOUT IT.
I DIDN'T KNOW THAT IT WAS ACTUALLY HAUNTED.
I WAS BEING DRAMATIC.

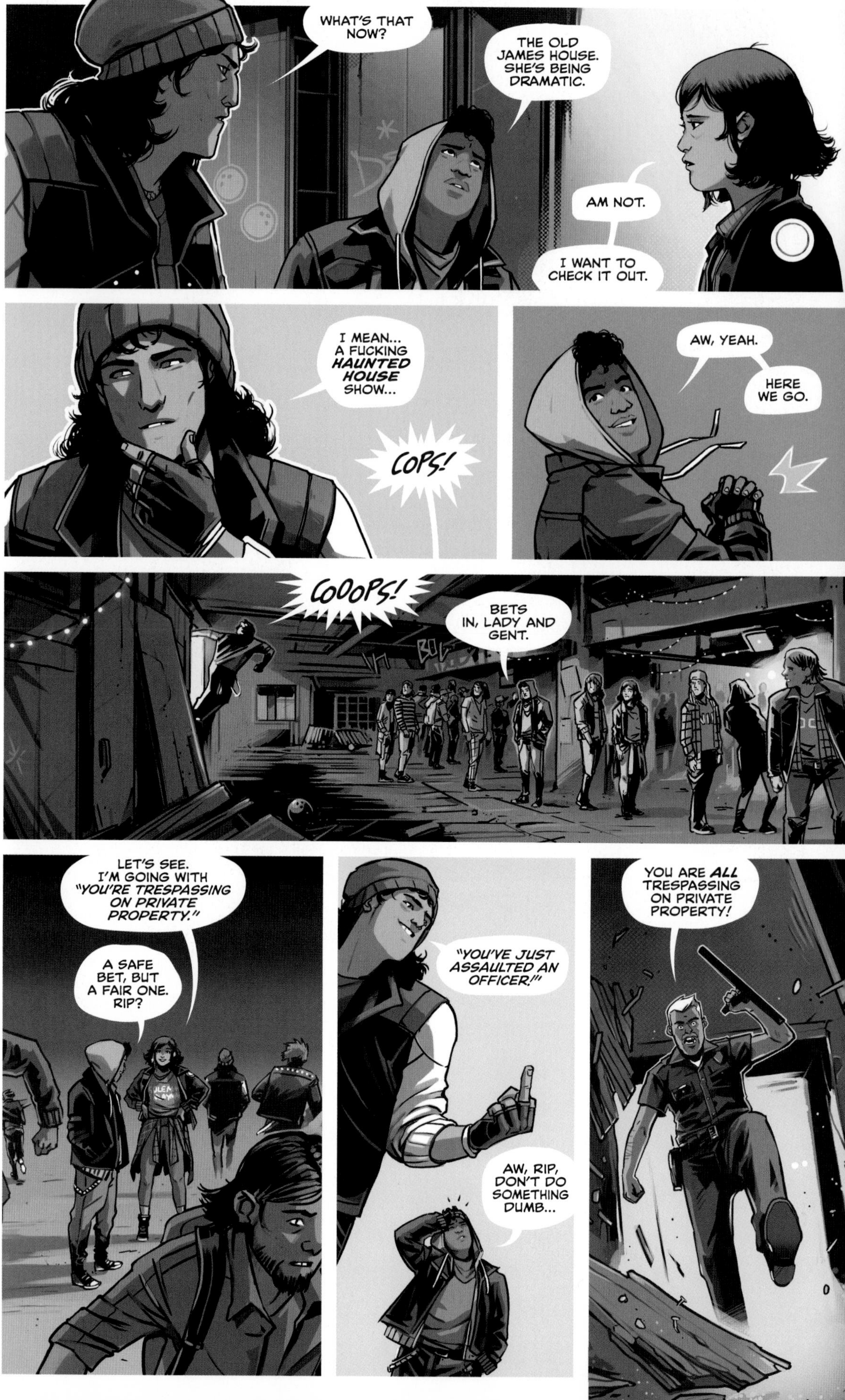
WHAT'S THAT NOW?
THE OLD JAMES HOUSE. SHE'S BEING DRAMATIC.
AM NOT.
I WANT TO CHECK IT OUT.
I MEAN... A FUCKING HAUNTED HOUSE SHOW...
AW, YEAH.
HERE WE GO.
COPS!
COOOPS!
BETS IN, LADY AND GENT.
LET'S SEE. I'M GOING WITH "YOU'RE TRESPASSING ON PRIVATE PROPERTY."
A SAFE BET, BUT A FAIR ONE. RIP?
"YOU'VE JUST ASSAULTED AN OFFICER!"
AW, RIP, DON'T DO SOMETHING DUMB...
YOU ARE ALL TRESPASSING ON PRIVATE PROPERTY!

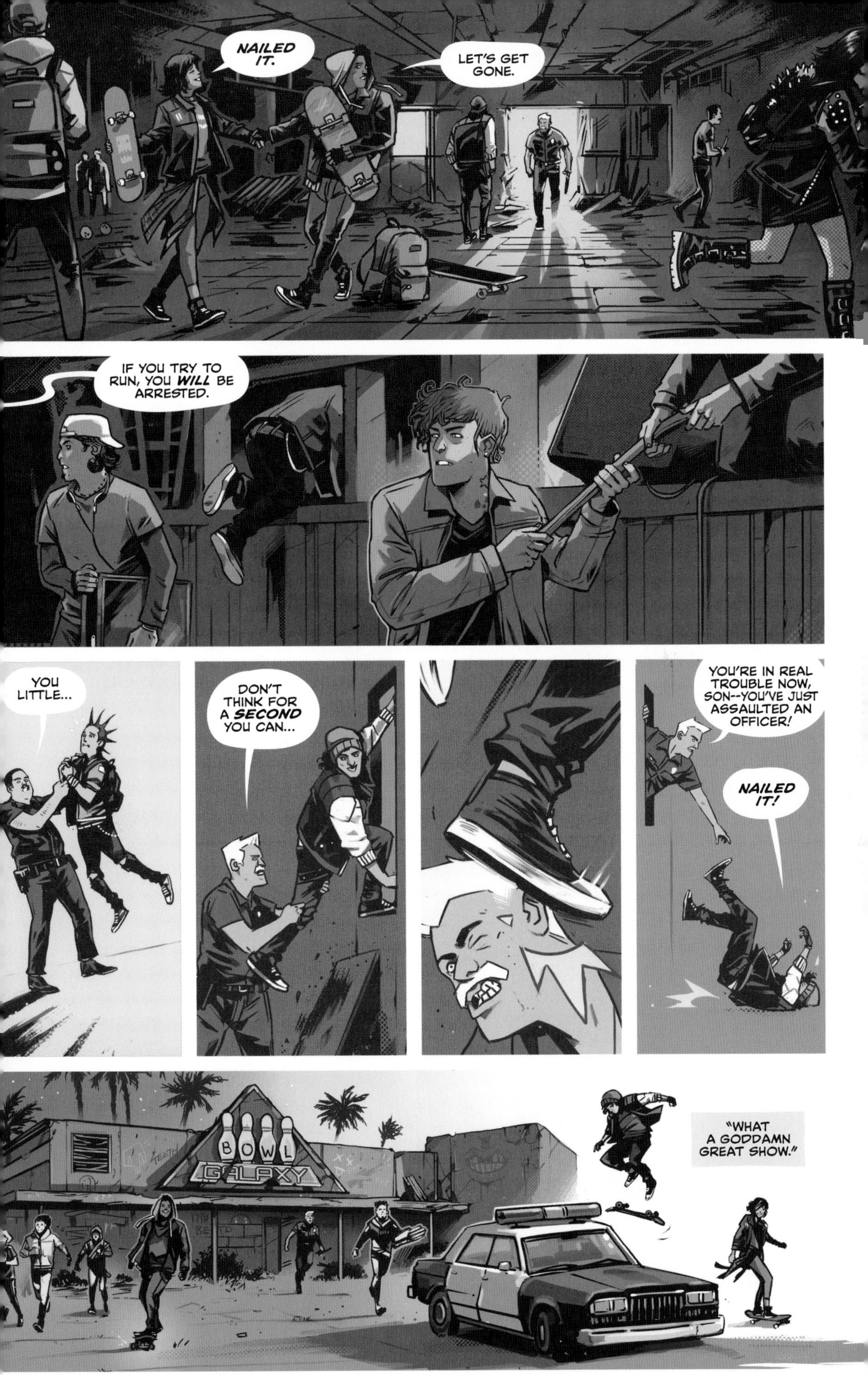
NAILED IT.
LET'S GET GONE.
IF YOU TRY TO RUN, YOU WILL BE ARRESTED.
YOU LITTLE...
DON'T THINK FOR A SECOND YOU CAN...
YOU'RE IN REAL TROUBLE NOW, SON--YOU'VE JUST ASSAULTED AN OFFICER!
NAILED IT!
BOWL
GALAXY
"WHAT A GODDAMN GREAT SHOW."

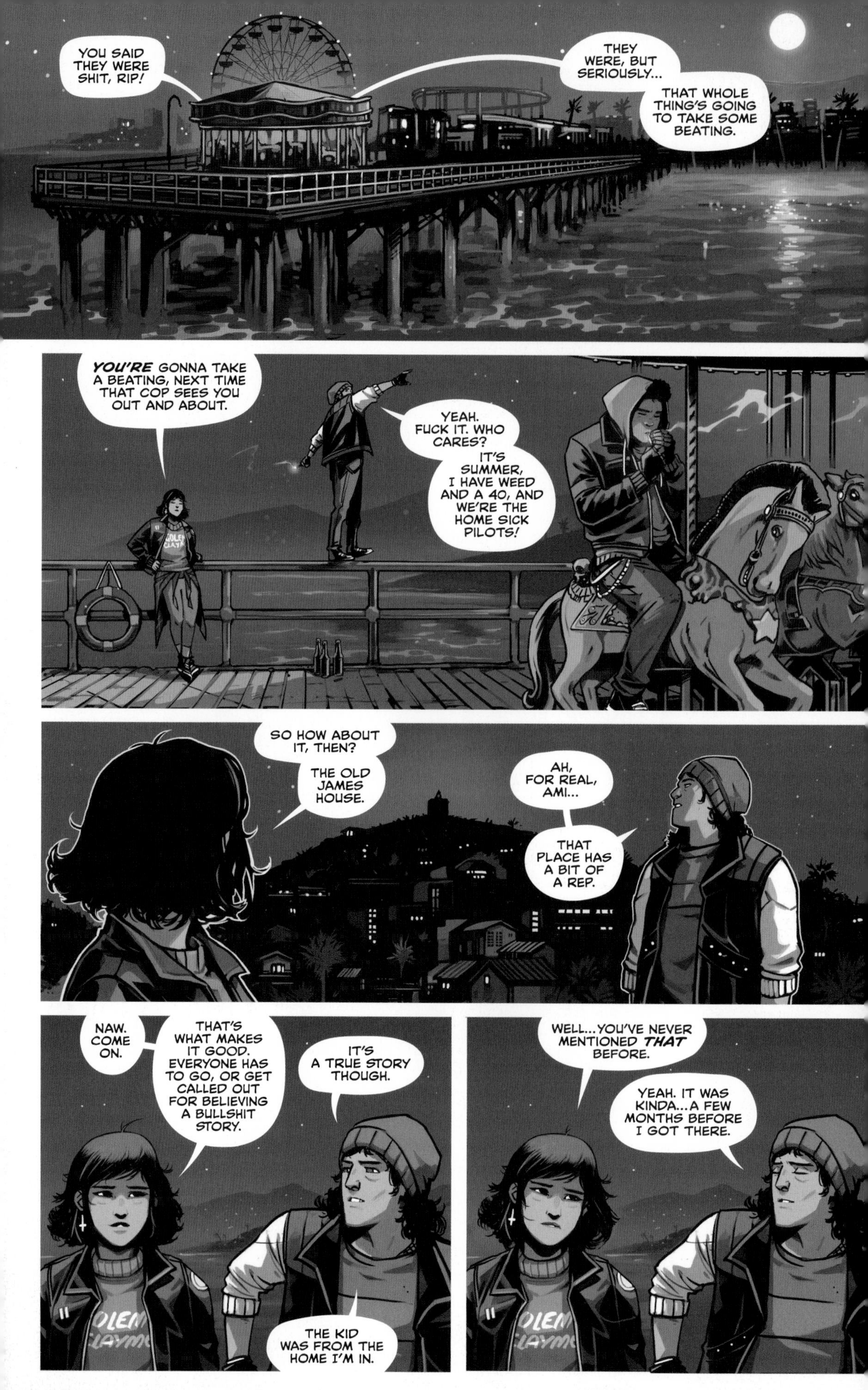
YOU SAID THEY WERE SHIT, RIP!
THEY WERE, BUT SERIOUSLY...
THAT WHOLE THING'S GOING TO TAKE SOME BEATING.
YOU'RE GONNA TAKE A BEATING, NEXT TIME THAT COP SEES YOU OUT AND ABOUT.
YEAH. FUCK IT. WHO CARES?
IT'S SUMMER, I HAVE WEED AND A 40, AND WE'RE THE HOME SICK PILOTS!
SO HOW ABOUT IT, THEN?
THE OLD JAMES HOUSE.
AH, FOR REAL, AMI...
THAT PLACE HAS A BIT OF A REP.
NAW. COME ON.
THAT'S WHAT MAKES IT GOOD. EVERYONE HAS TO GO, OR GET CALLED OUT FOR BELIEVING A BULLSHIT STORY.
IT'S A TRUE STORY THOUGH.
THE KID WAS FROM THE HOME I'M IN.
WELL...YOU'VE NEVER MENTIONED THAT BEFORE.
YEAH. IT WAS KINDA...A FEW MONTHS BEFORE I GOT THERE.

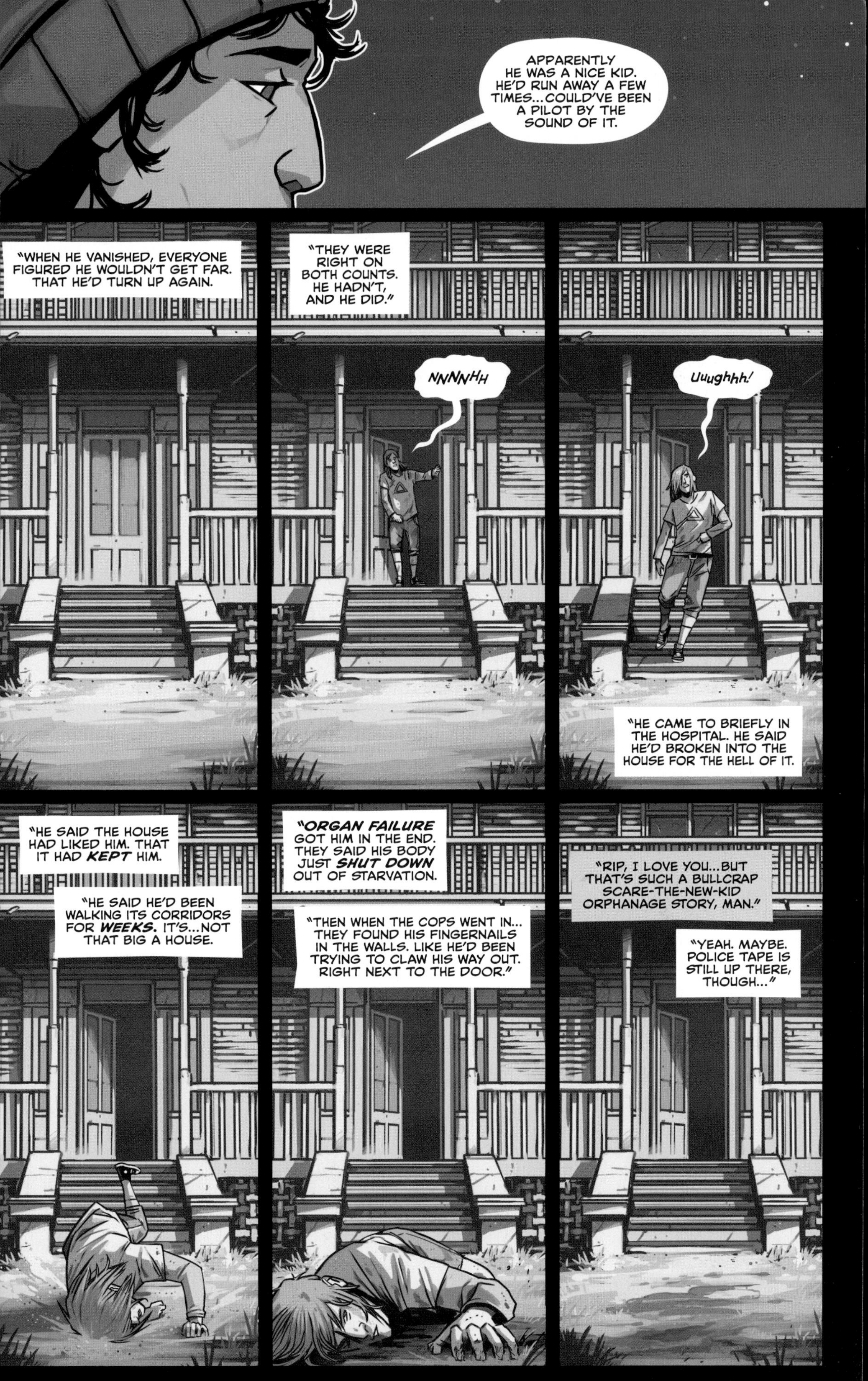
APPARENTLY HE WAS A NICE KID. HE'D RUN AWAY A FEW TIMES...COULD'VE BEEN A PILOT BY THE SOUND OF IT.
"WHEN HE VANISHED, EVERYONE FIGURED HE WOULDN'T GET FAR. THAT HE'D TURN UP AGAIN.
"THEY WERE RIGHT ON BOTH COUNTS. HE HADN'T, AND HE DID."
NNNNHH
Uuughhh!
"HE CAME TO BRIEFLY IN THE HOSPITAL. HE SAID HE'D BROKEN INTO THE HOUSE FOR THE HELL OF IT.
"HE SAID THE HOUSE HAD LIKED HIM. THAT IT HAD KEPT HIM.
"HE SAID HE'D BEEN WALKING ITS CORRIDORS FOR WEEKS. IT'S...NOT THAT BIG A HOUSE.
"ORGAN FAILURE GOT HIM IN THE END. THEY SAID HIS BODY JUST SHUT DOWN OUT OF STARVATION.
"THEN WHEN THE COPS WENT IN... THEY FOUND HIS FINGERNAILS IN THE WALLS. LIKE HE'D BEEN TRYING TO CLAW HIS WAY OUT. RIGHT NEXT TO THE DOOR."
"RIP, I LOVE YOU...BUT THAT'S SUCH A BULLCRAP SCARE-THE-NEW-KID ORPHANAGE STORY, MAN."
"YEAH. MAYBE. POLICE TAPE IS STILL UP THERE, THOUGH..."

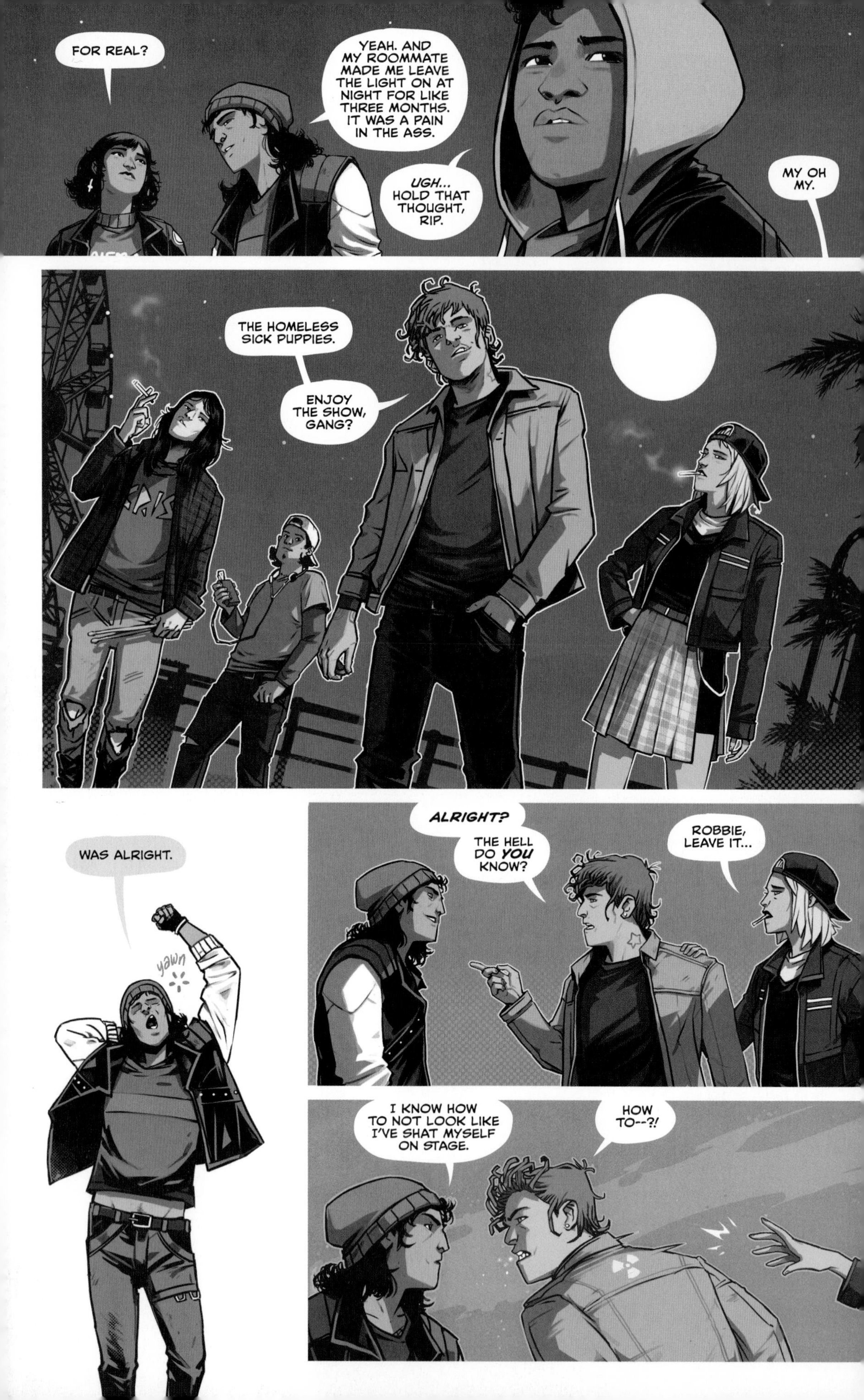
FOR REAL?
YEAH. AND MY ROOMMATE MADE ME LEAVE THE LIGHT ON AT NIGHT FOR LIKE THREE MONTHS. IT WAS A PAIN IN THE ASS.
UGH... HOLD THAT THOUGHT, RIP.
MY OH MY.
THE HOMELESS SICK PUPPIES.
ENJOY THE SHOW, GANG?
WAS ALRIGHT.
yawn
ALRIGHT?
THE HELL DO YOU KNOW?
ROBBIE, LEAVE IT...
I KNOW HOW TO NOT LOOK LIKE I'VE SHAT MYSELF ON STAGE.
HOW TO--?!

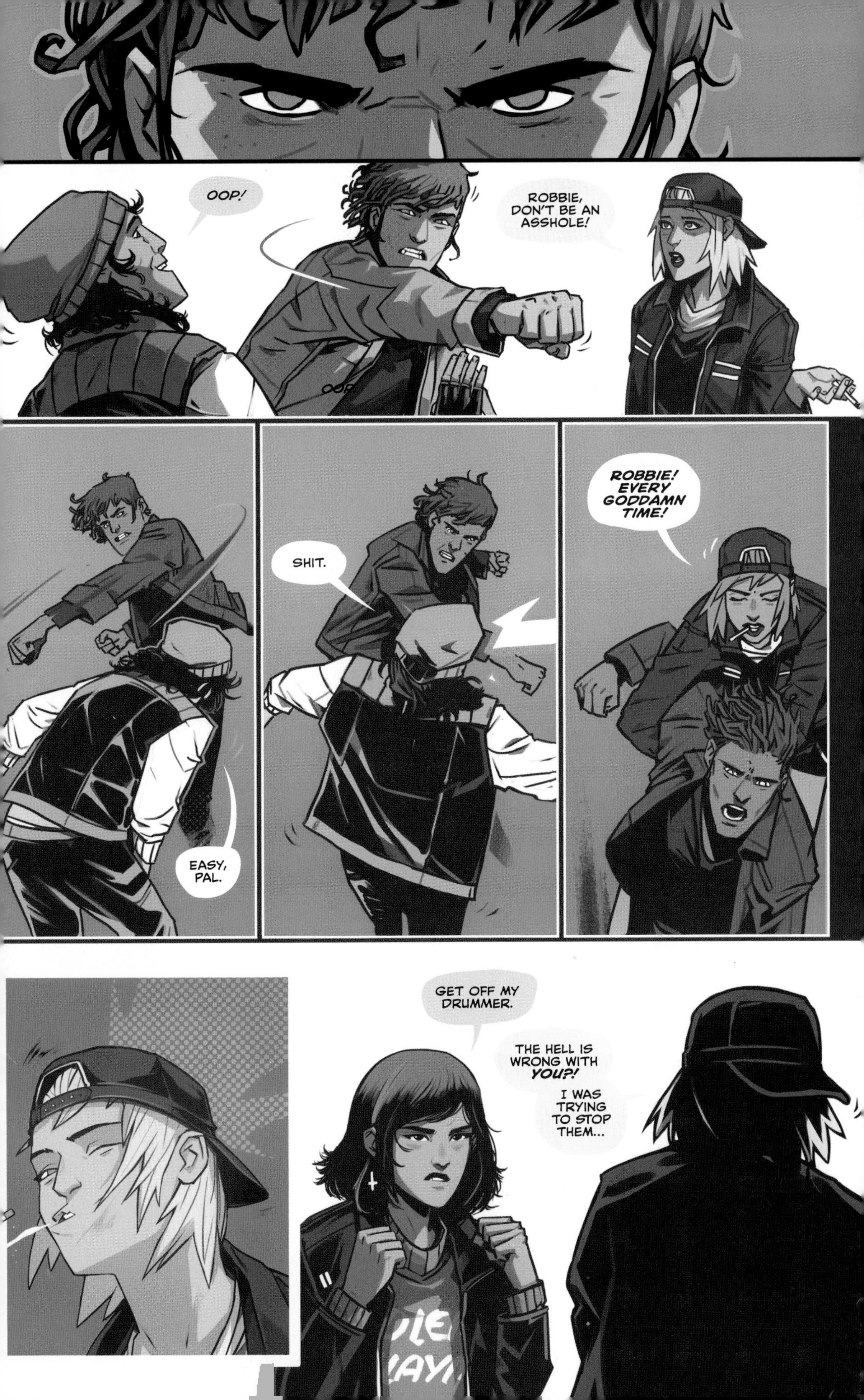
OOP!
ROBBIE, DON'T BE AN ASSHOLE!
EASY, PAL.
SHIT.
ROBBIE! EVERY GODDAMN TIME!
GET OFF MY DRUMMER.
THE HELL IS WRONG WITH YOU?!
I WAS TRYING TO STOP THEM...

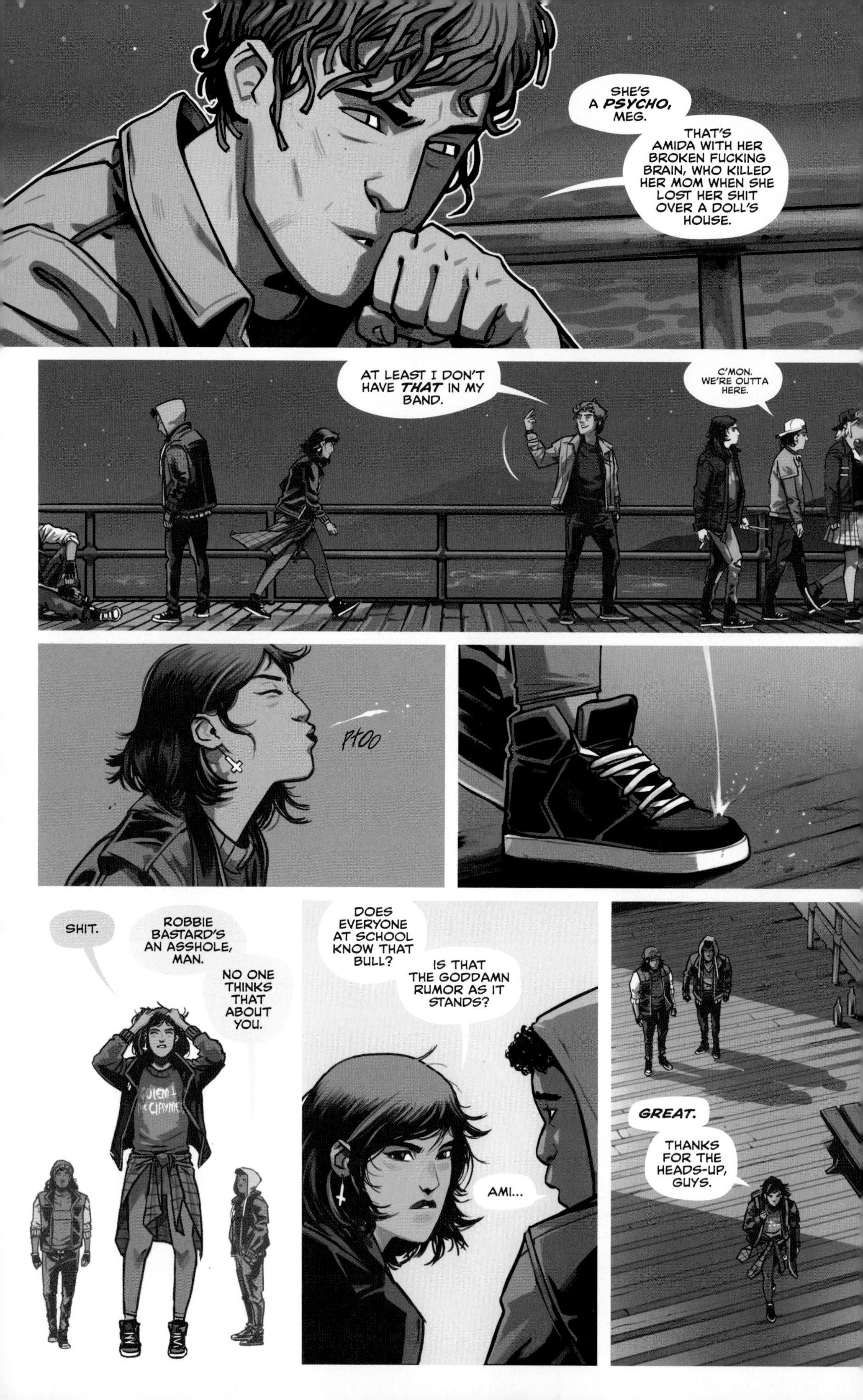
SHE'S A PSYCHO, MEG.
THAT'S AMIDA WITH HER BROKEN FUCKING BRAIN, WHO KILLED HER MOM WHEN SHE LOST HER SHIT OVER A DOLL'S HOUSE.
AT LEAST I DON'T HAVE THAT IN MY BAND.
C'MON. WE'RE OUTTA HERE.
PTOO
SHIT.
ROBBIE BASTARD'S AN ASSHOLE, MAN.
NO ONE THINKS THAT ABOUT YOU.
DOES EVERYONE AT SCHOOL KNOW THAT BULL?
IS THAT THE GODDAMN RUMOR AS IT STANDS?
AMI...
GREAT.
THANKS FOR THE HEADS-UP, GUYS.

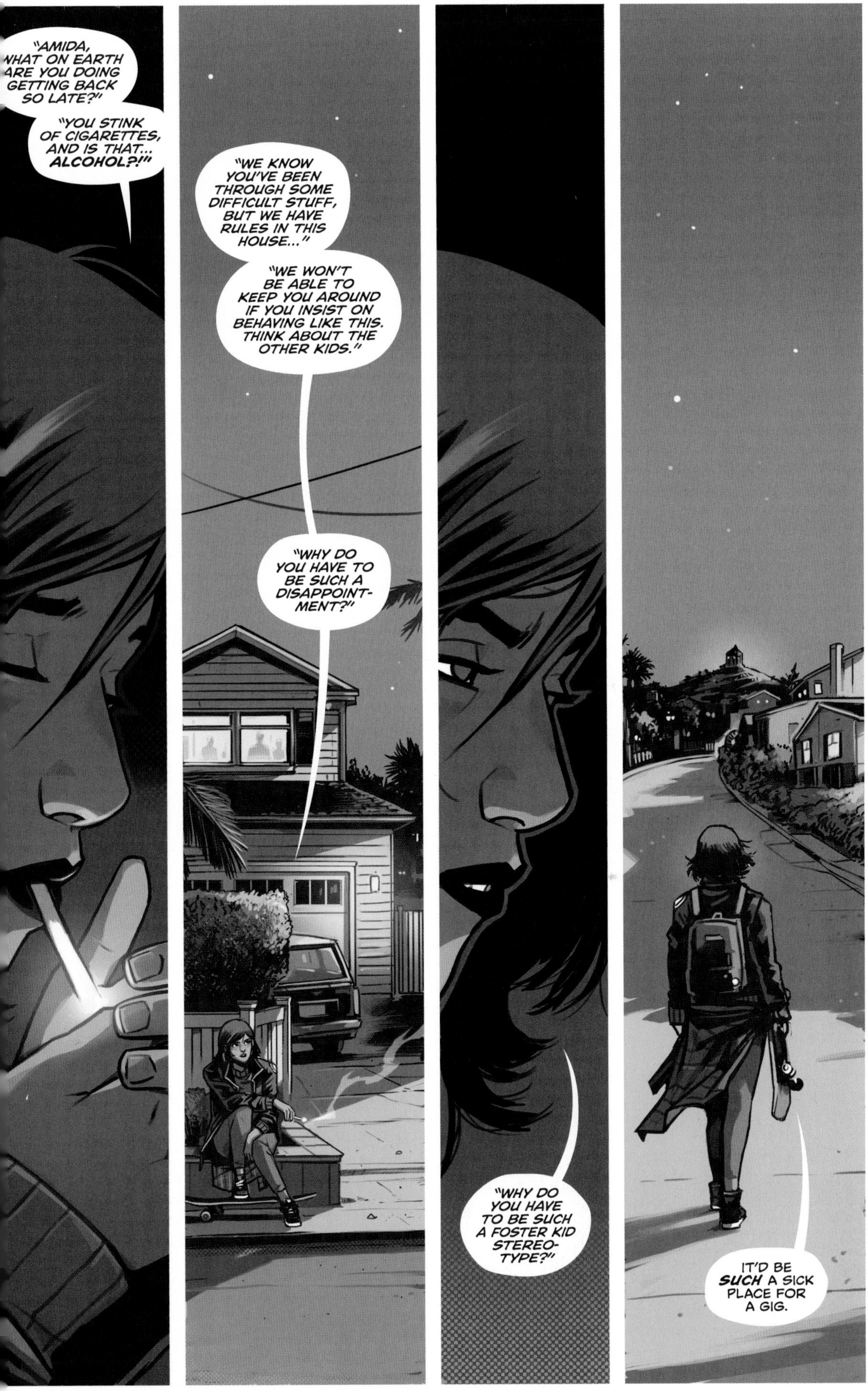
"AMIDA, WHAT ON EARTH ARE YOU DOING GETTING BACK SO LATE?"
"YOU STINK OF CIGARETTES, AND IS THAT... ALCOHOL?!"
"WE KNOW YOU'VE BEEN THROUGH SOME DIFFICULT STUFF, BUT WE HAVE RULES IN THIS HOUSE..."
"WE WON'T BE ABLE TO KEEP YOU AROUND IF YOU INSIST ON BEHAVING LIKE THIS. THINK ABOUT THE OTHER KIDS."
"WHY DO YOU HAVE TO BE SUCH A DISAPPOINT-MENT?"
"WHY DO YOU HAVE TO BE SUCH A FOSTER KID STEREO-TYPE?"
IT'D BE SUCH A SICK PLACE FOR A GIG.

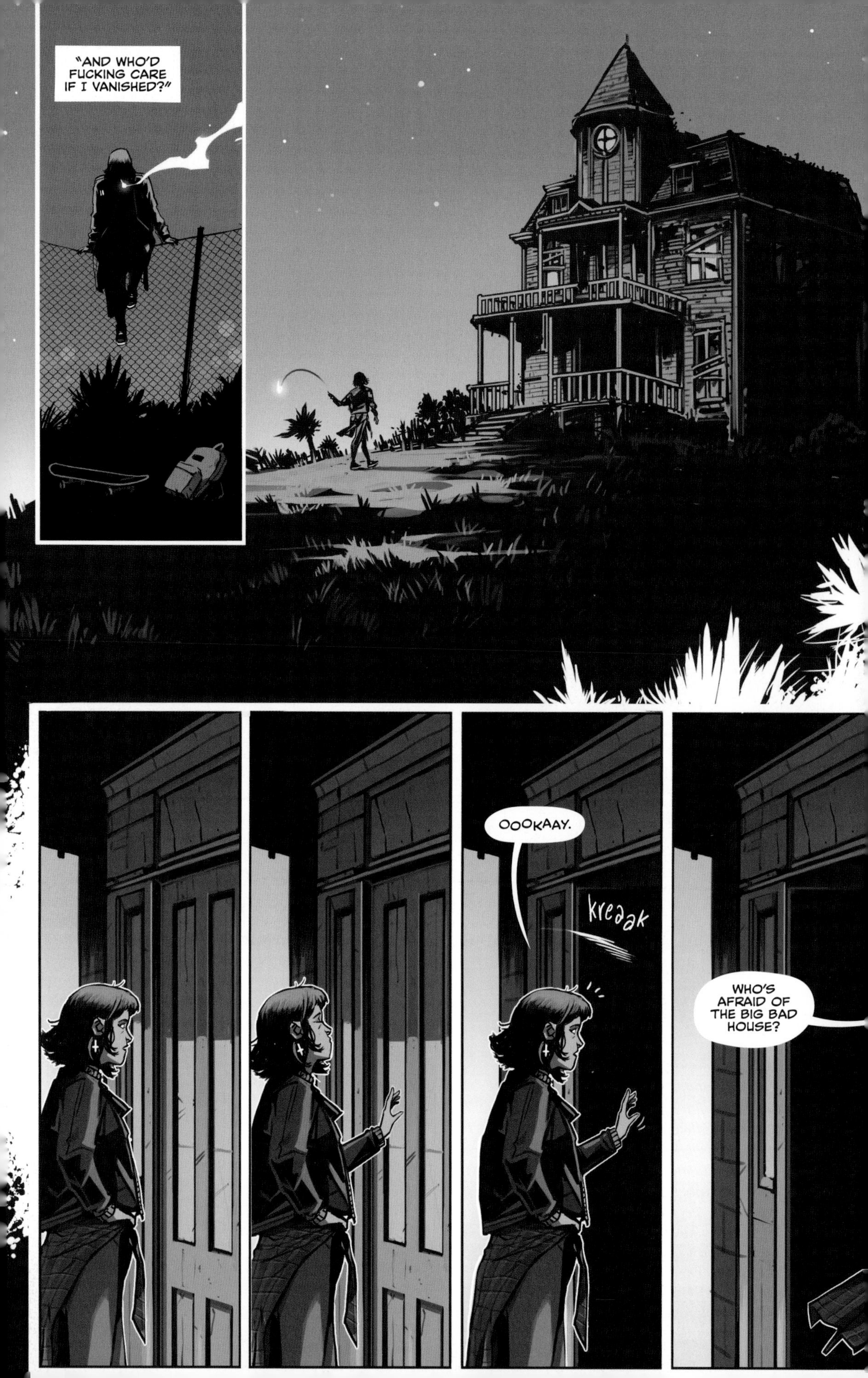
"AND WHO'D FUCKING CARE IF I VANISHED?"
OOOKAAY.
kreaak
WHO'S AFRAID OF THE BIG BAD HOUSE?

I WAS, IN ALL
HONESTY, QUITE
AFRAID OF THE
BIG BAD HOUSE.

IT WAS ROTTING AND
CREAKING AND DOING
ALL THE THINGS HOUSES
DO WHEN THEY AREN'T
LIVED IN--BUT WORST
OF ALL, IT WAS *EMPTY.*

I REMEMBERED BEING
EMPTY, TOO. I REMEMBERED
WHEN MOM DIED AND I LOST
EVERYTHING.

CAN YOU IMAGINE
BEING *STRIPPED*
OF ALL THE THINGS
THAT YOU THINK
MAKE *YOU* A *YOU?*
IT WAS SOMETHING
I'D HOPED NEVER
TO FEEL AGAIN.

IT WAS SOMETHING
I COULD FEEL IN
THAT HOUSE.

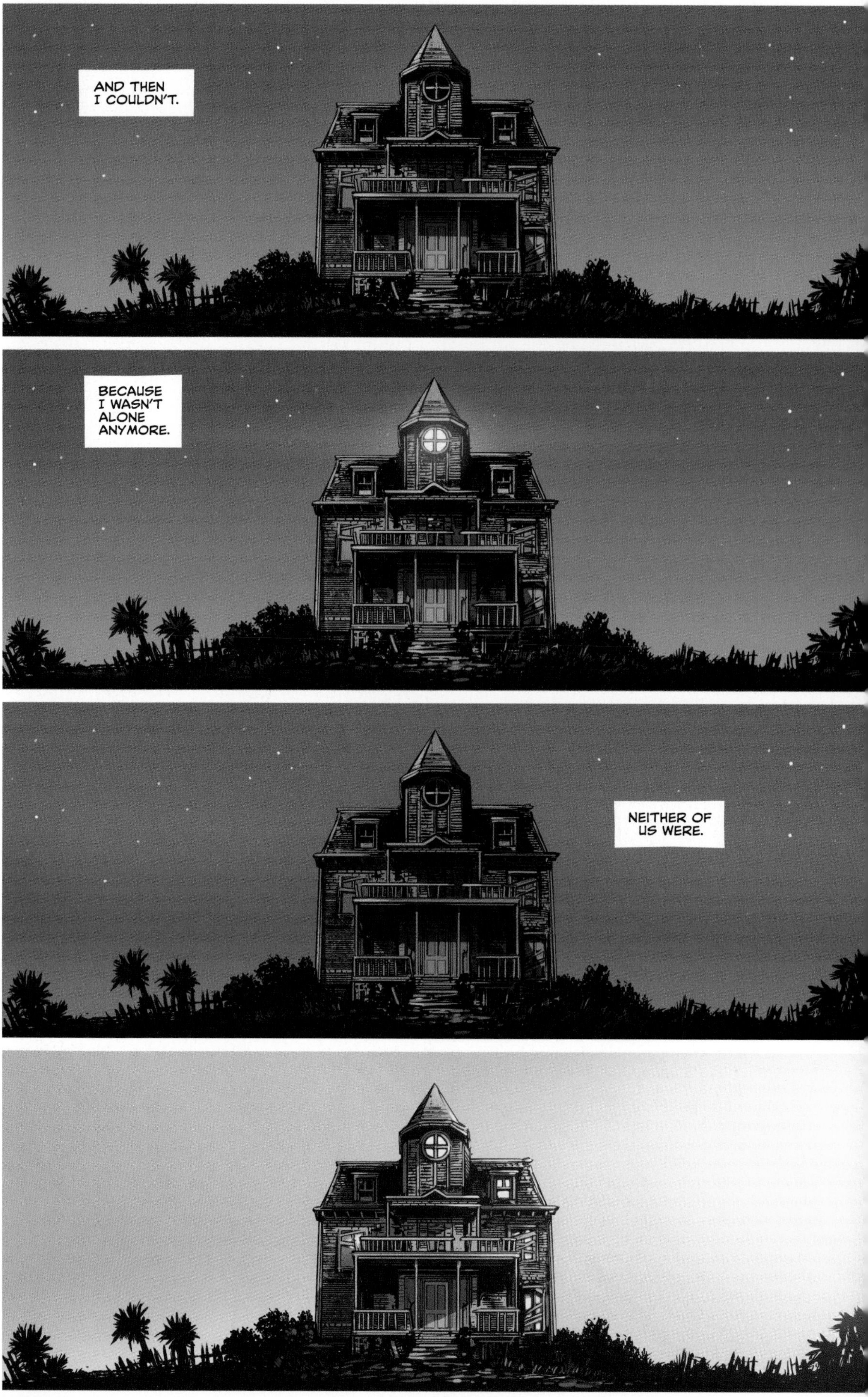
AND THEN
I COULDN'T.
BECAUSE
I WASN'T
ALONE
ANYMORE.
NEITHER OF
US WERE.

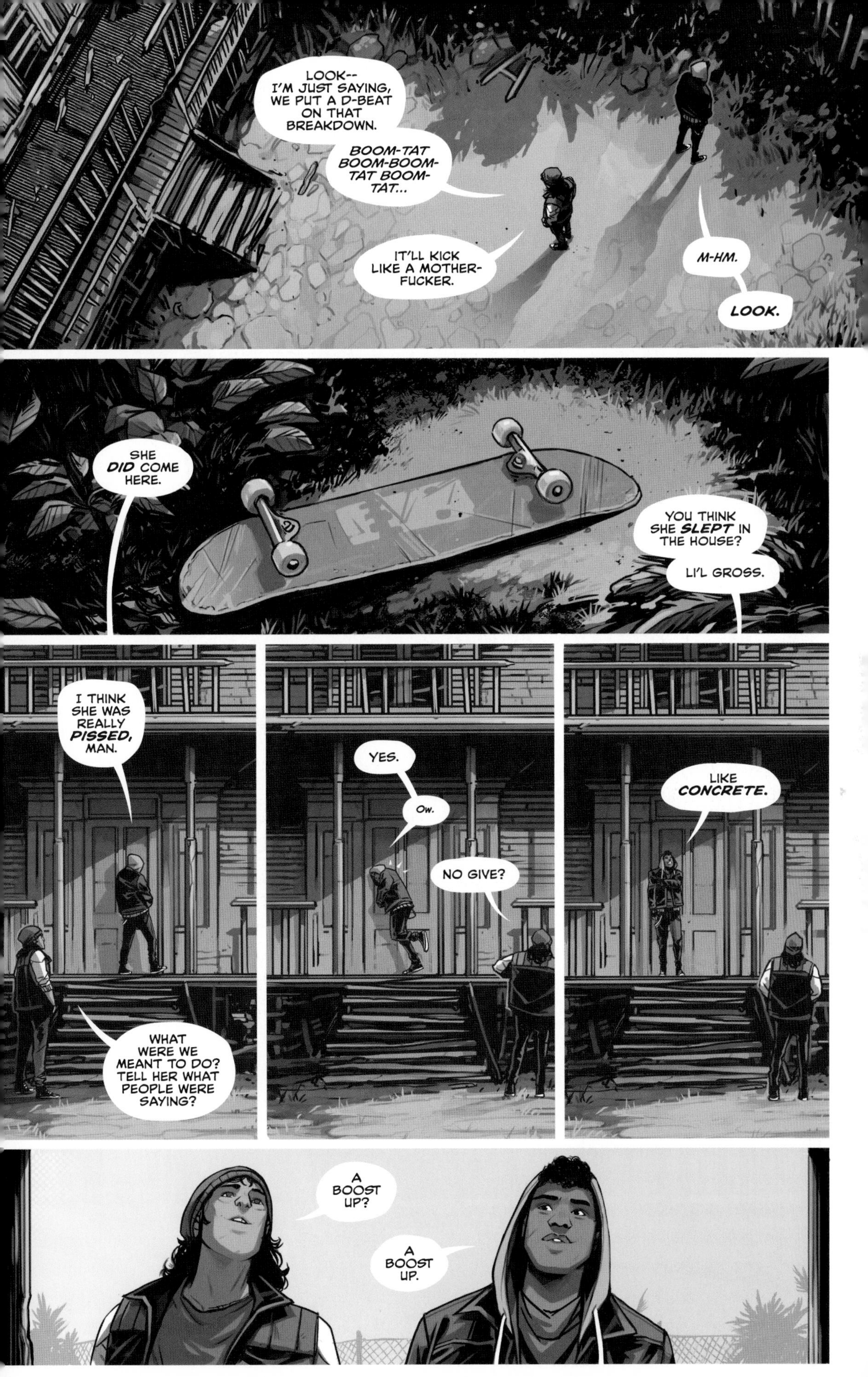
LOOK-- I'M JUST SAYING, WE PUT A D-BEAT ON THAT BREAKDOWN.
BOOM-TAT BOOM-BOOM-TAT BOOM-TAT...
IT'LL KICK LIKE A MOTHER-FUCKER.
M-HM.
LOOK.
SHE DID COME HERE.
YOU THINK SHE SLEPT IN THE HOUSE?
LI'L GROSS.
I THINK SHE WAS REALLY PISSED, MAN.
WHAT WERE WE MEANT TO DO? TELL HER WHAT PEOPLE WERE SAYING?
YES.
Ow.
NO GIVE?
LIKE CONCRETE.
A BOOST UP?
A BOOST UP.

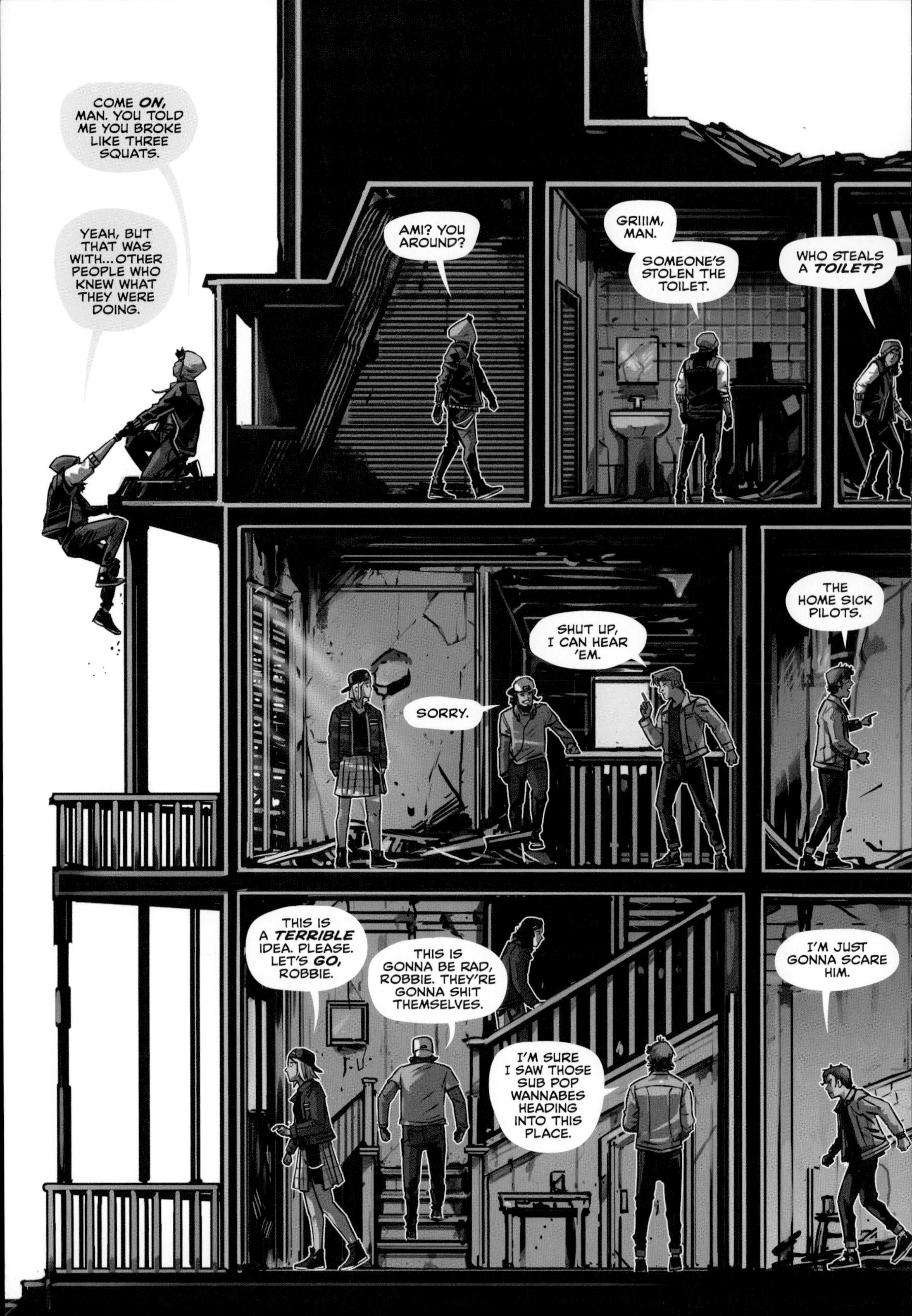
COME ON, MAN. YOU TOLD ME YOU BROKE LIKE THREE SQUATS.
YEAH, BUT THAT WAS WITH...OTHER PEOPLE WHO KNEW WHAT THEY WERE DOING.
AMI? YOU AROUND?
GRIIIM, MAN.
SOMEONE'S STOLEN THE TOILET.
WHO STEALS A TOILET?
SHUT UP, I CAN HEAR 'EM.
SORRY.
THE HOME SICK PILOTS.
THIS IS A TERRIBLE IDEA. PLEASE. LET'S GO, ROBBIE.
THIS IS GONNA BE RAD, ROBBIE. THEY'RE GONNA SHIT THEMSELVES.
I'M SURE I SAW THOSE SUB POP WANNABES HEADING INTO THIS PLACE.
I'M JUST GONNA SCARE HIM.

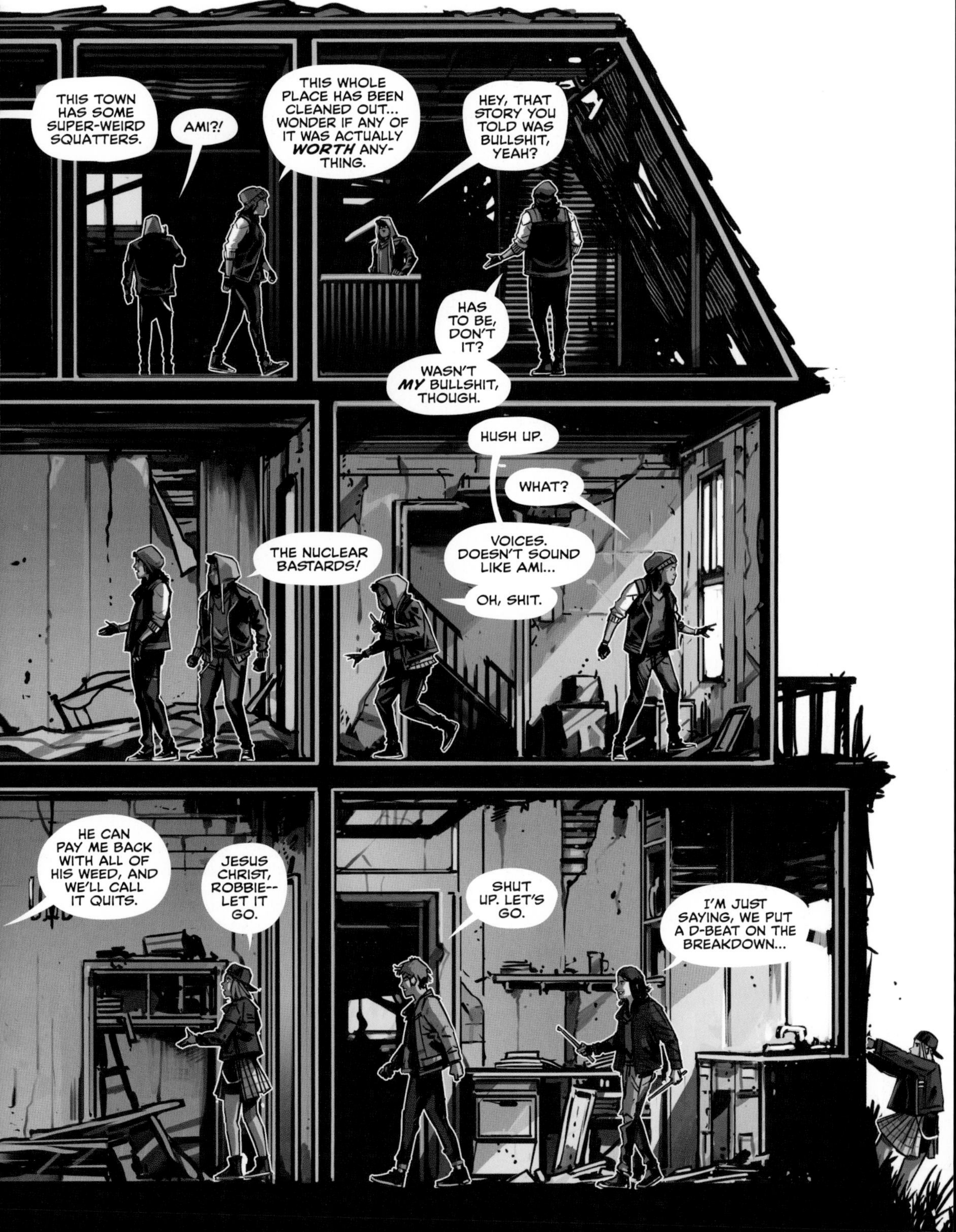

THIS TOWN HAS SOME SUPER-WEIRD SQUATTERS.
AMI?!
THIS WHOLE PLACE HAS BEEN CLEANED OUT... WONDER IF ANY OF IT WAS ACTUALLY WORTH ANY-THING.
HEY, THAT STORY YOU TOLD WAS BULLSHIT, YEAH?
HAS TO BE, DON'T IT?
WASN'T MY BULLSHIT, THOUGH.
THE NUCLEAR BASTARDS!
HUSH UP.
WHAT?
VOICES. DOESN'T SOUND LIKE AMI...
OH, SHIT.
HE CAN PAY ME BACK WITH ALL OF HIS WEED, AND WE'LL CALL IT QUITS.
JESUS CHRIST, ROBBIE-- LET IT GO.
SHUT UP. LET'S GO.
I'M JUST SAYING, WE PUT A D-BEAT ON THE BREAKDOWN...

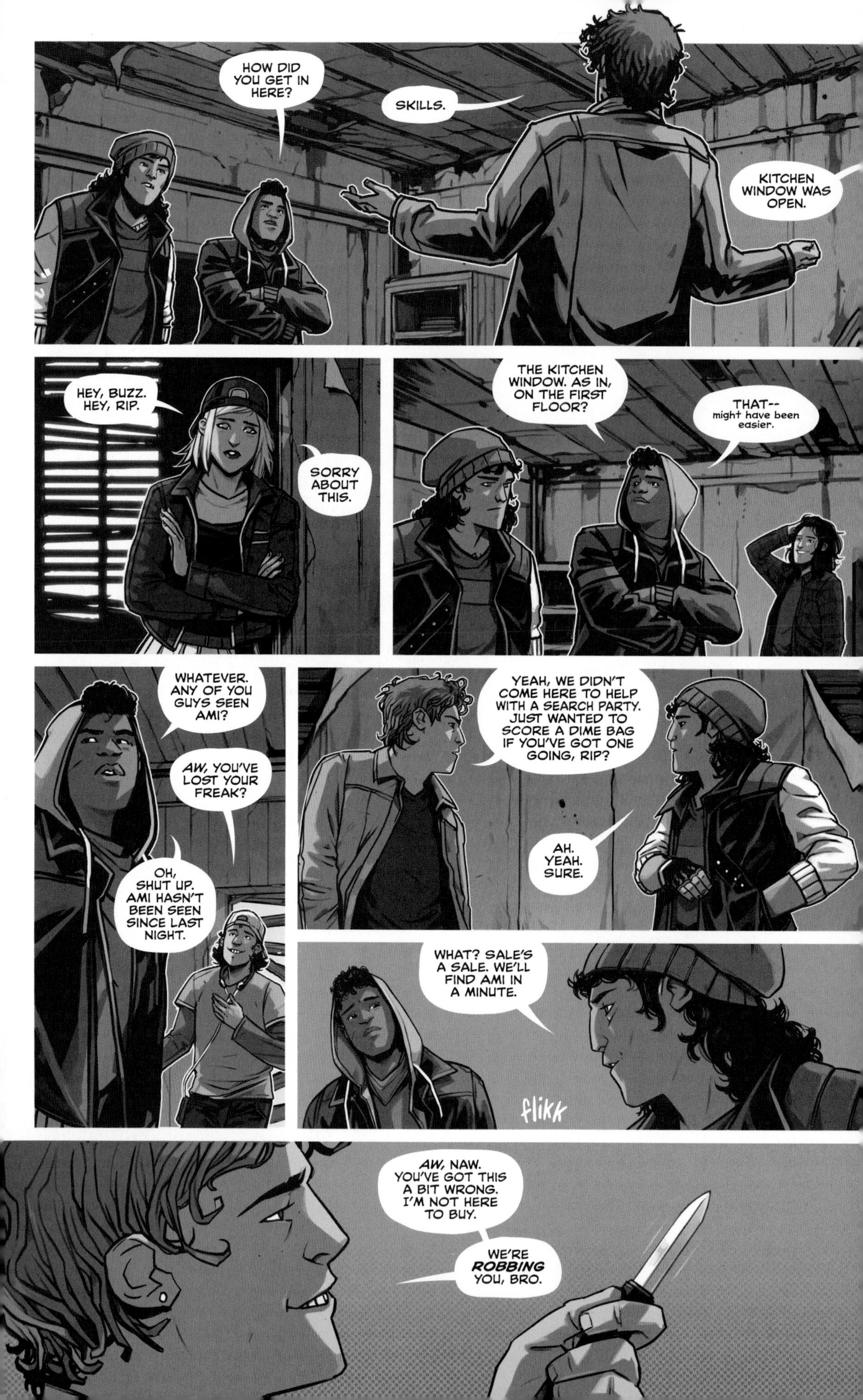
HOW DID YOU GET IN HERE?
SKILLS.
KITCHEN WINDOW WAS OPEN.
HEY, BUZZ. HEY, RIP.
SORRY ABOUT THIS.
THE KITCHEN WINDOW. AS IN, ON THE FIRST FLOOR?
THAT-- might have been easier.
WHATEVER. ANY OF YOU GUYS SEEN AMI?
AW, YOU'VE LOST YOUR FREAK?
OH, SHUT UP. AMI HASN'T BEEN SEEN SINCE LAST NIGHT.
YEAH, WE DIDN'T COME HERE TO HELP WITH A SEARCH PARTY. JUST WANTED TO SCORE A DIME BAG IF YOU'VE GOT ONE GOING, RIP?
AH. YEAH. SURE.
WHAT? SALE'S A SALE. WE'LL FIND AMI IN A MINUTE.
flikk
AW, NAW. YOU'VE GOT THIS A BIT WRONG. I'M NOT HERE TO BUY.
WE'RE ROBBING YOU, BRO.

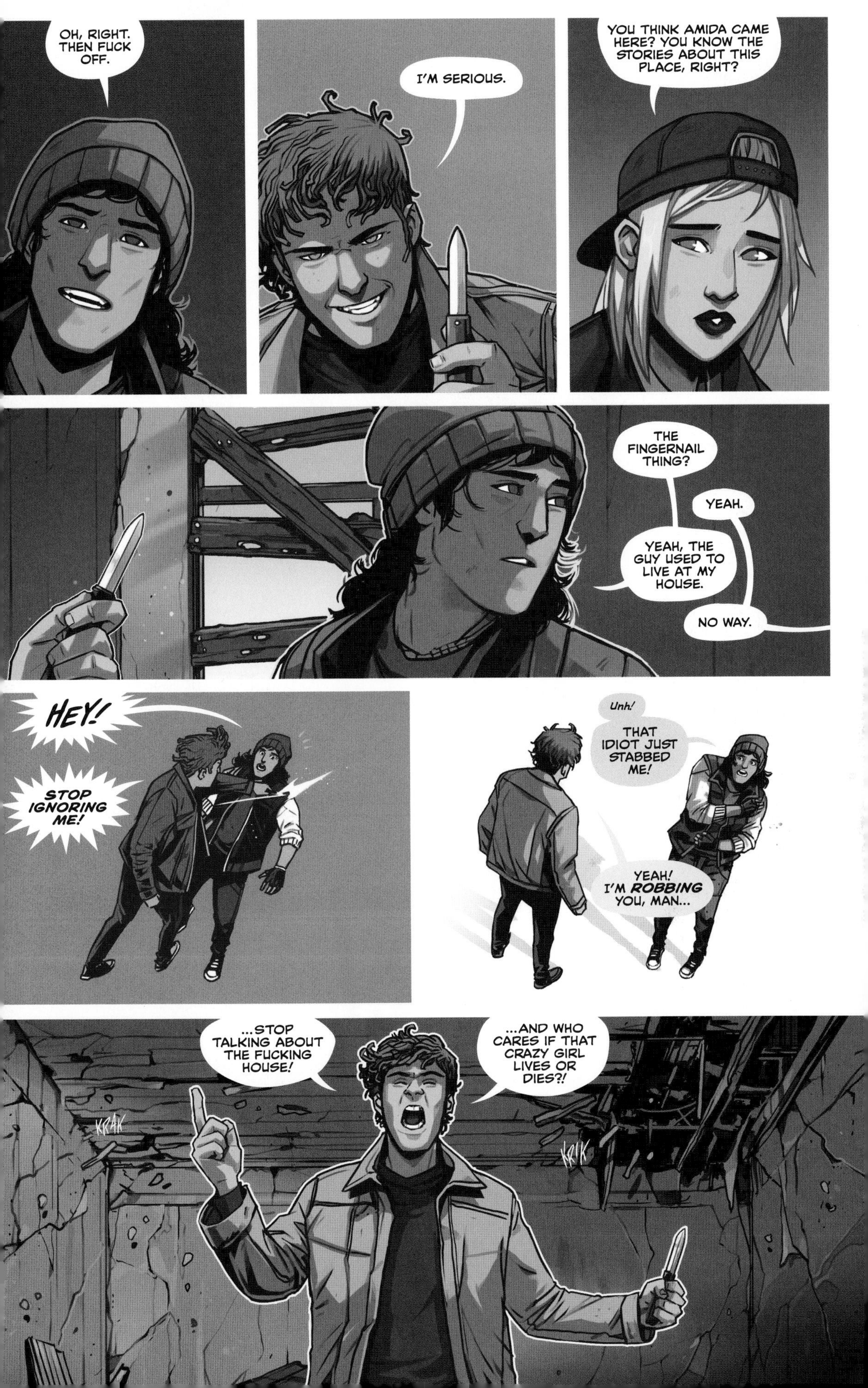
OH, RIGHT. THEN FUCK OFF.
I'M SERIOUS.
YOU THINK AMIDA CAME HERE? YOU KNOW THE STORIES ABOUT THIS PLACE, RIGHT?
THE FINGERNAIL THING?
YEAH.
YEAH, THE GUY USED TO LIVE AT MY HOUSE.
NO WAY.
HEY!
STOP IGNORING ME!
Unh!
THAT IDIOT JUST STABBED ME!
YEAH! I'M ROBBING YOU, MAN...
...STOP TALKING ABOUT THE FUCKING HOUSE!
...AND WHO CARES IF THAT CRAZY GIRL LIVES OR DIES?!
KRAK
KRIK

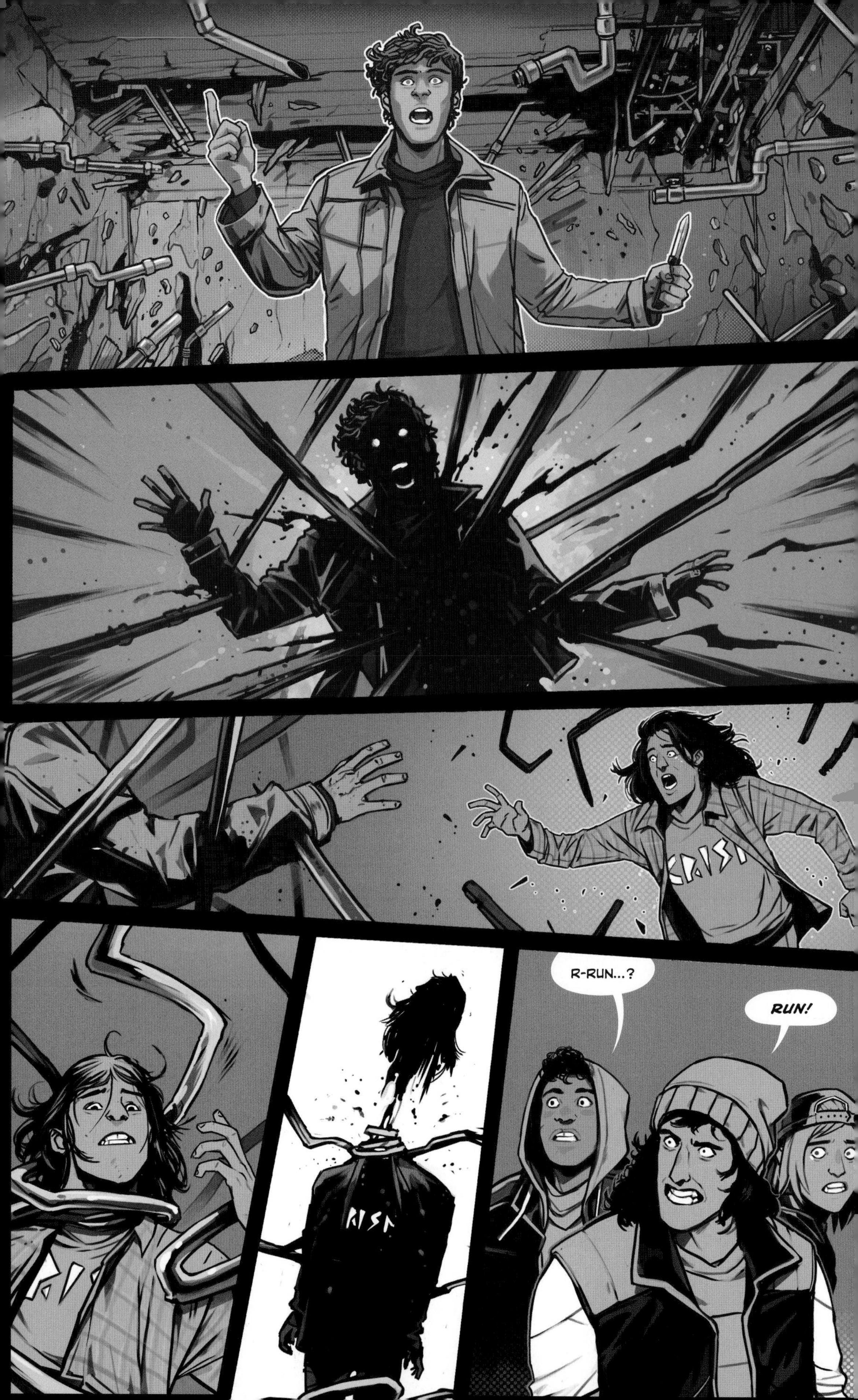
R-RUN...?
RUN!

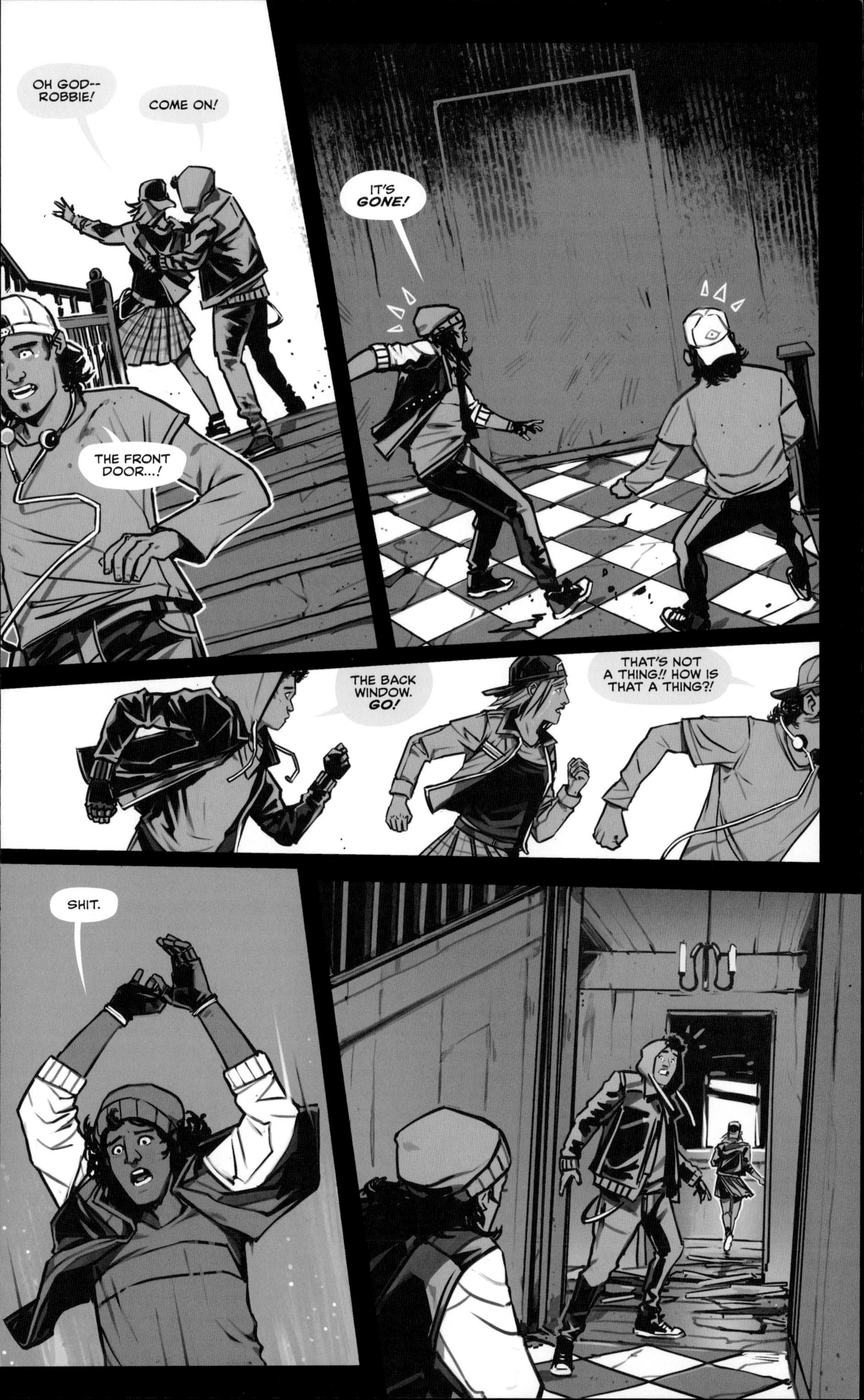
OH GOD--
ROBBIE!
COME ON!
THE FRONT
DOOR...!
IT'S
GONE!
THE BACK
WINDOW.
GO!
THAT'S NOT
A THING!! HOW IS
THAT A THING?!
SHIT.

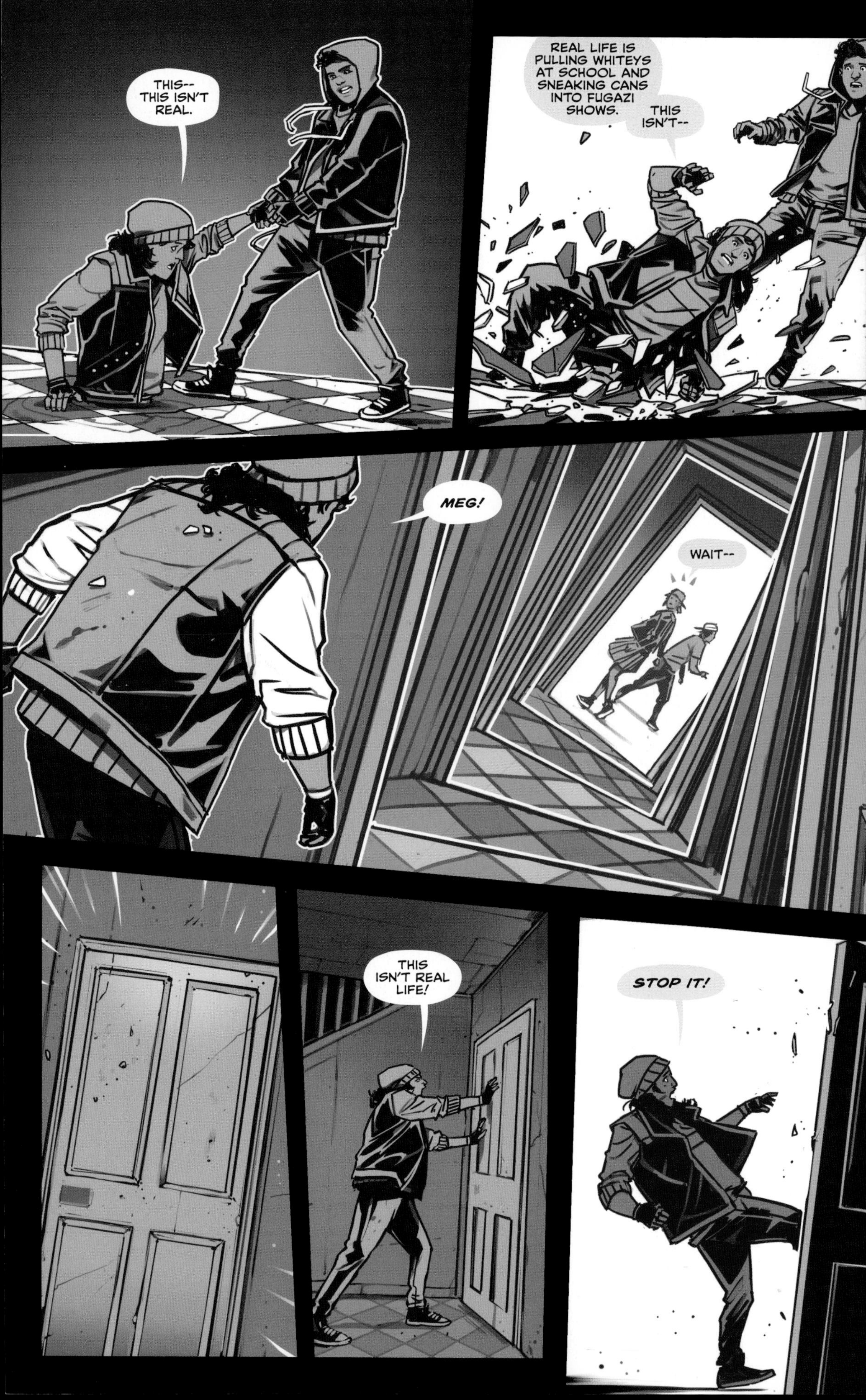
THIS--
THIS ISN'T
REAL.
REAL LIFE IS
PULLING WHITEYS
AT SCHOOL AND
SNEAKING CANS
INTO FUGAZI
SHOWS.
THIS
ISN'T--
MEG!
WAIT--
THIS
ISN'T REAL
LIFE!
STOP IT!

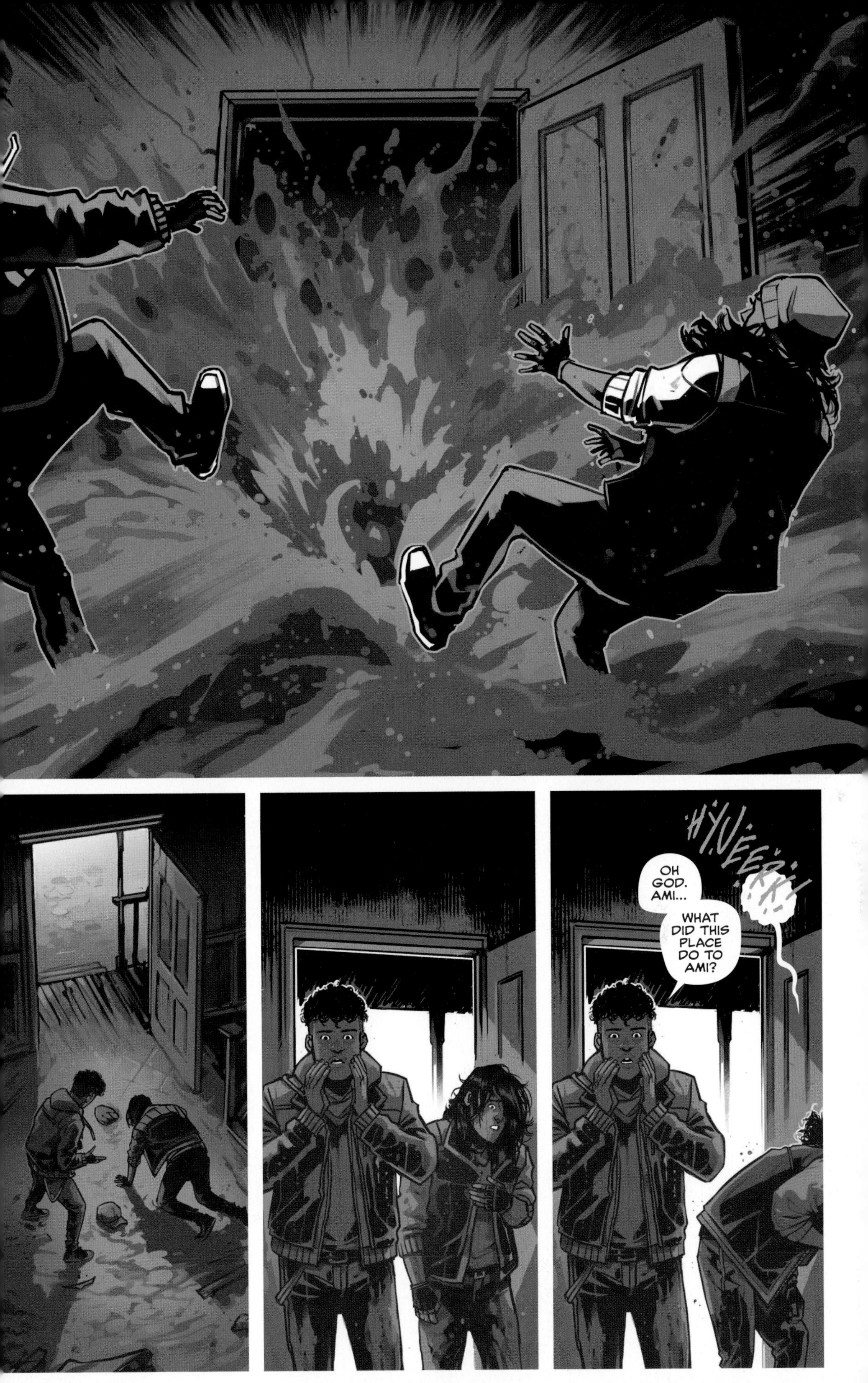
HYUEERK!
OH GOD. AMI...
WHAT DID THIS PLACE DO TO AMI?

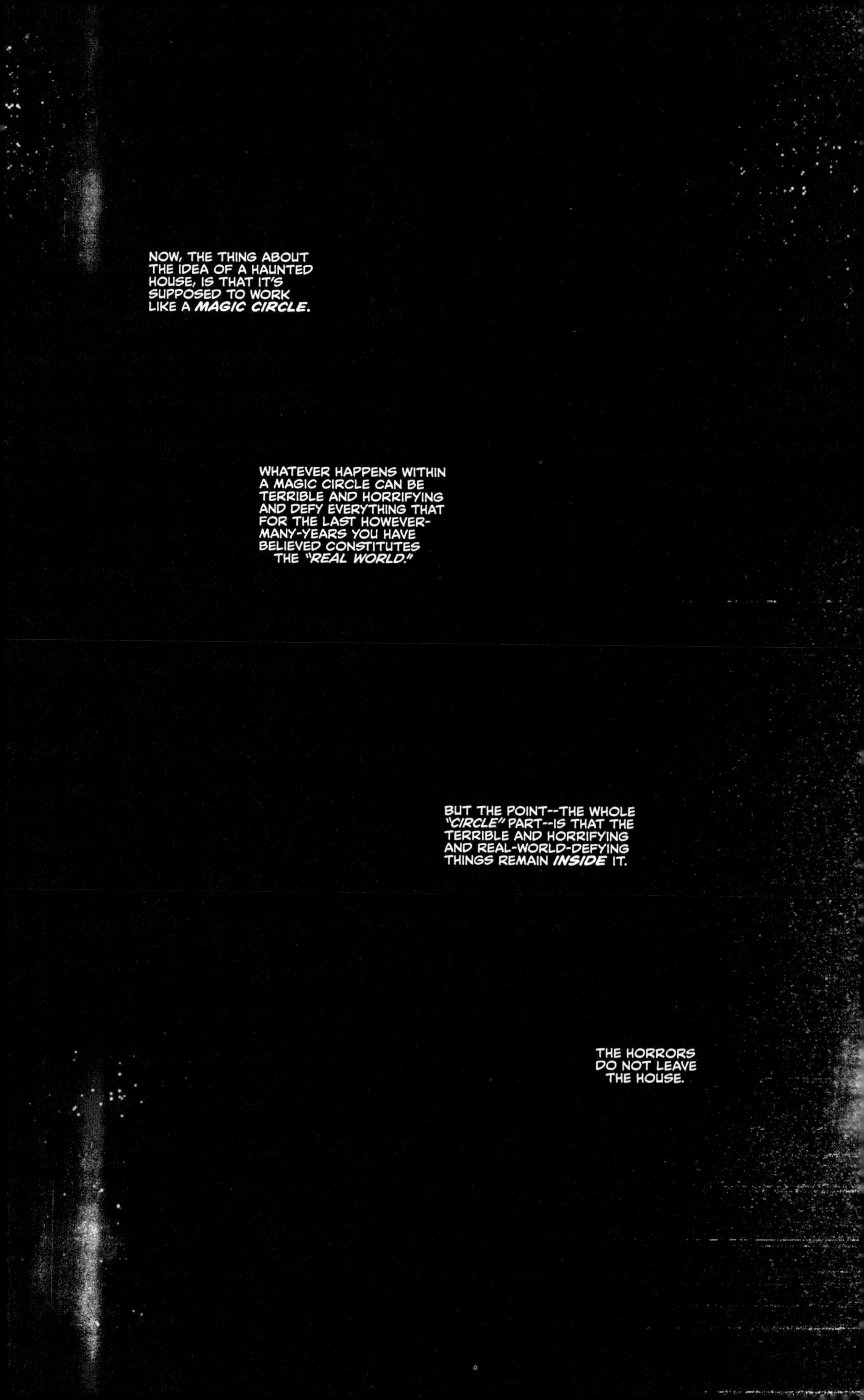
NOW, THE THING ABOUT THE IDEA OF A HAUNTED HOUSE, IS THAT IT'S SUPPOSED TO WORK LIKE A MAGIC CIRCLE.
WHATEVER HAPPENS WITHIN A MAGIC CIRCLE CAN BE TERRIBLE AND HORRIFYING AND DEFY EVERYTHING THAT FOR THE LAST HOWEVER-MANY-YEARS YOU HAVE BELIEVED CONSTITUTES THE "REAL WORLD."
BUT THE POINT--THE WHOLE "CIRCLE" PART--IS THAT THE TERRIBLE AND HORRIFYING AND REAL-WORLD-DEFYING THINGS REMAIN INSIDE IT.
THE HORRORS DO NOT LEAVE THE HOUSE.

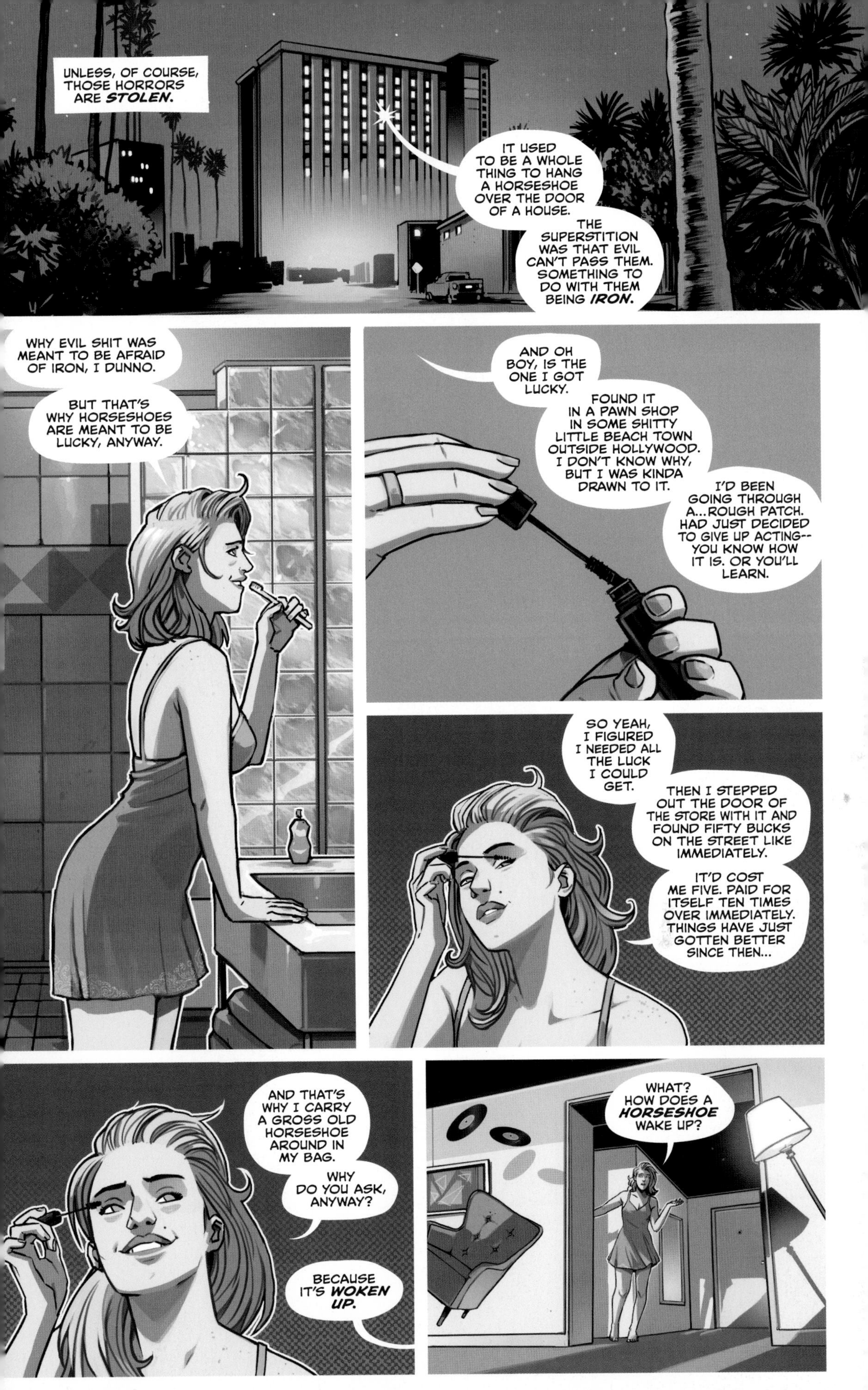
UNLESS, OF COURSE, THOSE HORRORS ARE **STOLEN.**
IT USED TO BE A WHOLE THING TO HANG A HORSESHOE OVER THE DOOR OF A HOUSE.
THE SUPERSTITION WAS THAT EVIL CAN'T PASS THEM. SOMETHING TO DO WITH THEM BEING **IRON.**
WHY EVIL SHIT WAS MEANT TO BE AFRAID OF IRON, I DUNNO.
BUT THAT'S WHY HORSESHOES ARE MEANT TO BE LUCKY, ANYWAY.
AND OH BOY, IS THE ONE I GOT LUCKY.
FOUND IT IN A PAWN SHOP IN SOME SHITTY LITTLE BEACH TOWN OUTSIDE HOLLYWOOD. I DON'T KNOW WHY, BUT I WAS KINDA DRAWN TO IT.
I'D BEEN GOING THROUGH A...ROUGH PATCH. HAD JUST DECIDED TO GIVE UP ACTING-- YOU KNOW HOW IT IS. OR YOU'LL LEARN.
SO YEAH, I FIGURED I NEEDED ALL THE LUCK I COULD GET.
THEN I STEPPED OUT THE DOOR OF THE STORE WITH IT AND FOUND FIFTY BUCKS ON THE STREET LIKE IMMEDIATELY.
IT'D COST ME FIVE. PAID FOR ITSELF TEN TIMES OVER IMMEDIATELY. THINGS HAVE JUST GOTTEN BETTER SINCE THEN...
AND THAT'S WHY I CARRY A GROSS OLD HORSESHOE AROUND IN MY BAG.
WHY DO YOU ASK, ANYWAY?
BECAUSE IT'S **WOKEN UP.**
WHAT? HOW DOES A **HORSESHOE** WAKE UP?

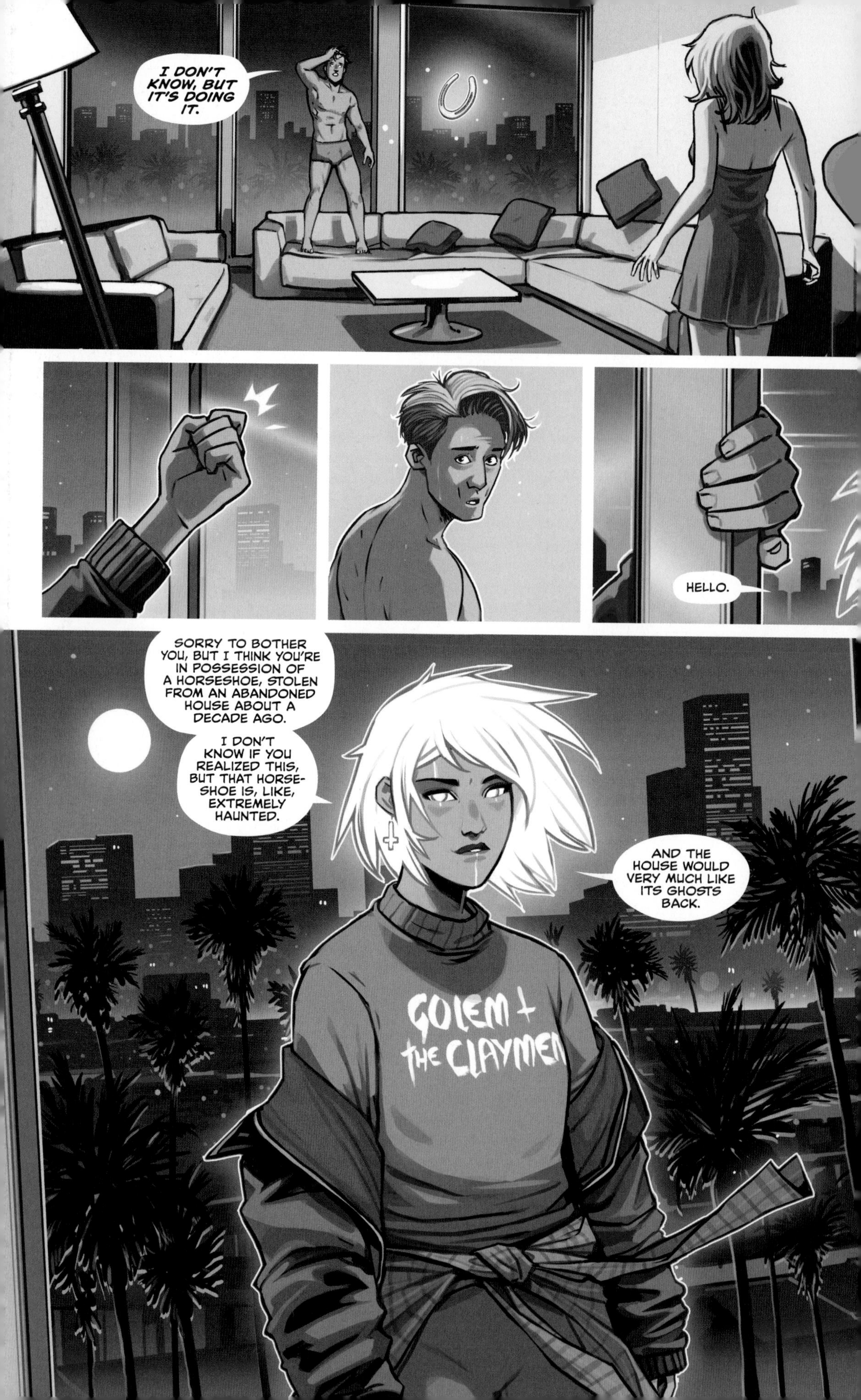
I DON'T KNOW, BUT IT'S DOING IT.
HELLO.
SORRY TO BOTHER YOU, BUT I THINK YOU'RE IN POSSESSION OF A HORSESHOE, STOLEN FROM AN ABANDONED HOUSE ABOUT A DECADE AGO.
I DON'T KNOW IF YOU REALIZED THIS, BUT THAT HORSE-SHOE IS, LIKE, EXTREMELY HAUNTED.
AND THE HOUSE WOULD VERY MUCH LIKE ITS GHOSTS BACK.
GOLEM + THE CLAYMEN

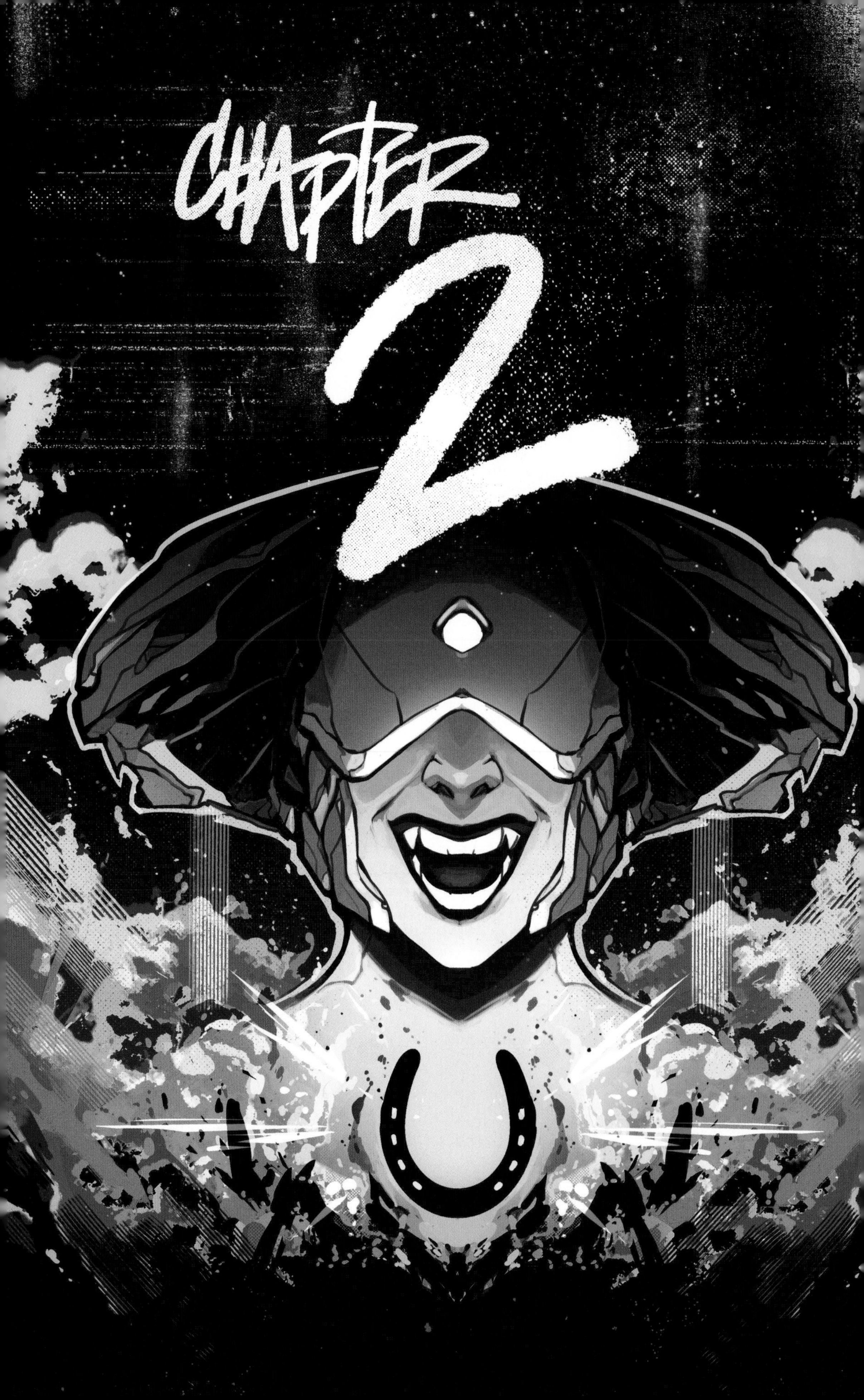
CHAPTER
2

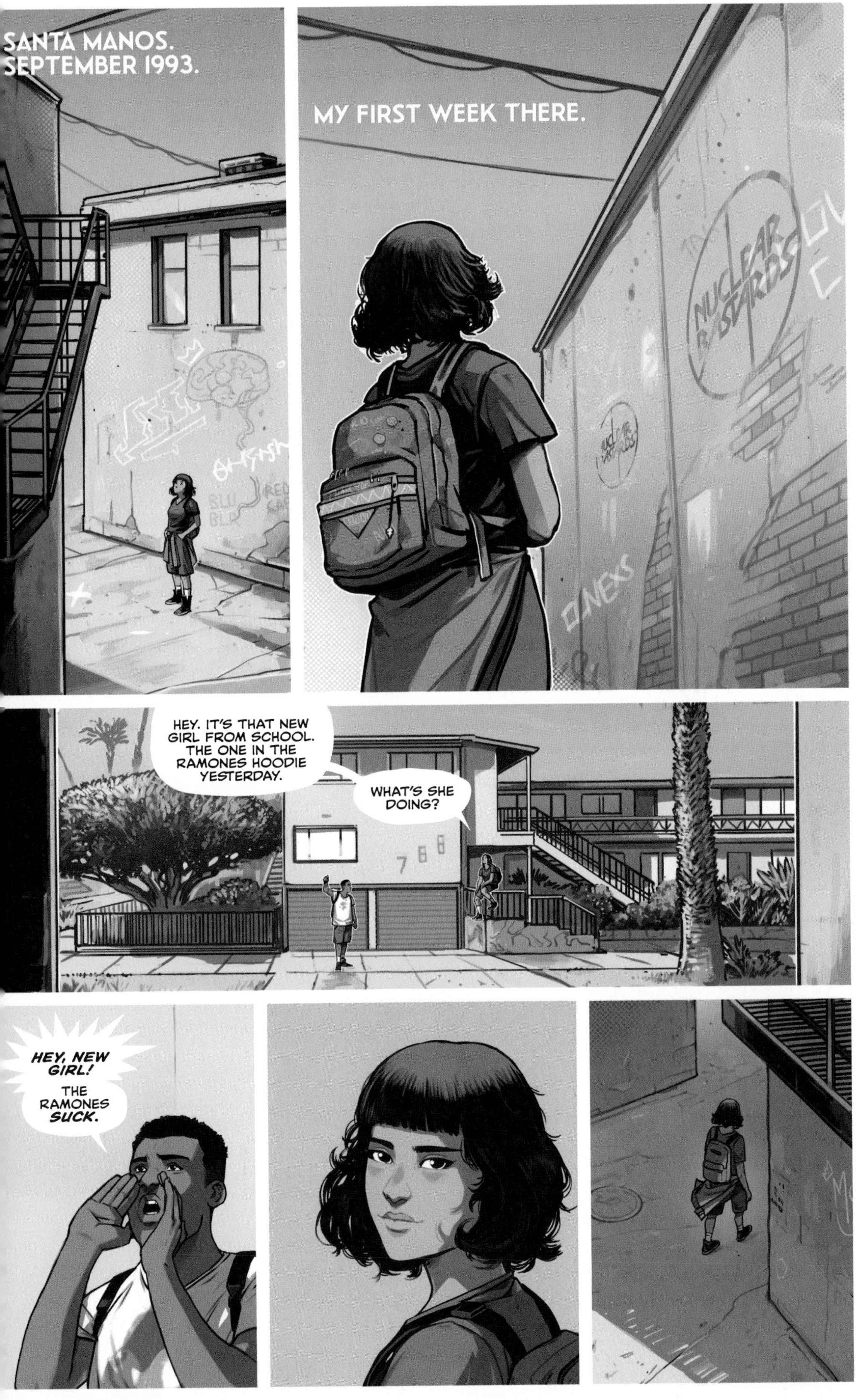
SANTA MANOS.
SEPTEMBER 1993.
MY FIRST WEEK THERE.
NUCLEAR BASTARDS
HEY. IT'S THAT NEW GIRL FROM SCHOOL. THE ONE IN THE RAMONES HOODIE YESTERDAY.
WHAT'S SHE DOING?
HEY, NEW GIRL!
THE RAMONES SUCK.

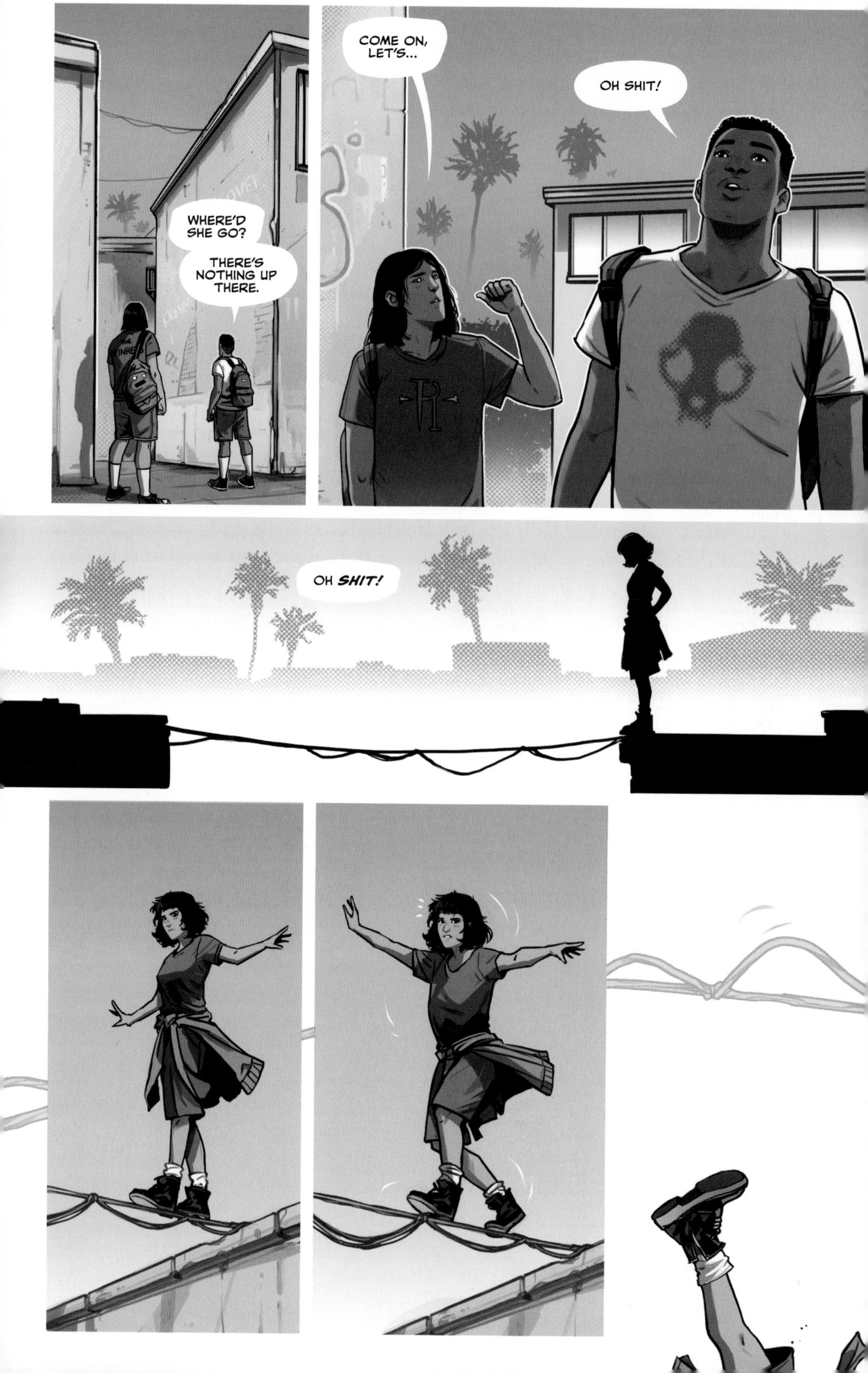
WHERE'D SHE GO?
THERE'S NOTHING UP THERE.
COME ON, LET'S...
OH SHIT!
OH **SHIT!**

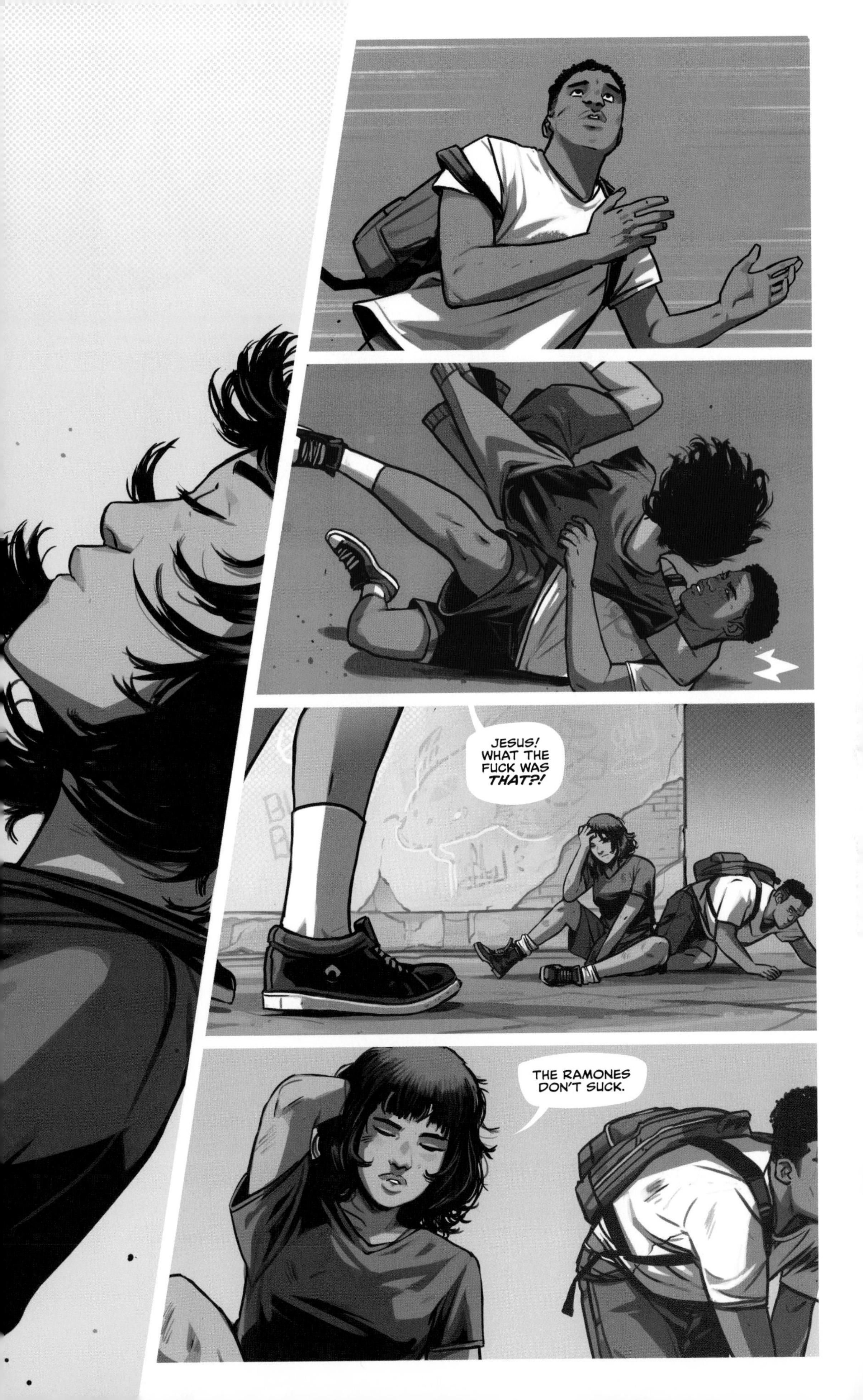
JESUS! WHAT THE FUCK WAS THAT?!
THE RAMONES DON'T SUCK.

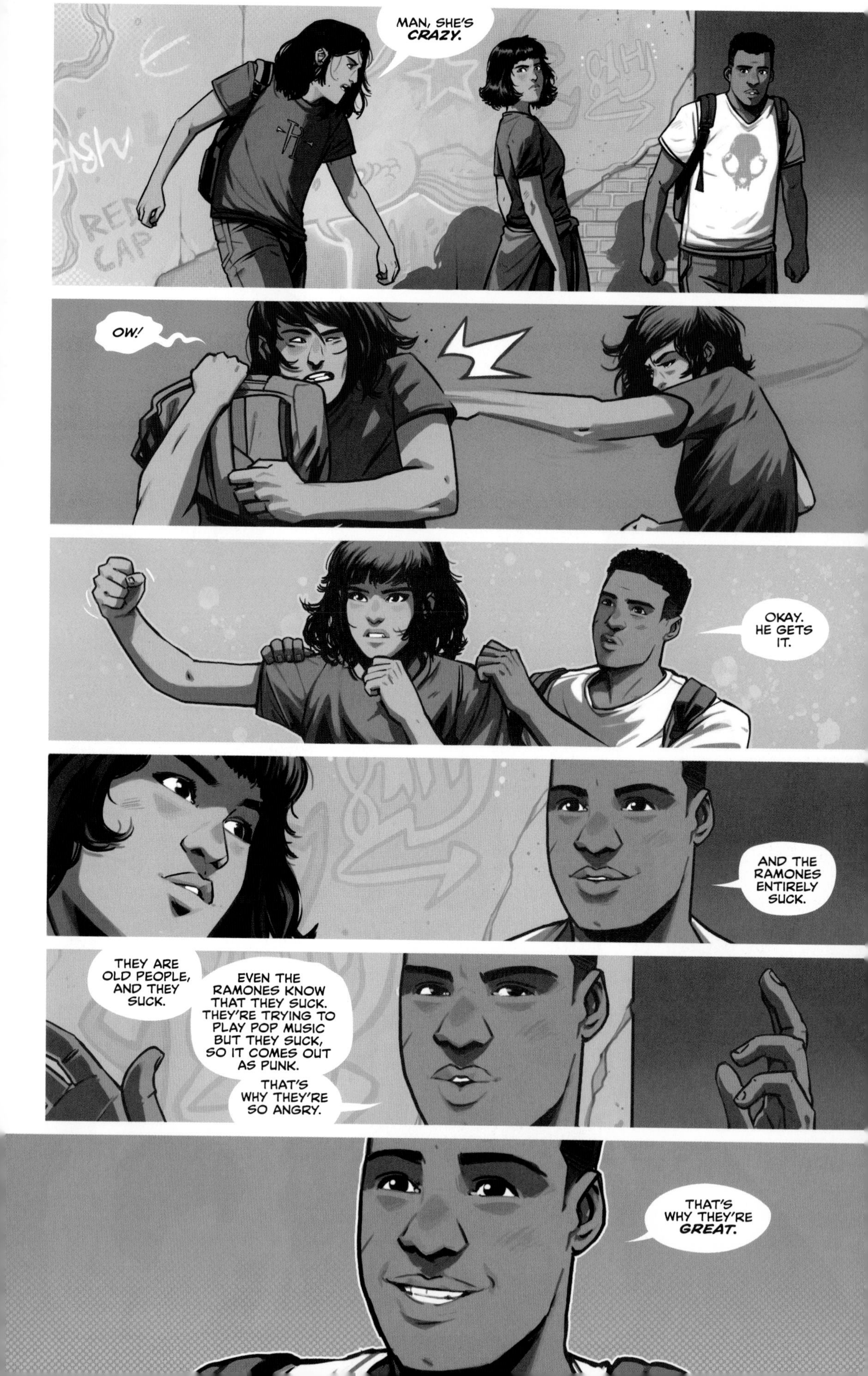
MAN, SHE'S *CRAZY.*
OW!
OKAY. HE GETS IT.
AND THE RAMONES ENTIRELY SUCK.
THEY ARE OLD PEOPLE, AND THEY SUCK.
EVEN THE RAMONES KNOW THAT THEY SUCK. THEY'RE TRYING TO PLAY POP MUSIC BUT THEY SUCK, SO IT COMES OUT AS PUNK.
THAT'S WHY THEY'RE SO ANGRY.
THAT'S WHY THEY'RE *GREAT.*

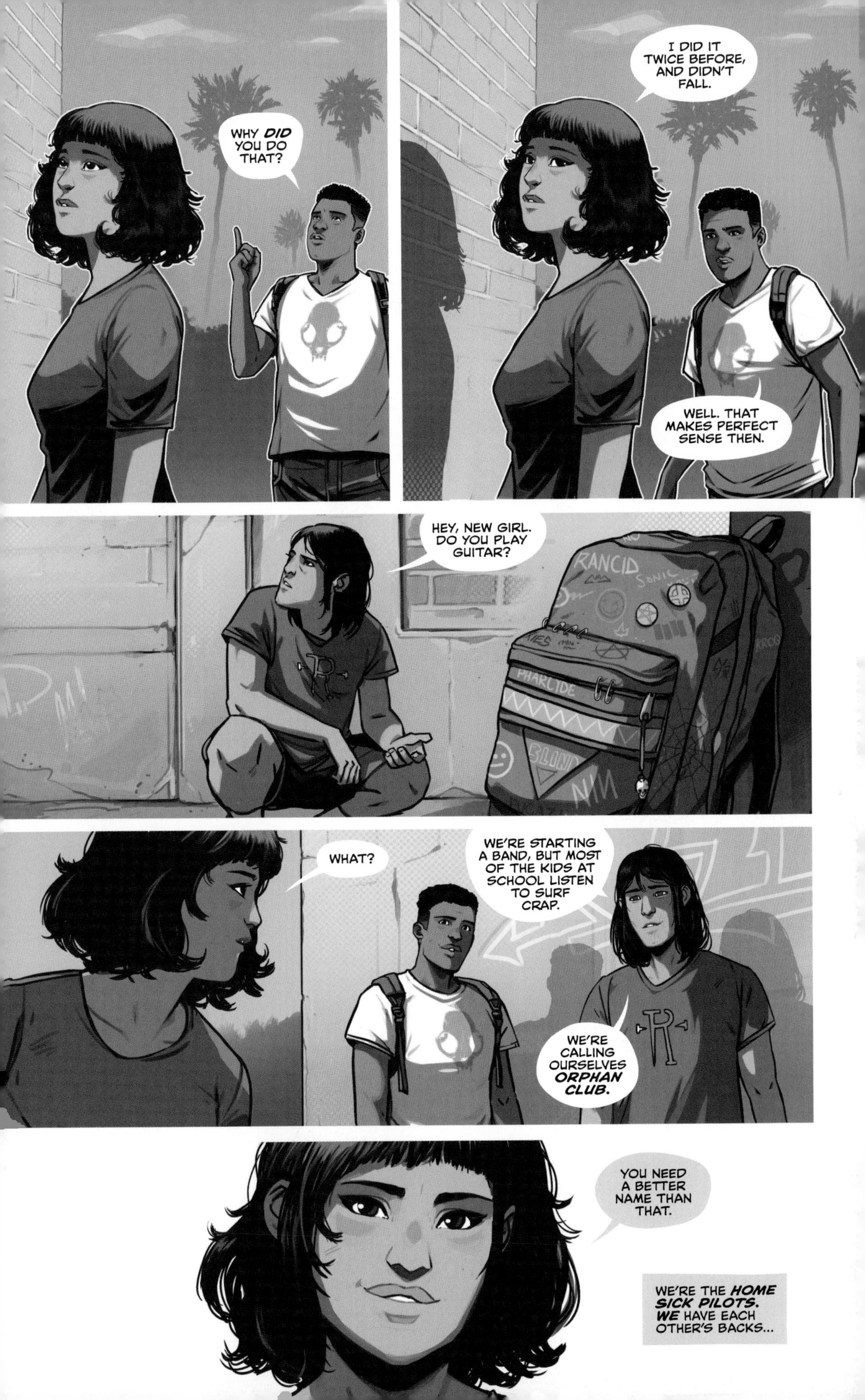
WHY DID YOU DO THAT?
I DID IT TWICE BEFORE, AND DIDN'T FALL.
WELL. THAT MAKES PERFECT SENSE THEN.
HEY, NEW GIRL. DO YOU PLAY GUITAR?
WHAT?
WE'RE STARTING A BAND, BUT MOST OF THE KIDS AT SCHOOL LISTEN TO SURF CRAP.
WE'RE CALLING OURSELVES ORPHAN CLUB.
YOU NEED A BETTER NAME THAN THAT.
WE'RE THE HOME SICK PILOTS. WE HAVE EACH OTHER'S BACKS...

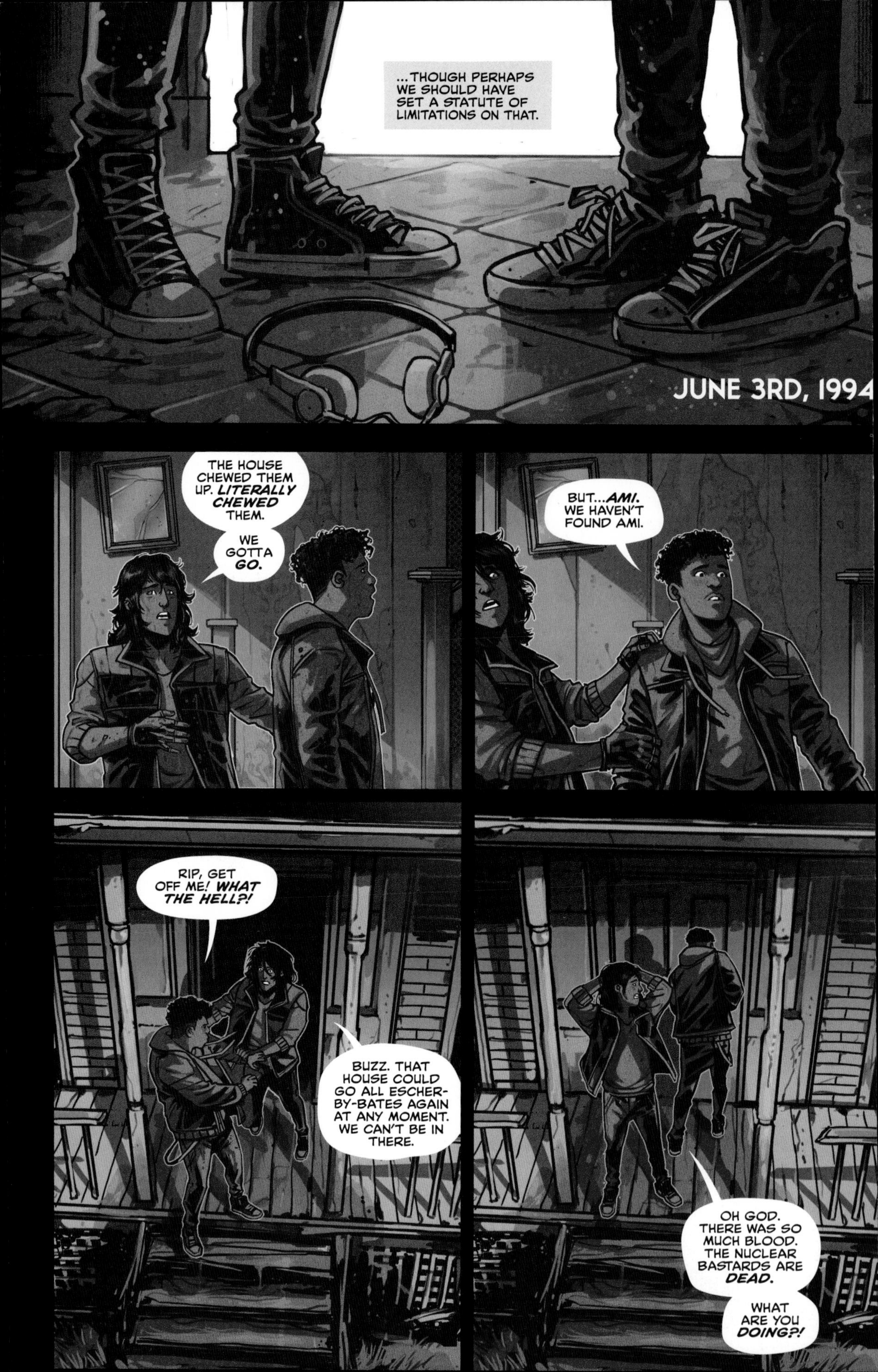
...THOUGH PERHAPS WE SHOULD HAVE SET A STATUTE OF LIMITATIONS ON THAT.
JUNE 3RD, 1994
THE HOUSE CHEWED THEM UP. LITERALLY CHEWED THEM.
WE GOTTA GO.
BUT...AMI. WE HAVEN'T FOUND AMI.
RIP, GET OFF ME! WHAT THE HELL?!
BUZZ. THAT HOUSE COULD GO ALL ESCHER-BY-BATES AGAIN AT ANY MOMENT. WE CAN'T BE IN THERE.
OH GOD. THERE WAS SO MUCH BLOOD. THE NUCLEAR BASTARDS ARE DEAD.
WHAT ARE YOU DOING?!

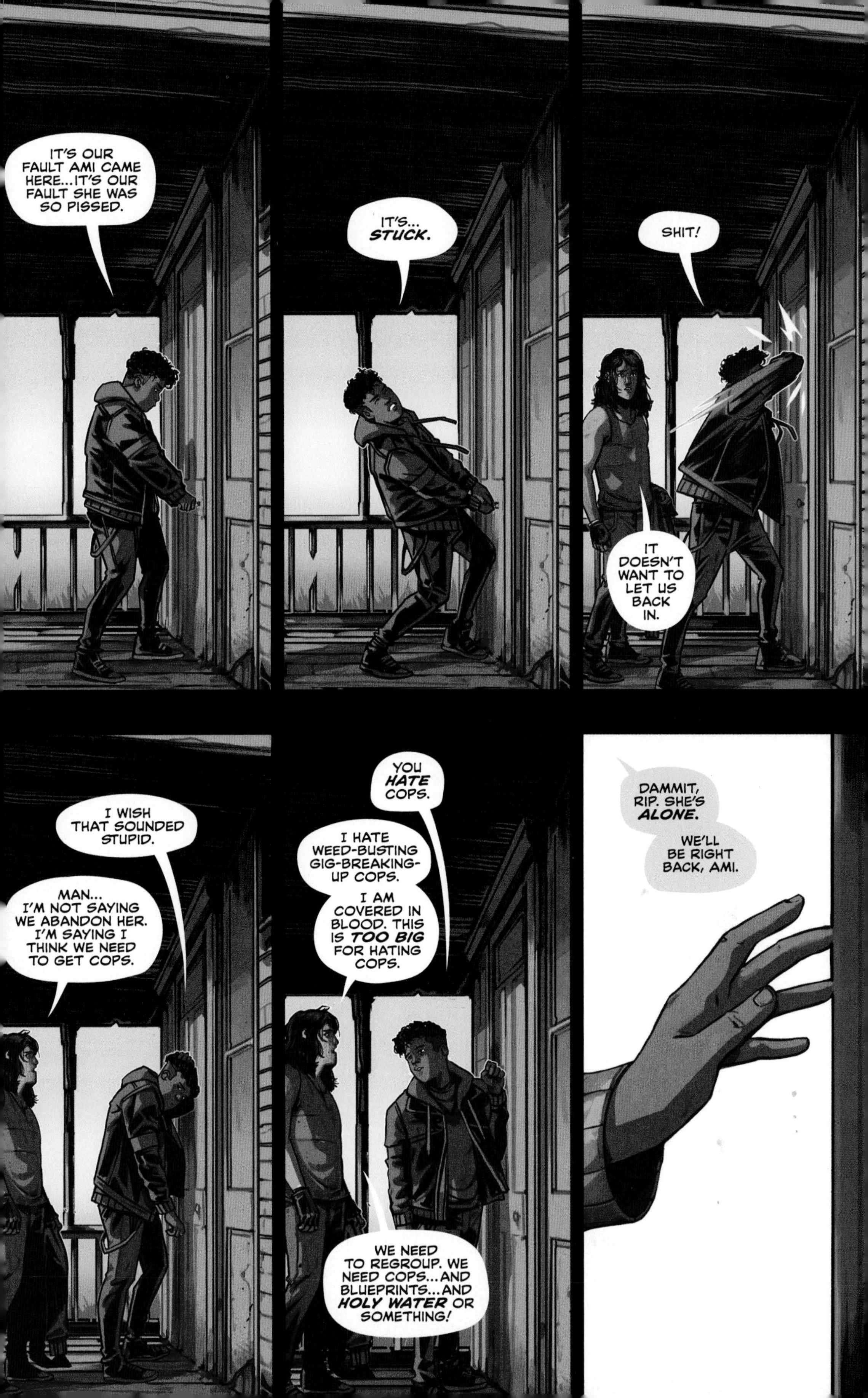
IT'S OUR FAULT AMI CAME HERE...IT'S OUR FAULT SHE WAS SO PISSED.
IT'S... *STUCK.*
SHIT!
IT DOESN'T WANT TO LET US BACK IN.
I WISH THAT SOUNDED STUPID.
MAN... I'M NOT SAYING WE ABANDON HER. I'M SAYING I THINK WE NEED TO GET COPS.
YOU *HATE* COPS.
I HATE WEED-BUSTING GIG-BREAKING-UP COPS.
I AM COVERED IN BLOOD. THIS IS *TOO BIG* FOR HATING COPS.
WE NEED TO REGROUP. WE NEED COPS...AND BLUEPRINTS...AND *HOLY WATER* OR SOMETHING!
DAMMIT, RIP. SHE'S *ALONE.*
WE'LL BE RIGHT BACK, AMI.

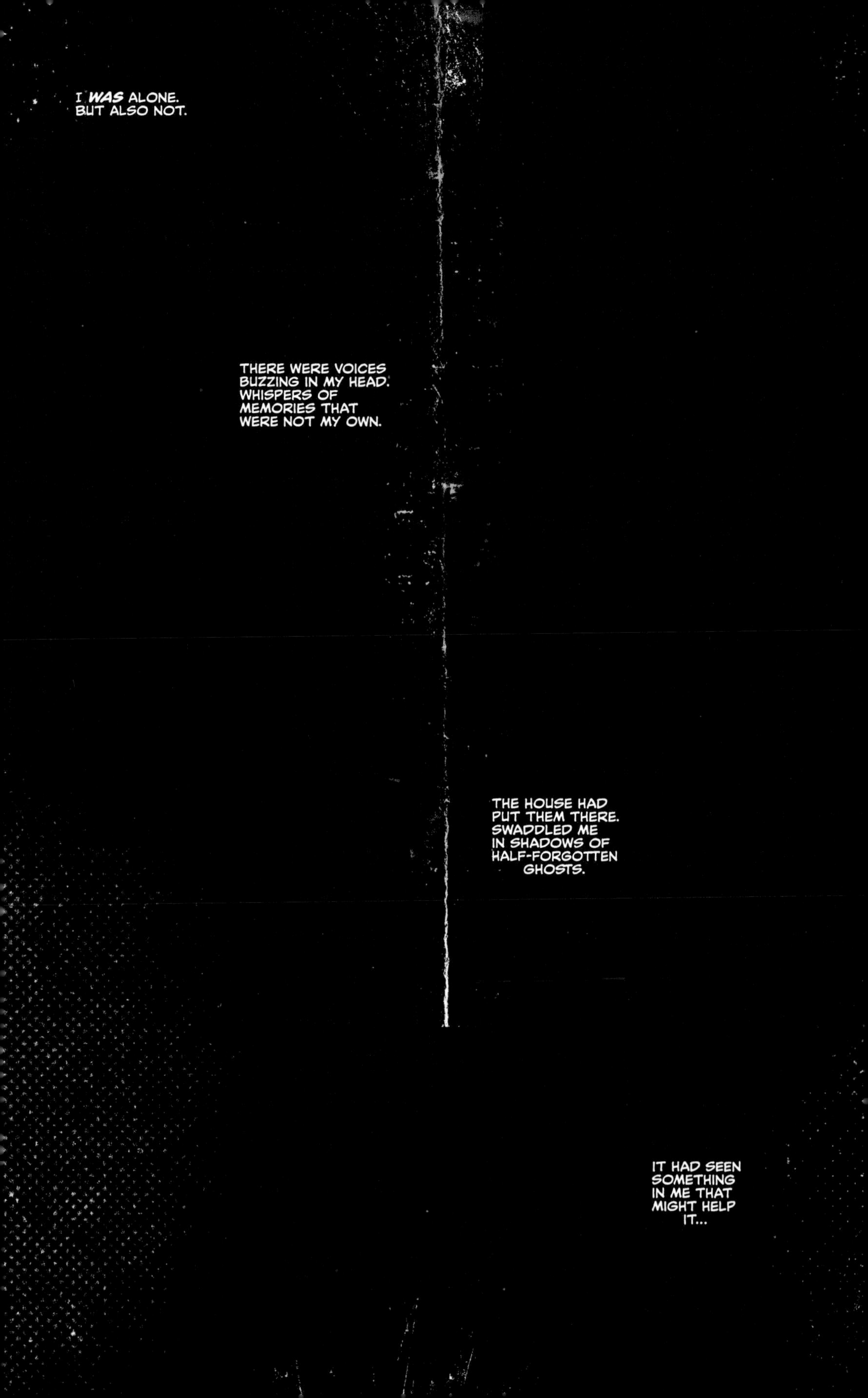
I *WAS* ALONE. BUT ALSO NOT.
THERE WERE VOICES BUZZING IN MY HEAD. WHISPERS OF MEMORIES THAT WERE NOT MY OWN.
THE HOUSE HAD PUT THEM THERE. SWADDLED ME IN SHADOWS OF HALF-FORGOTTEN GHOSTS.
IT HAD SEEN SOMETHING IN ME THAT MIGHT HELP IT...

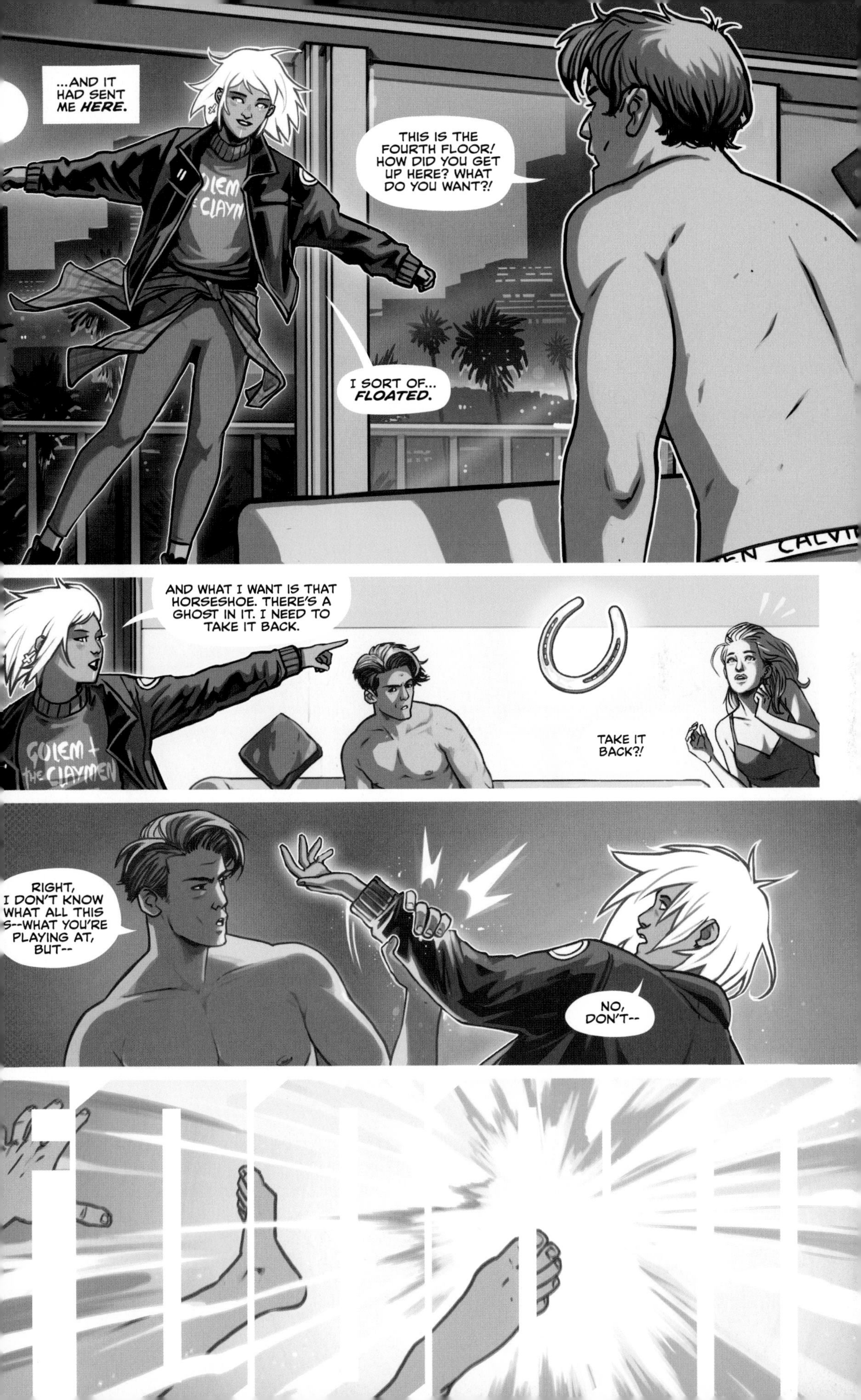
...AND IT HAD SENT ME *HERE.*
THIS IS THE FOURTH FLOOR! HOW DID YOU GET UP HERE? WHAT DO YOU WANT?!
I SORT OF... *FLOATED.*
AND WHAT I WANT IS THAT HORSESHOE. THERE'S A GHOST IN IT. I NEED TO TAKE IT BACK.
TAKE IT BACK?!
RIGHT, I DON'T KNOW WHAT ALL THIS S--WHAT YOU'RE PLAYING AT, BUT--
NO, DON'T--

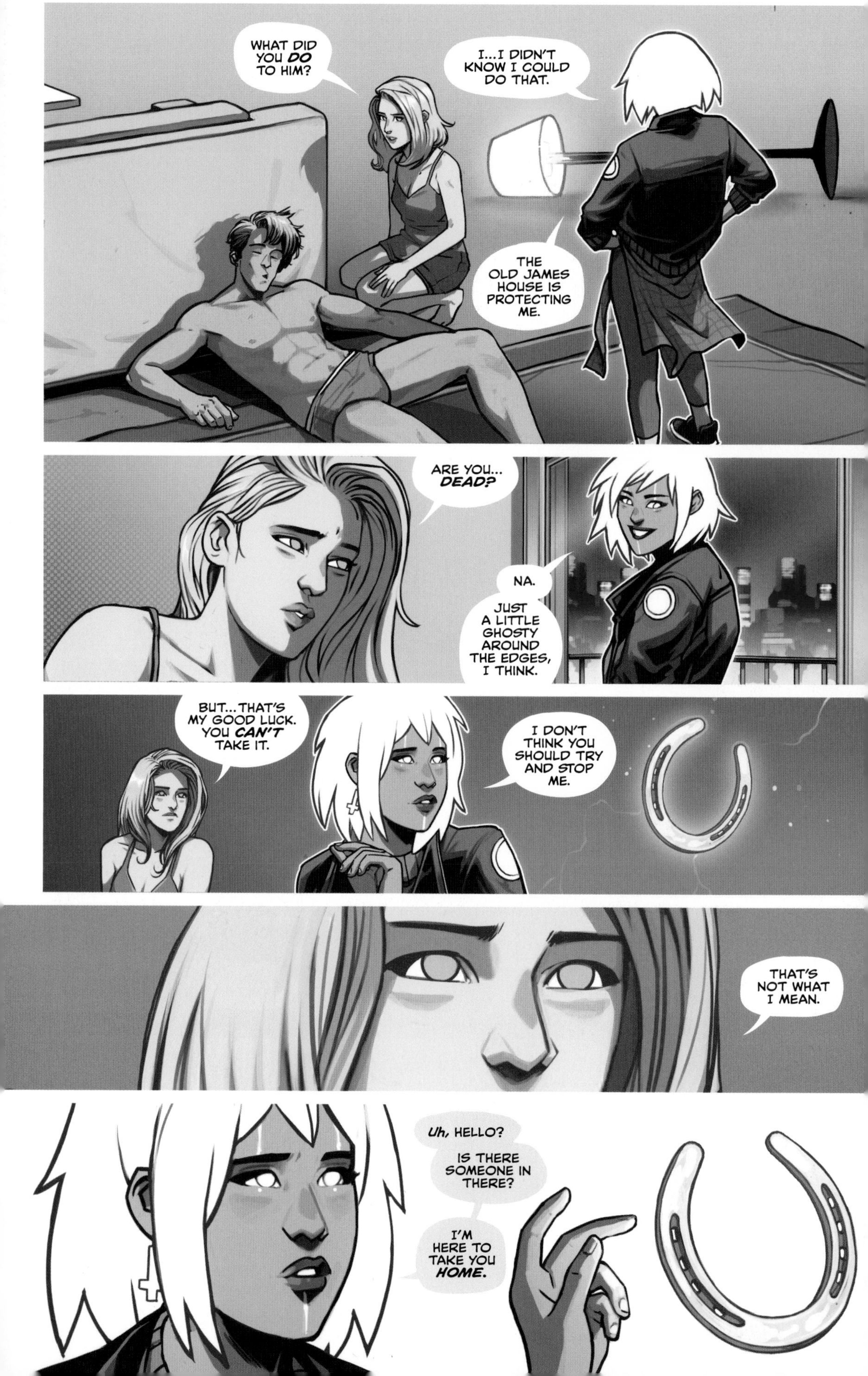
WHAT DID YOU *DO* TO HIM?
I...I DIDN'T KNOW I COULD DO THAT.
THE OLD JAMES HOUSE IS PROTECTING ME.
ARE YOU... *DEAD?*
NA.
JUST A LITTLE GHOSTY AROUND THE EDGES, I THINK.
BUT...THAT'S MY GOOD LUCK. YOU *CAN'T* TAKE IT.
I DON'T THINK YOU SHOULD TRY AND STOP ME.
THAT'S NOT WHAT I MEAN.
Uh, HELLO?
IS THERE SOMEONE IN THERE?
I'M HERE TO TAKE YOU *HOME.*

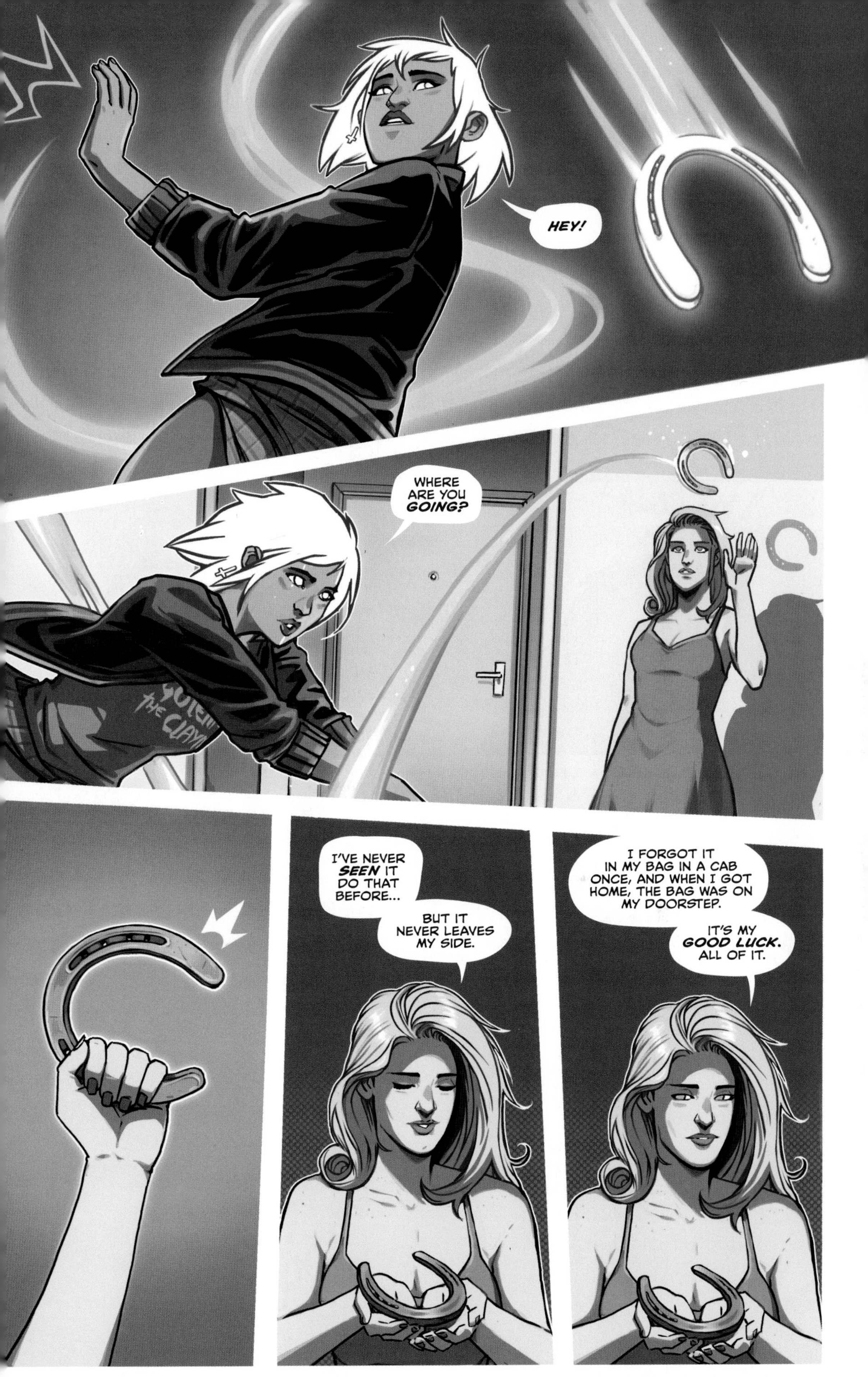
HEY!
WHERE ARE YOU GOING?
I'VE NEVER SEEN IT DO THAT BEFORE...
BUT IT NEVER LEAVES MY SIDE.
I FORGOT IT IN MY BAG IN A CAB ONCE, AND WHEN I GOT HOME, THE BAG WAS ON MY DOORSTEP.
IT'S MY GOOD LUCK. ALL OF IT.

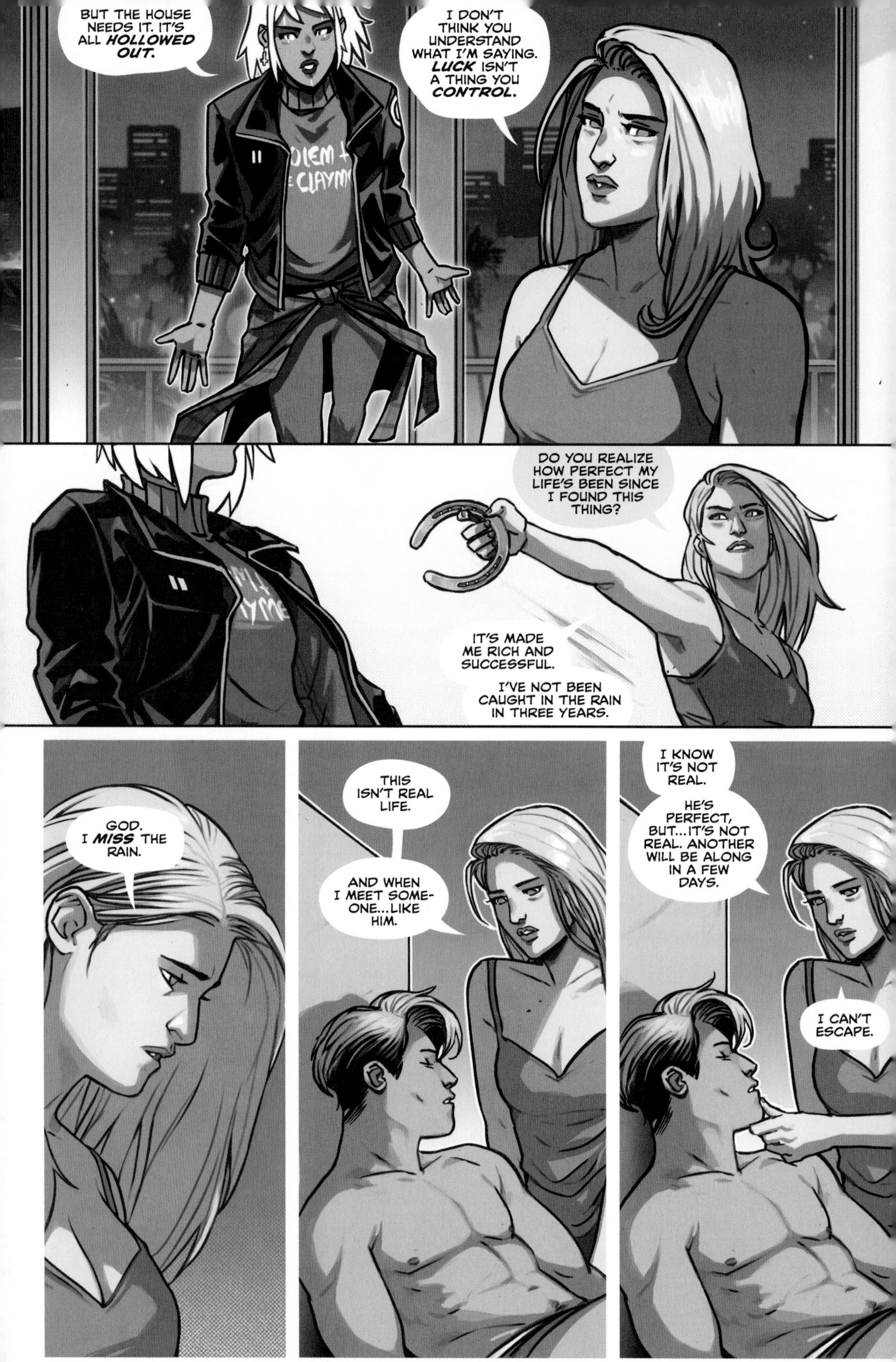
BUT THE HOUSE NEEDS IT. IT'S ALL *HOLLOWED OUT*.
I DON'T THINK YOU UNDERSTAND WHAT I'M SAYING. *LUCK* ISN'T A THING YOU *CONTROL*.
DO YOU REALIZE HOW PERFECT MY LIFE'S BEEN SINCE I FOUND THIS THING?
IT'S MADE ME RICH AND SUCCESSFUL.
I'VE NOT BEEN CAUGHT IN THE RAIN IN THREE YEARS.
GOD. I *MISS* THE RAIN.
THIS ISN'T REAL LIFE.
AND WHEN I MEET SOME-ONE...LIKE HIM.
I KNOW IT'S NOT REAL.
HE'S PERFECT, BUT...IT'S NOT REAL. ANOTHER WILL BE ALONG IN A FEW DAYS.
I CAN'T ESCAPE.

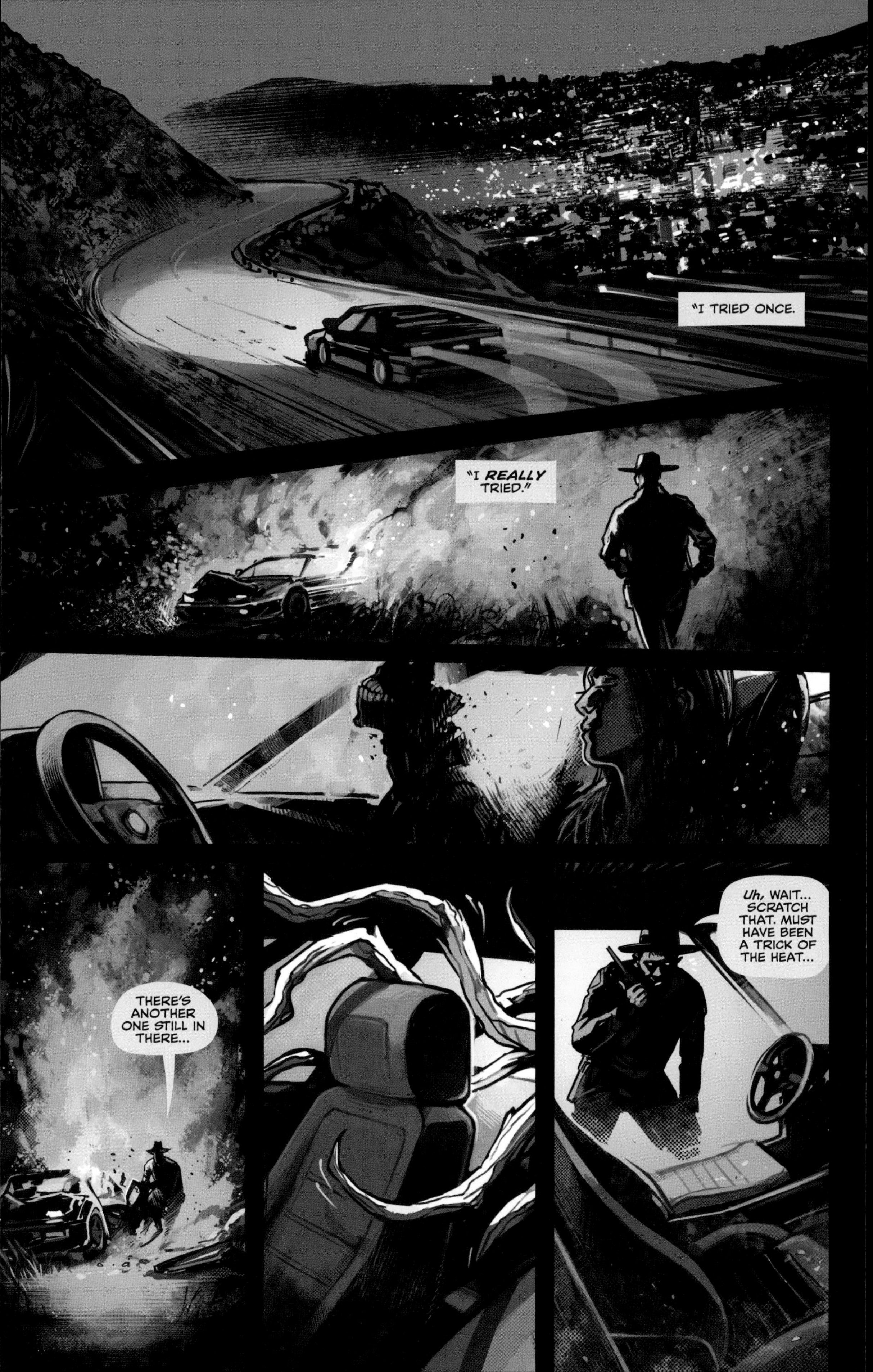
"I TRIED ONCE.
"I *REALLY* TRIED."
THERE'S ANOTHER ONE STILL IN THERE...
Uh, WAIT... SCRATCH THAT. MUST HAVE BEEN A TRICK OF THE HEAT...

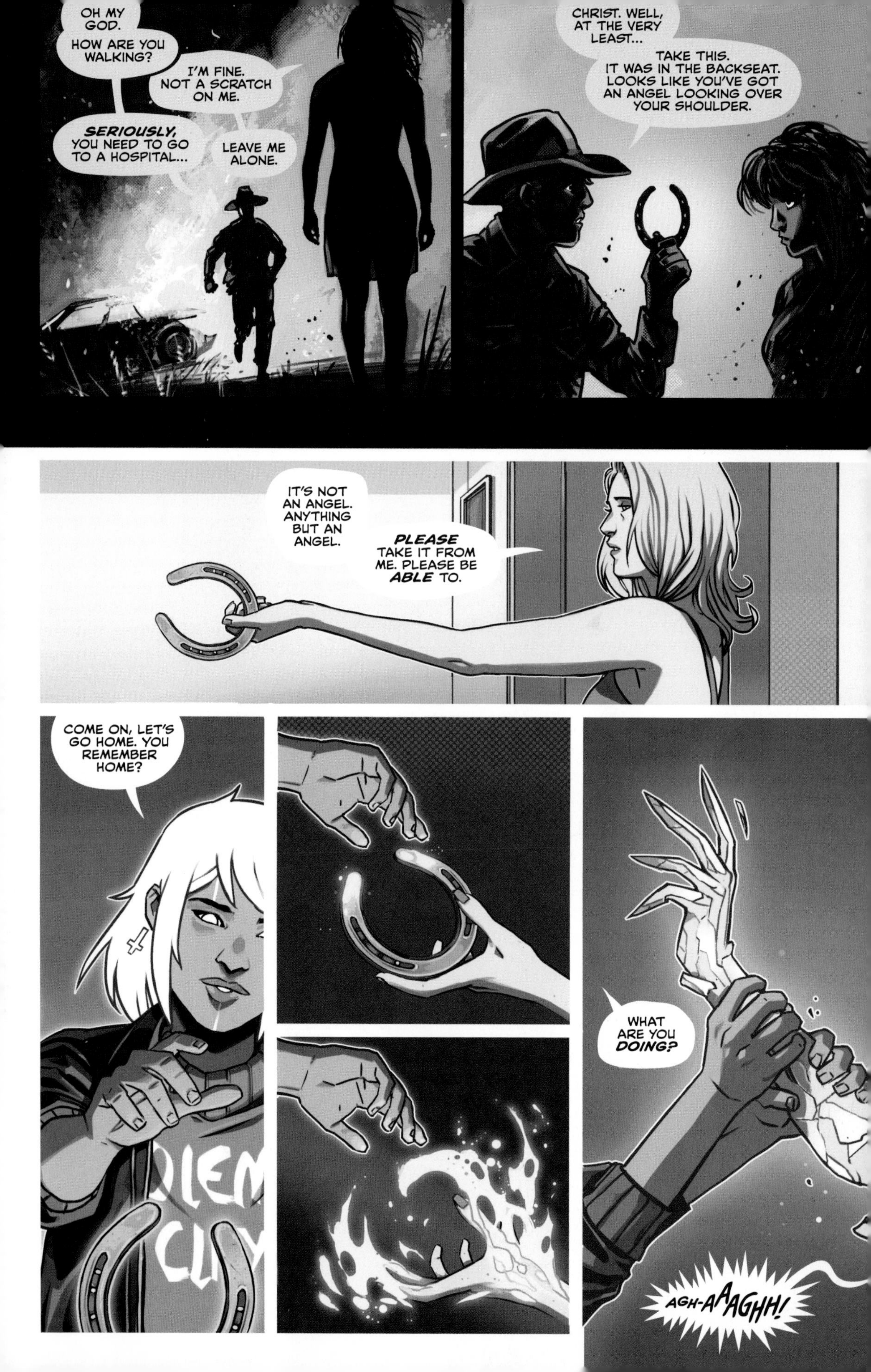
OH MY GOD.
HOW ARE YOU WALKING?
I'M FINE. NOT A SCRATCH ON ME.
SERIOUSLY, YOU NEED TO GO TO A HOSPITAL...
LEAVE ME ALONE.
CHRIST. WELL, AT THE VERY LEAST...
TAKE THIS. IT WAS IN THE BACKSEAT. LOOKS LIKE YOU'VE GOT AN ANGEL LOOKING OVER YOUR SHOULDER.
IT'S NOT AN ANGEL. ANYTHING BUT AN ANGEL.
PLEASE TAKE IT FROM ME. PLEASE BE ABLE TO.
COME ON, LET'S GO HOME. YOU REMEMBER HOME?
WHAT ARE YOU DOING?
AGH-AAAGHH!

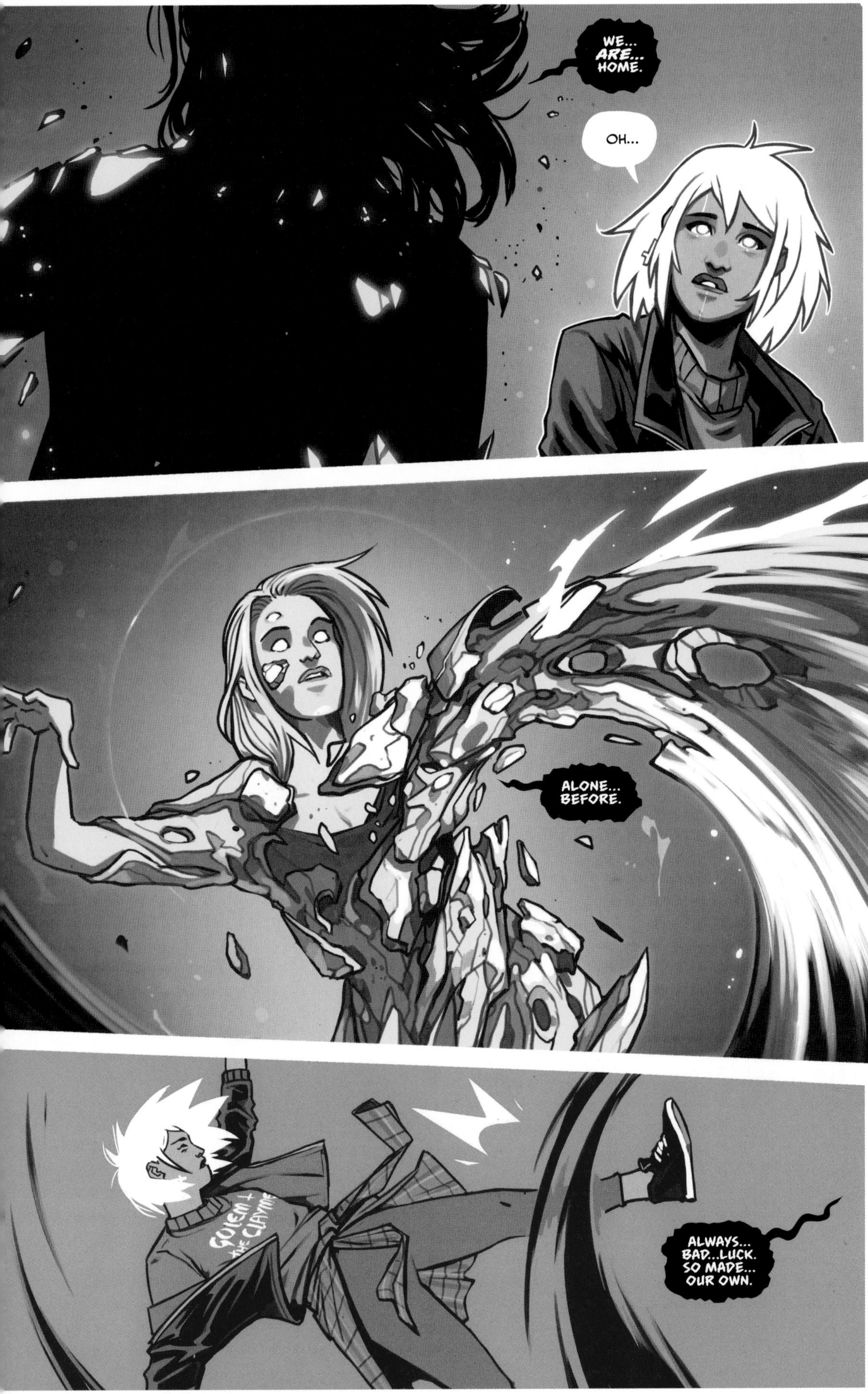
WE... ARE... HOME.
OH...
ALONE... BEFORE.
ALWAYS... BAD...LUCK. SO MADE... OUR OWN.

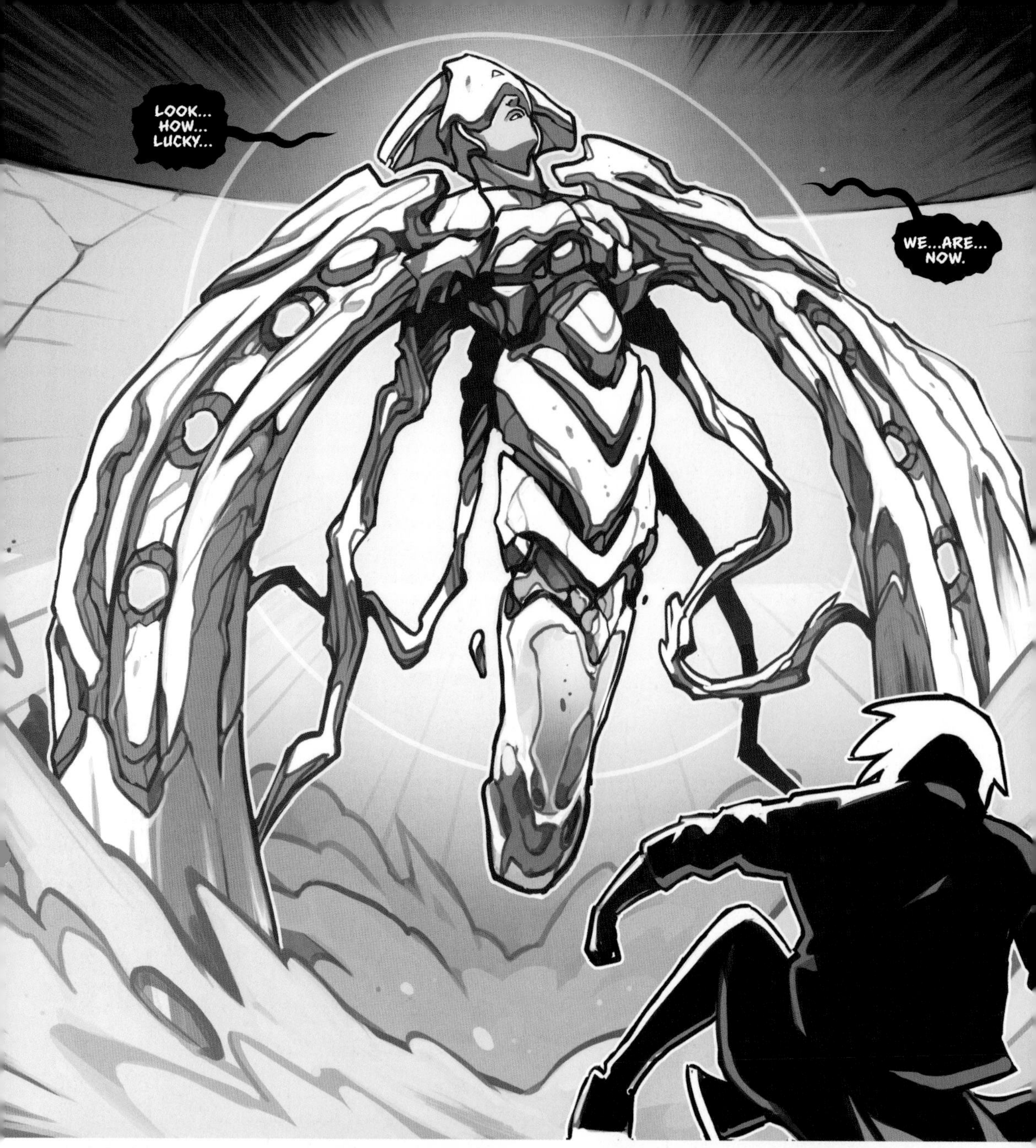
LOOK... HOW... LUCKY...
WE...ARE... NOW.

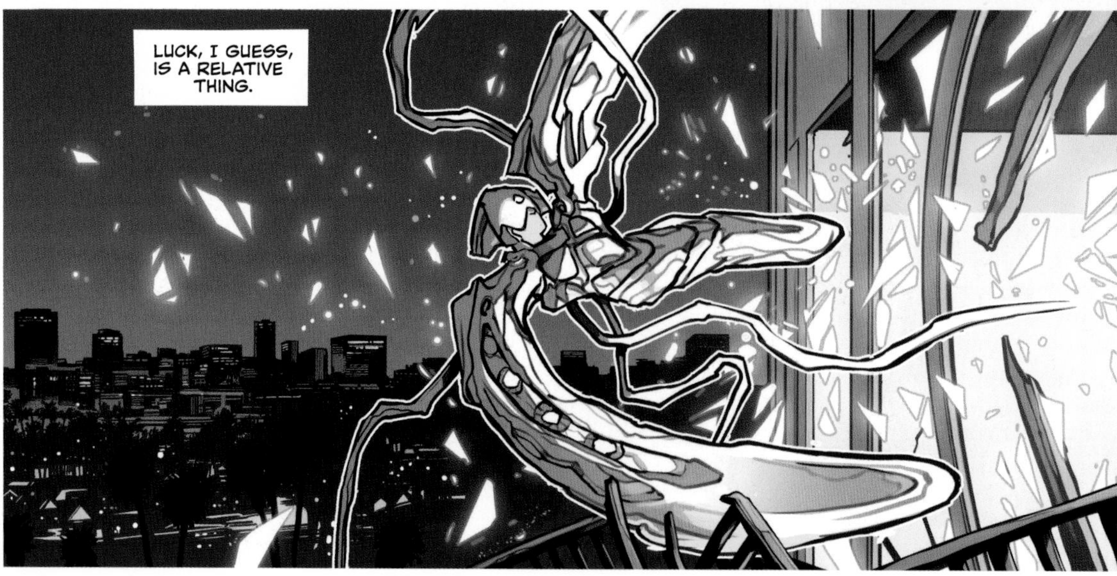
LUCK, I GUESS, IS A RELATIVE THING.

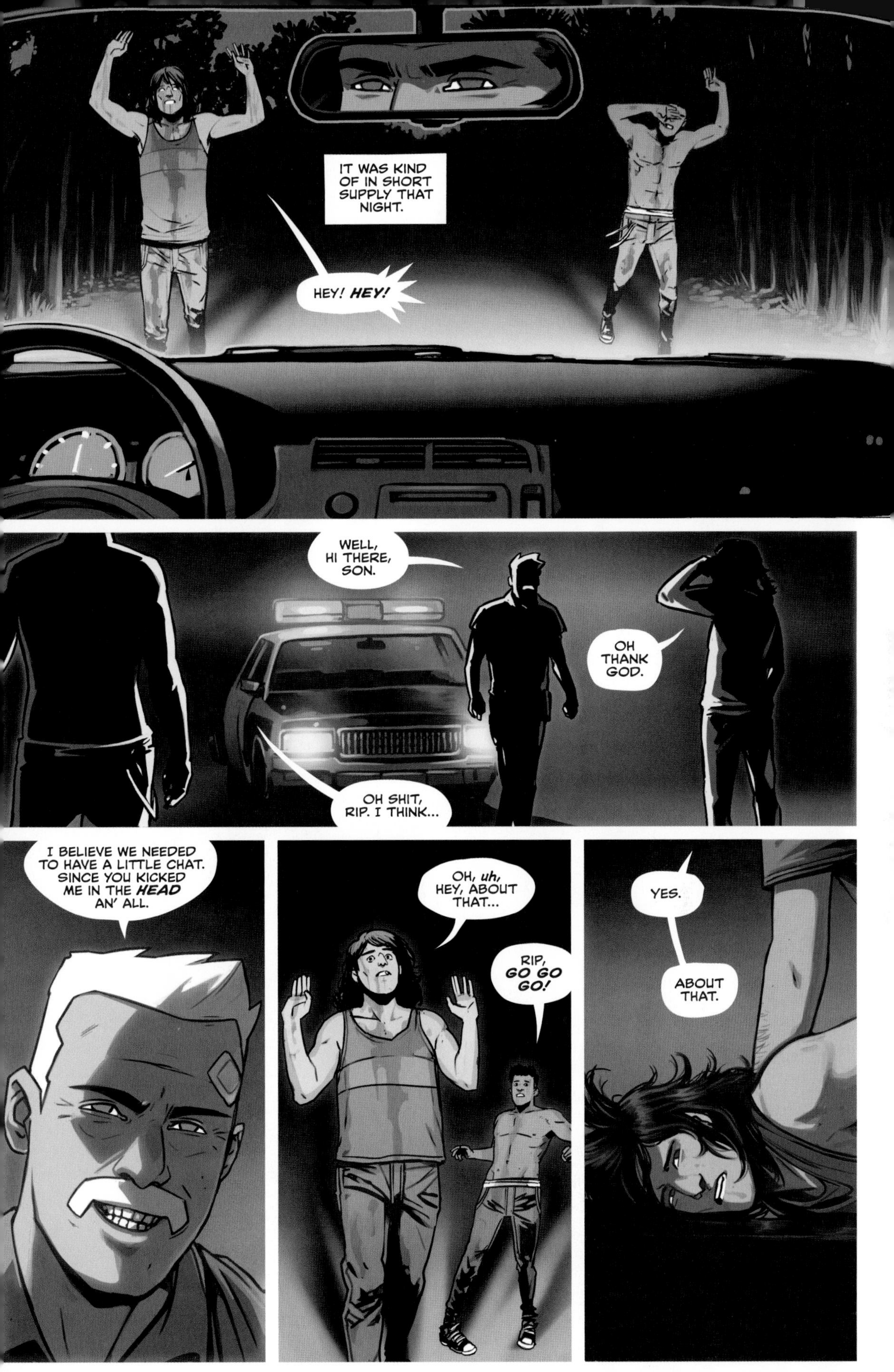
IT WAS KIND OF IN SHORT SUPPLY THAT NIGHT.
HEY! **HEY!**
WELL, HI THERE, SON.
OH THANK GOD.
OH SHIT, RIP. I THINK...
I BELIEVE WE NEEDED TO HAVE A LITTLE CHAT. SINCE YOU KICKED ME IN THE *HEAD* AN' ALL.
OH, *uh*, HEY, ABOUT THAT...
RIP, **GO GO GO!**
YES.
ABOUT THAT.

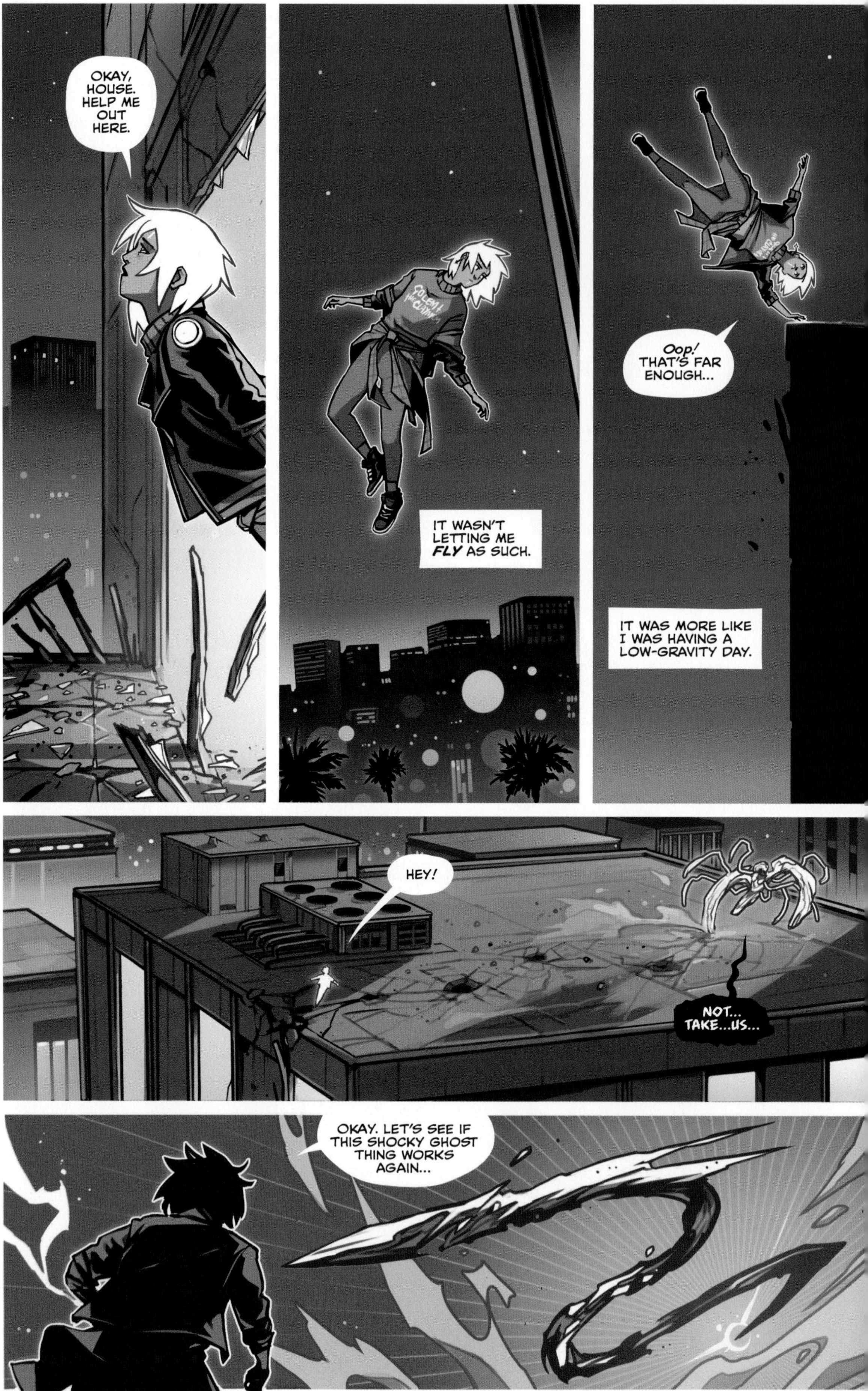
OKAY, HOUSE. HELP ME OUT HERE.
IT WASN'T LETTING ME *FLY* AS SUCH.
Oop! THAT'S FAR ENOUGH...
IT WAS MORE LIKE I WAS HAVING A LOW-GRAVITY DAY.
HEY!
NOT... TAKE...US...
OKAY. LET'S SEE IF THIS SHOCKY GHOST THING WORKS AGAIN...

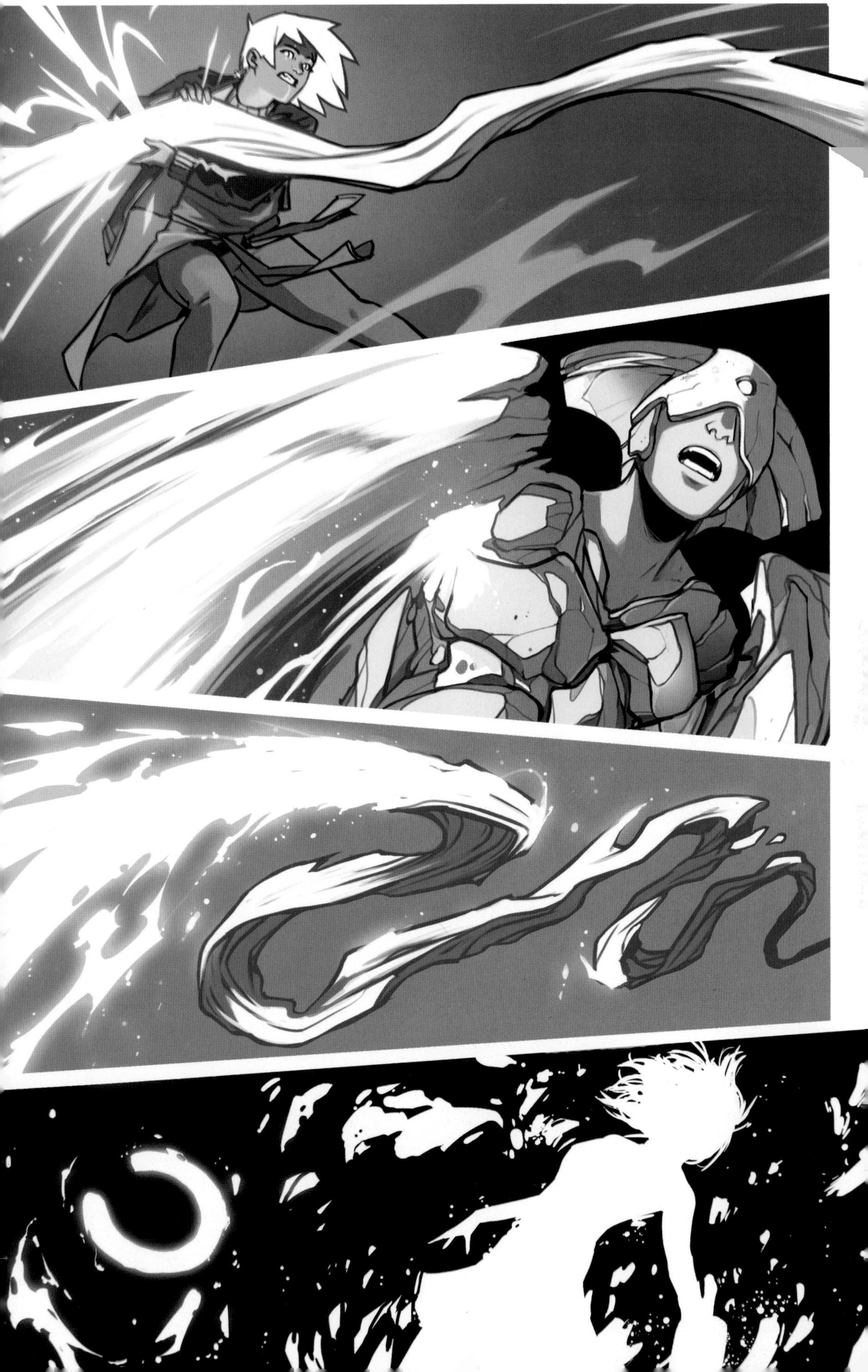

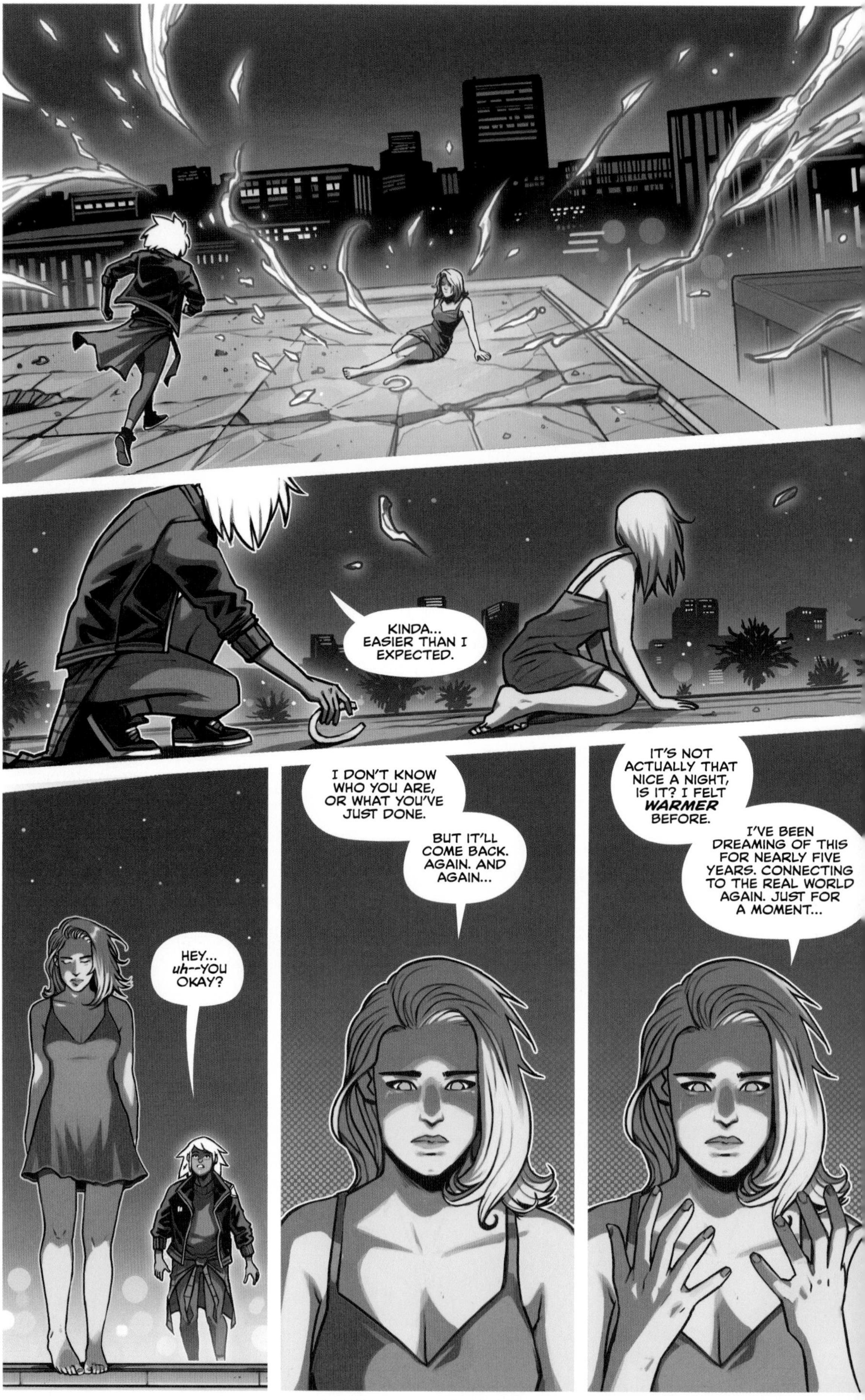
KINDA... EASIER THAN I EXPECTED.
HEY... uh--YOU OKAY?
I DON'T KNOW WHO YOU ARE, OR WHAT YOU'VE JUST DONE.
BUT IT'LL COME BACK. AGAIN. AND AGAIN...
IT'S NOT ACTUALLY THAT NICE A NIGHT, IS IT? I FELT WARMER BEFORE.
I'VE BEEN DREAMING OF THIS FOR NEARLY FIVE YEARS. CONNECTING TO THE REAL WORLD AGAIN. JUST FOR A MOMENT...

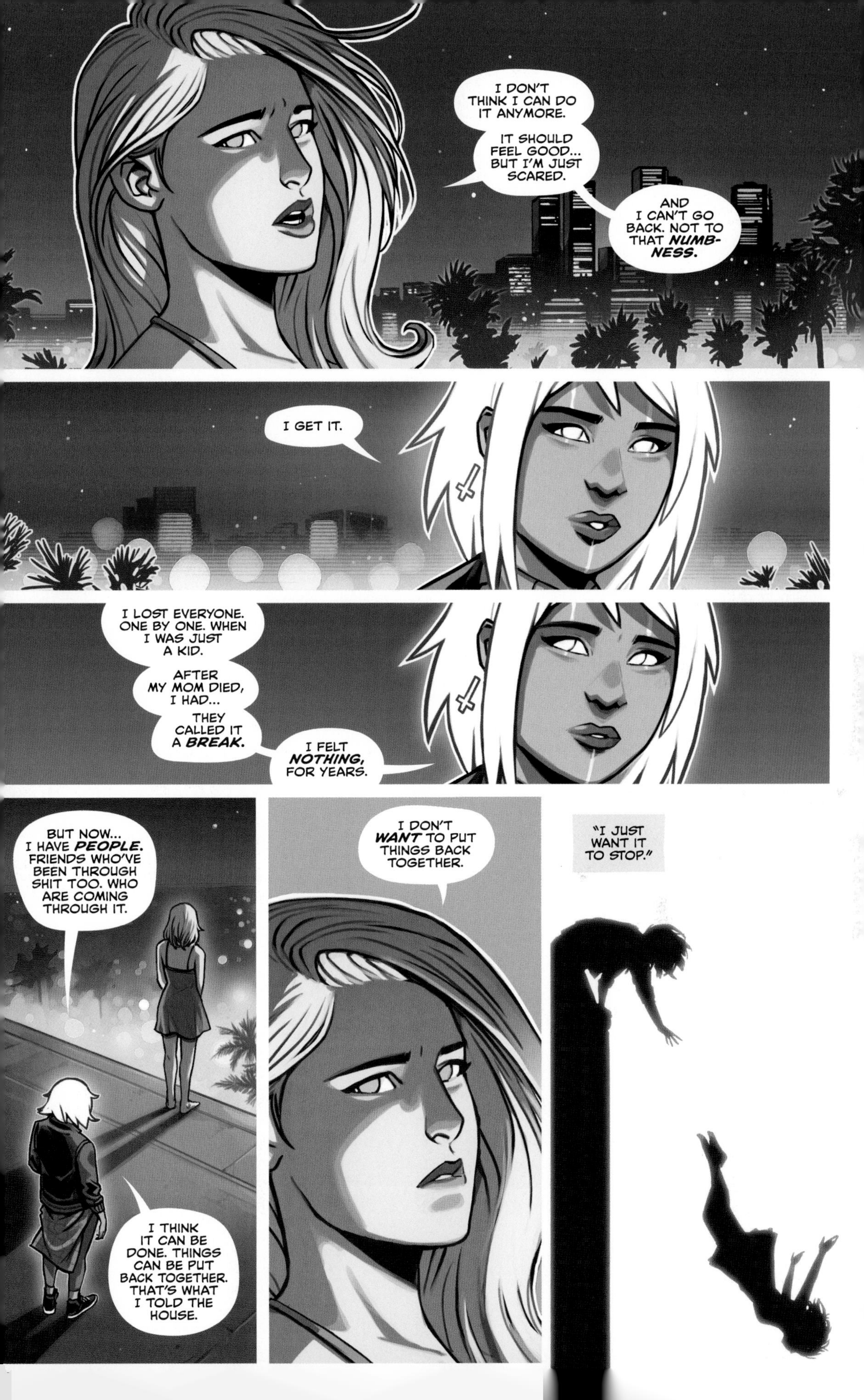
I DON'T THINK I CAN DO IT ANYMORE.
IT SHOULD FEEL GOOD... BUT I'M JUST SCARED.
AND I CAN'T GO BACK. NOT TO THAT ***NUMB-NESS.***
I GET IT.
I LOST EVERYONE. ONE BY ONE. WHEN I WAS JUST A KID.
AFTER MY MOM DIED, I HAD...
THEY CALLED IT A ***BREAK.***
I FELT ***NOTHING,*** FOR YEARS.
BUT NOW... I HAVE ***PEOPLE.*** FRIENDS WHO'VE BEEN THROUGH SHIT TOO. WHO ARE COMING THROUGH IT.
I THINK IT CAN BE DONE. THINGS CAN BE PUT BACK TOGETHER. THAT'S WHAT I TOLD THE HOUSE.
I DON'T ***WANT*** TO PUT THINGS BACK TOGETHER.
"I JUST WANT IT TO STOP."

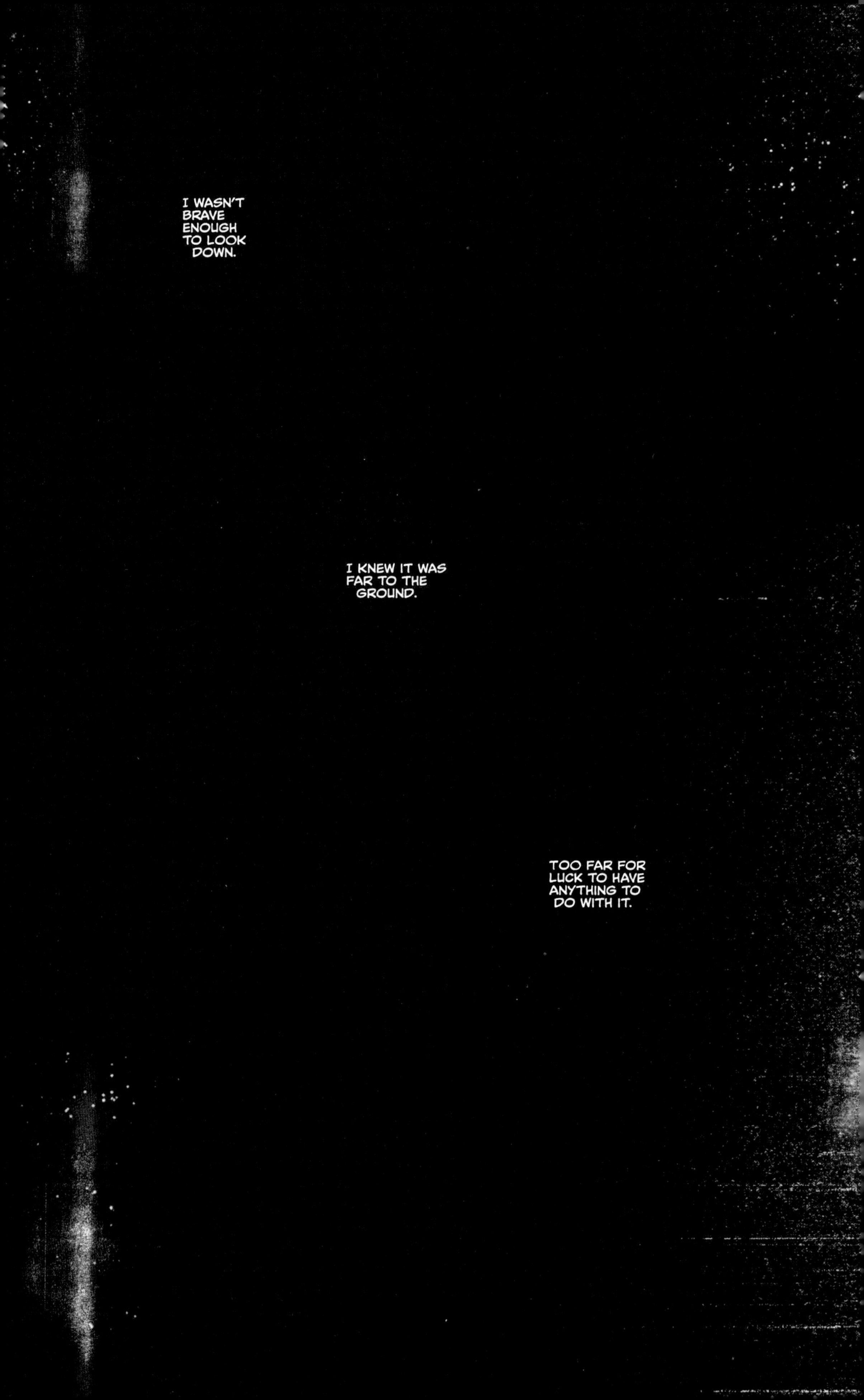
I WASN'T BRAVE ENOUGH TO LOOK DOWN.
I KNEW IT WAS FAR TO THE GROUND.
TOO FAR FOR LUCK TO HAVE ANYTHING TO DO WITH IT.

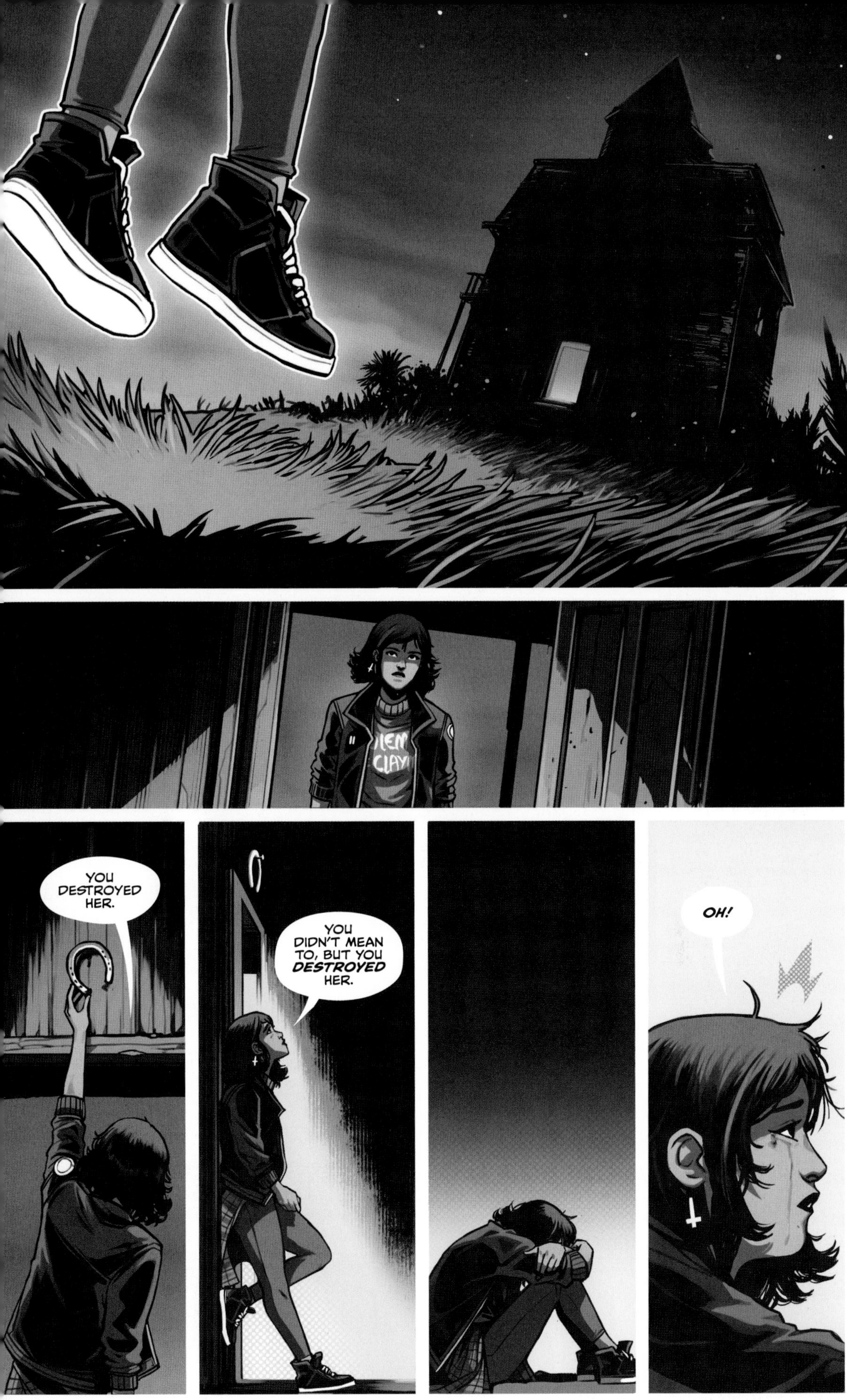
YOU DESTROYED HER.
YOU DIDN'T MEAN TO, BUT YOU *DESTROYED* HER.
OH!

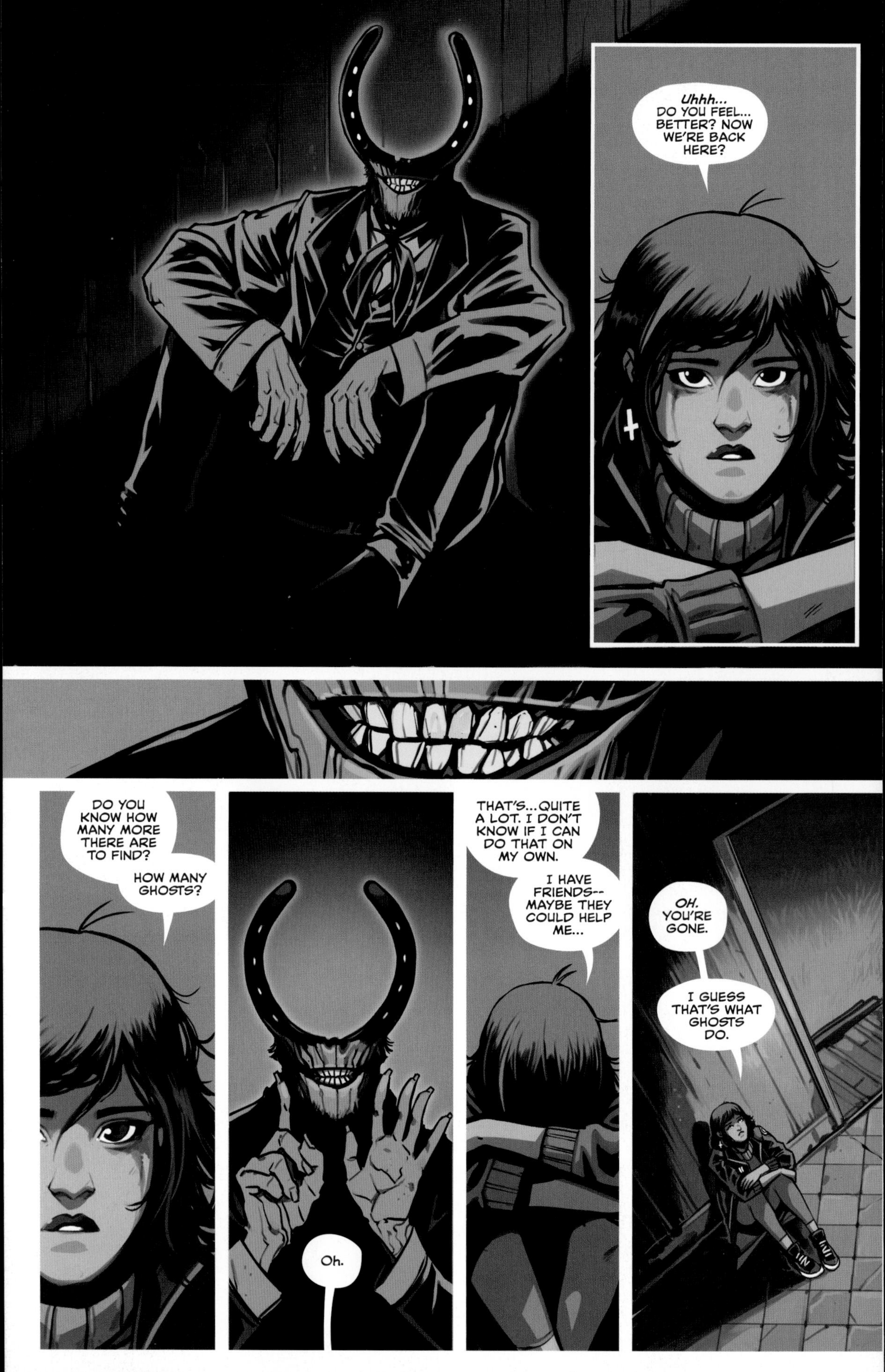
Uhhh... DO YOU FEEL... BETTER? NOW WE'RE BACK HERE?
DO YOU KNOW HOW MANY MORE THERE ARE TO FIND?
HOW MANY GHOSTS?
Oh.
THAT'S...QUITE A LOT. I DON'T KNOW IF I CAN DO THAT ON MY OWN.
I HAVE FRIENDS-- MAYBE THEY COULD HELP ME...
OH. YOU'RE GONE.
I GUESS THAT'S WHAT GHOSTS DO.

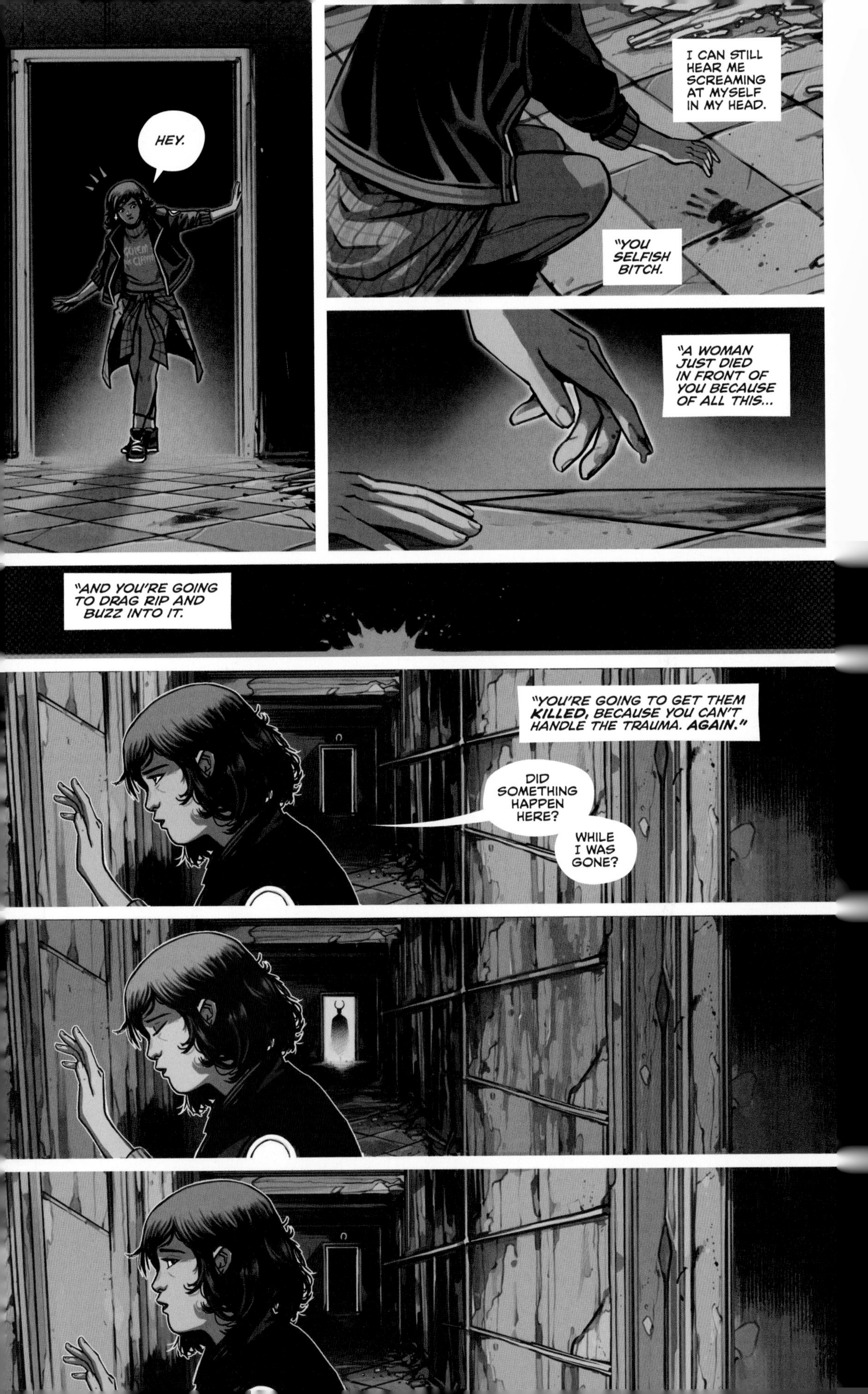
HEY.
I CAN STILL HEAR ME SCREAMING AT MYSELF IN MY HEAD.
"YOU SELFISH BITCH.
"A WOMAN JUST DIED IN FRONT OF YOU BECAUSE OF ALL THIS...
"AND YOU'RE GOING TO DRAG RIP AND BUZZ INTO IT.
"YOU'RE GOING TO GET THEM **KILLED**, BECAUSE YOU CAN'T HANDLE THE TRAUMA. **AGAIN.**"
DID SOMETHING HAPPEN HERE?
WHILE I WAS GONE?

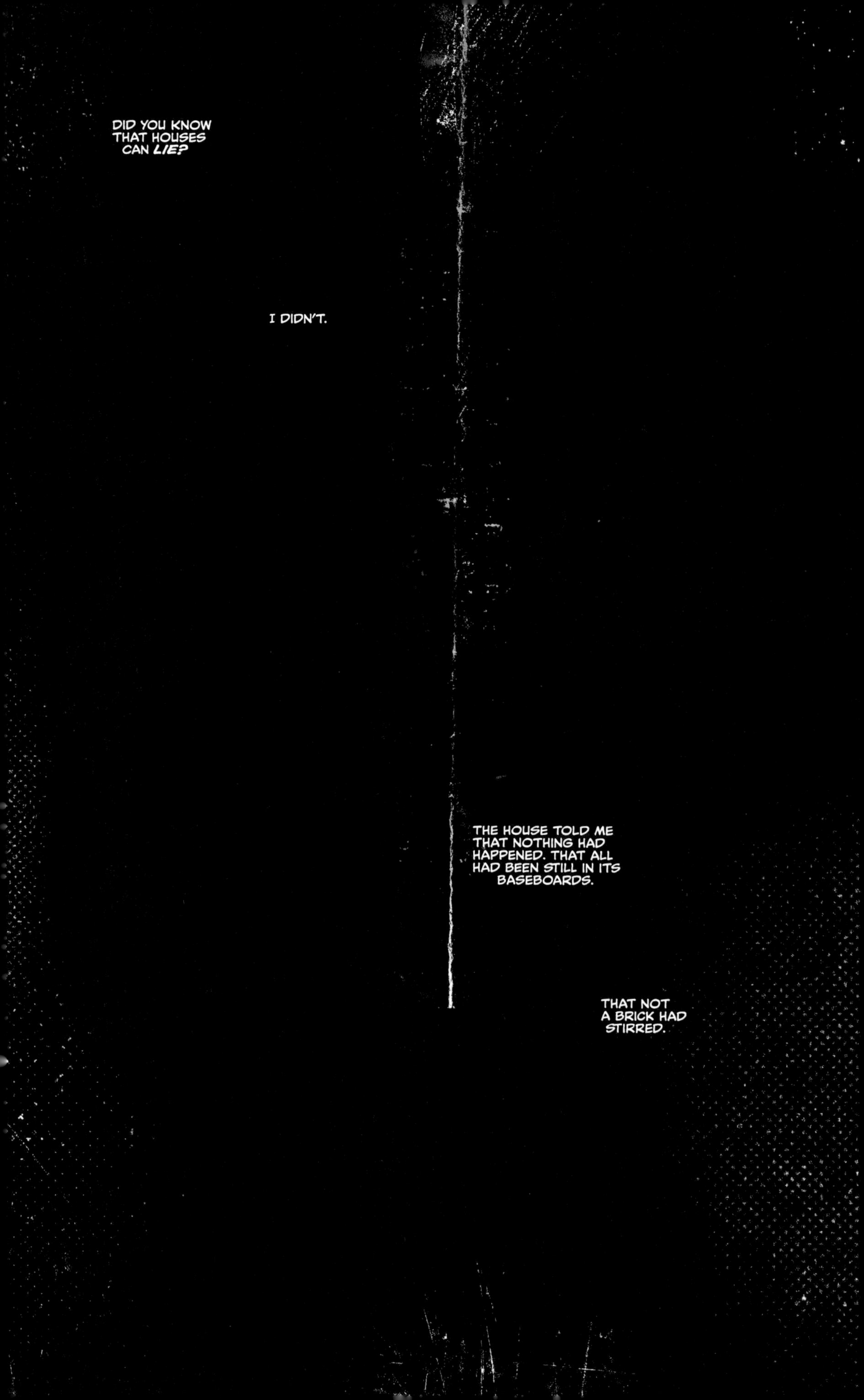
DID YOU KNOW THAT HOUSES CAN *LIE?*
I DIDN'T.
THE HOUSE TOLD ME THAT NOTHING HAD HAPPENED. THAT ALL HAD BEEN STILL IN ITS BASEBOARDS.
THAT NOT A BRICK HAD STIRRED.

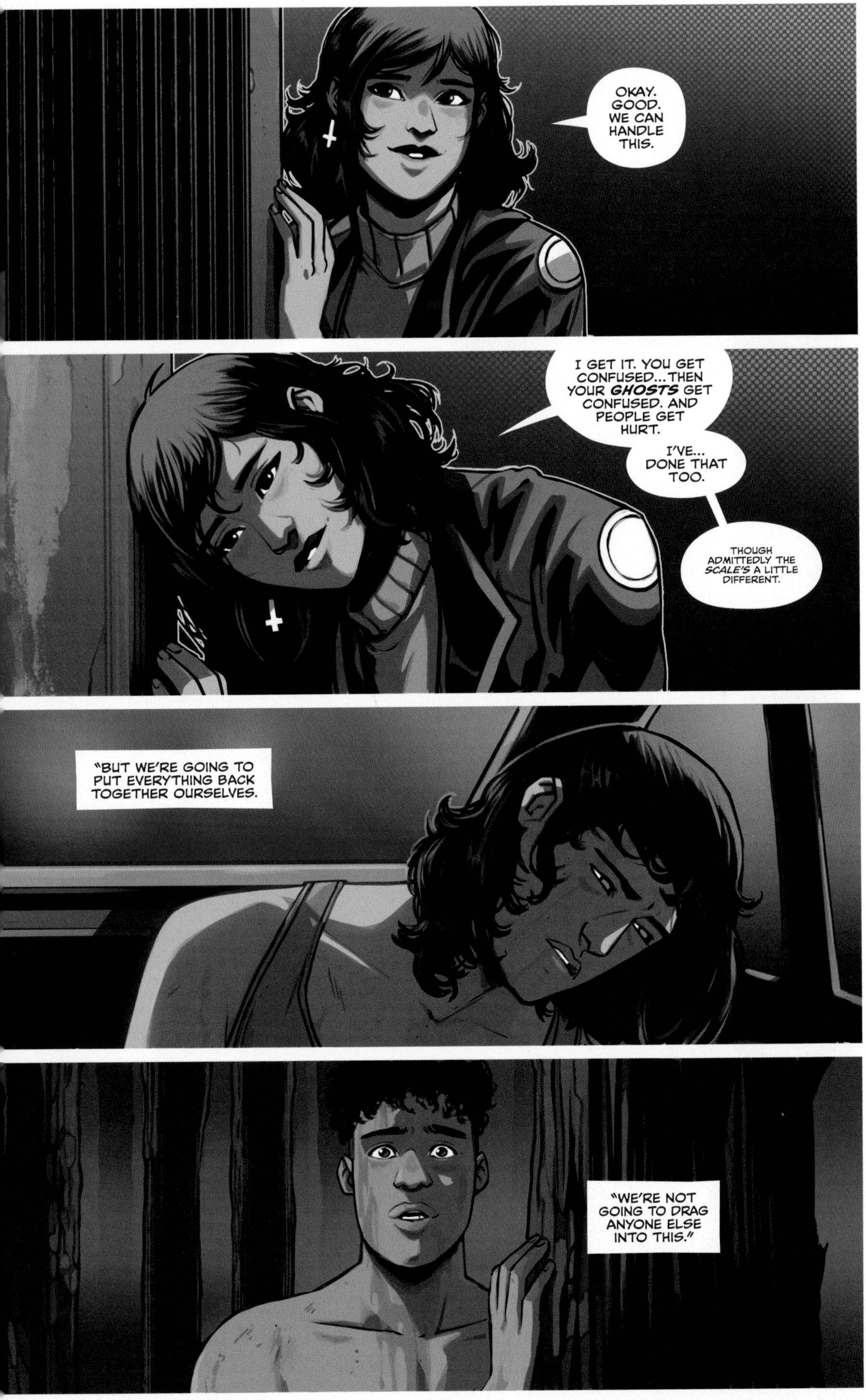
OKAY. GOOD. WE CAN HANDLE THIS.
I GET IT. YOU GET CONFUSED...THEN YOUR GHOSTS GET CONFUSED. AND PEOPLE GET HURT.
I'VE... DONE THAT TOO.
THOUGH ADMITTEDLY THE SCALE'S A LITTLE DIFFERENT.
"BUT WE'RE GOING TO PUT EVERYTHING BACK TOGETHER OURSELVES.
"WE'RE NOT GOING TO DRAG ANYONE ELSE INTO THIS."

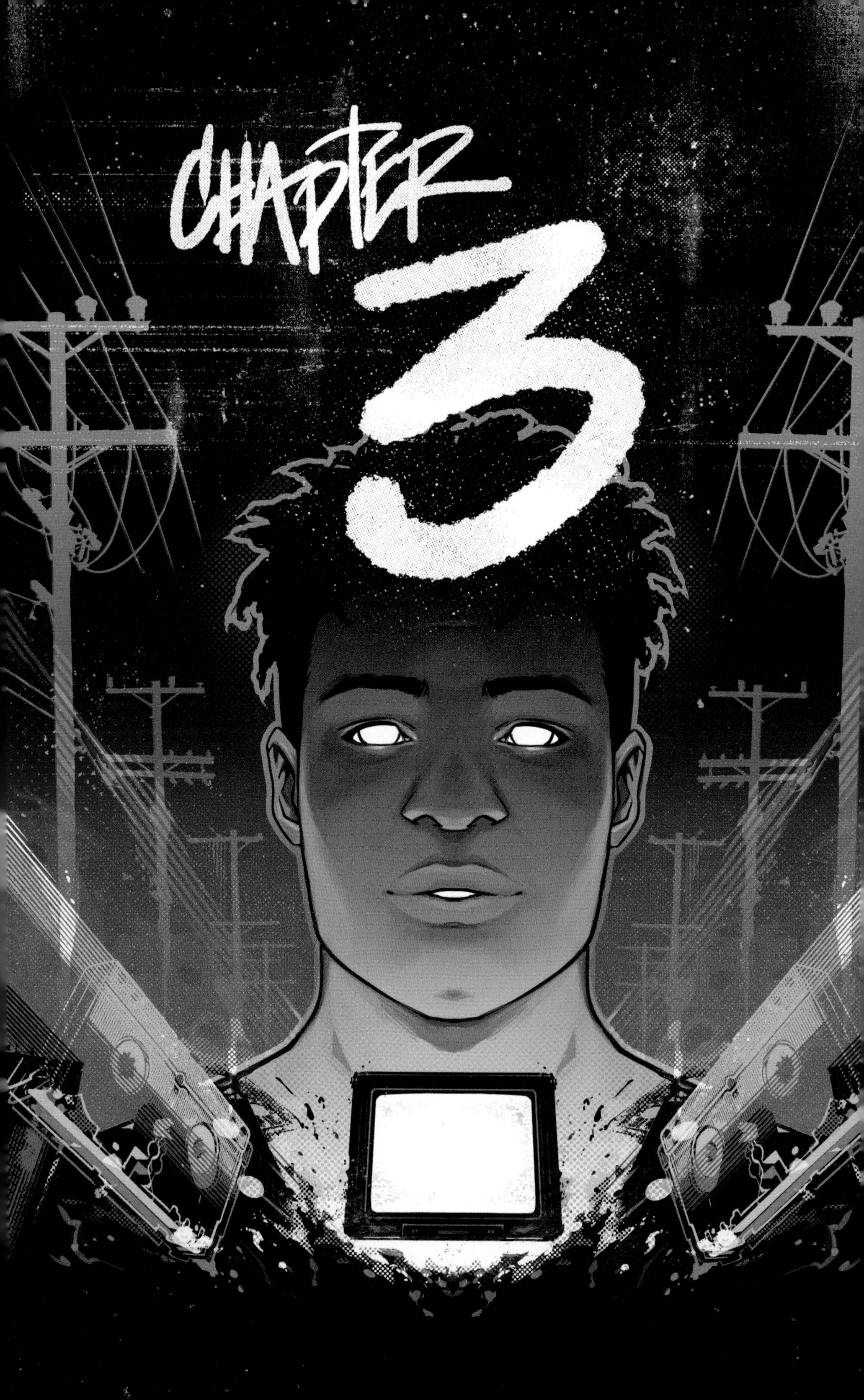
CHAPTER
3

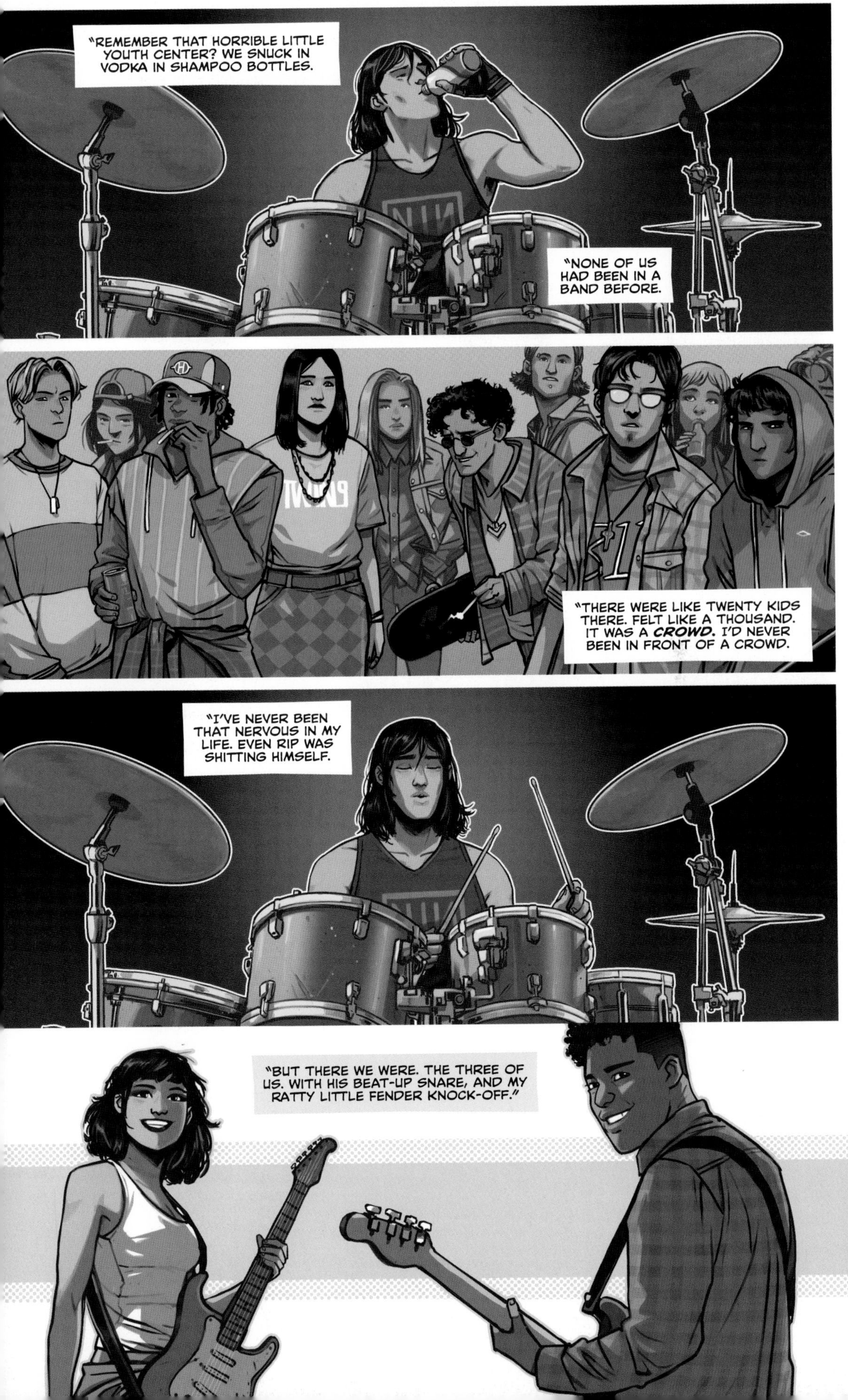
"REMEMBER THAT HORRIBLE LITTLE YOUTH CENTER? WE SNUCK IN VODKA IN SHAMPOO BOTTLES.
"NONE OF US HAD BEEN IN A BAND BEFORE.
"THERE WERE LIKE TWENTY KIDS THERE. FELT LIKE A THOUSAND. IT WAS A *CROWD.* I'D NEVER BEEN IN FRONT OF A CROWD.
"I'VE NEVER BEEN THAT NERVOUS IN MY LIFE. EVEN RIP WAS SHITTING HIMSELF.
"BUT THERE WE WERE. THE THREE OF US. WITH HIS BEAT-UP SNARE, AND MY RATTY LITTLE FENDER KNOCK-OFF."

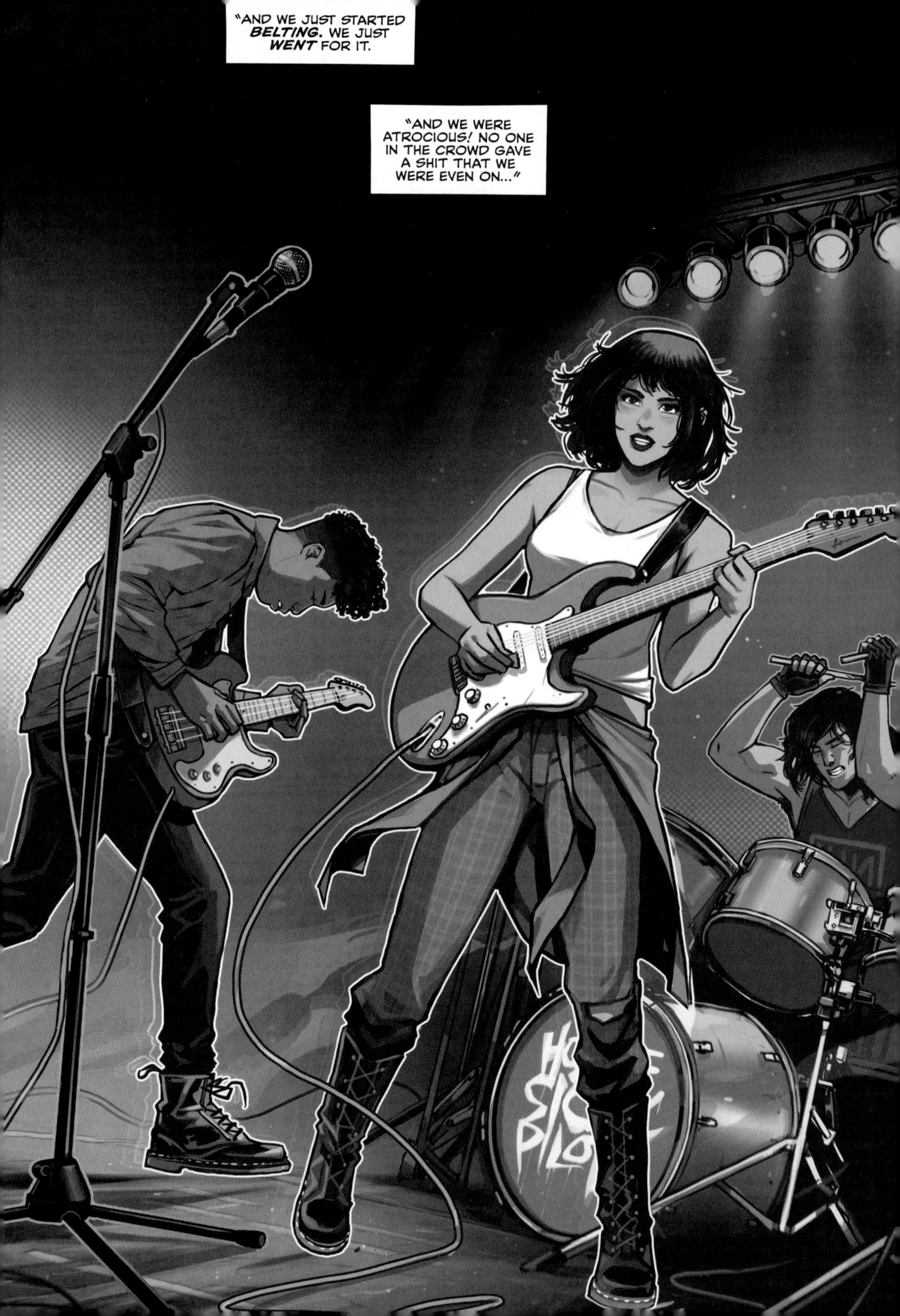
"AND WE JUST STARTED BELTING. WE JUST WENT FOR IT.
"AND WE WERE ATROCIOUS! NO ONE IN THE CROWD GAVE A SHIT THAT WE WERE EVEN ON..."

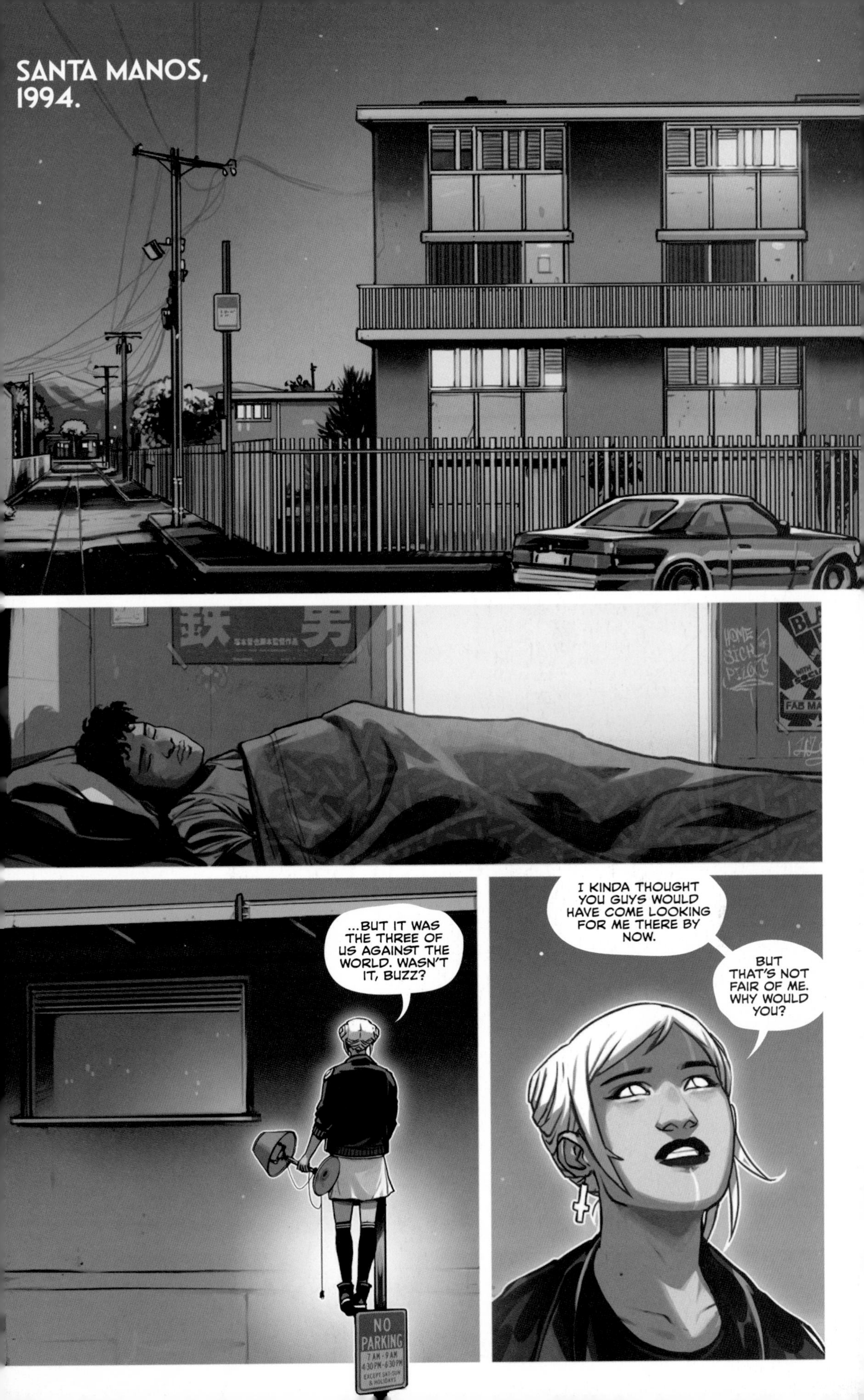
SANTA MANOS, 1994.
...BUT IT WAS THE THREE OF US AGAINST THE WORLD. WASN'T IT, BUZZ?
NO PARKING 7 AM - 9 AM 4:30 PM - 6:30 PM EXCEPT SAT-SUN & HOLIDAYS
I KINDA THOUGHT YOU GUYS WOULD HAVE COME LOOKING FOR ME THERE BY NOW.
BUT THAT'S NOT FAIR OF ME. WHY WOULD YOU?

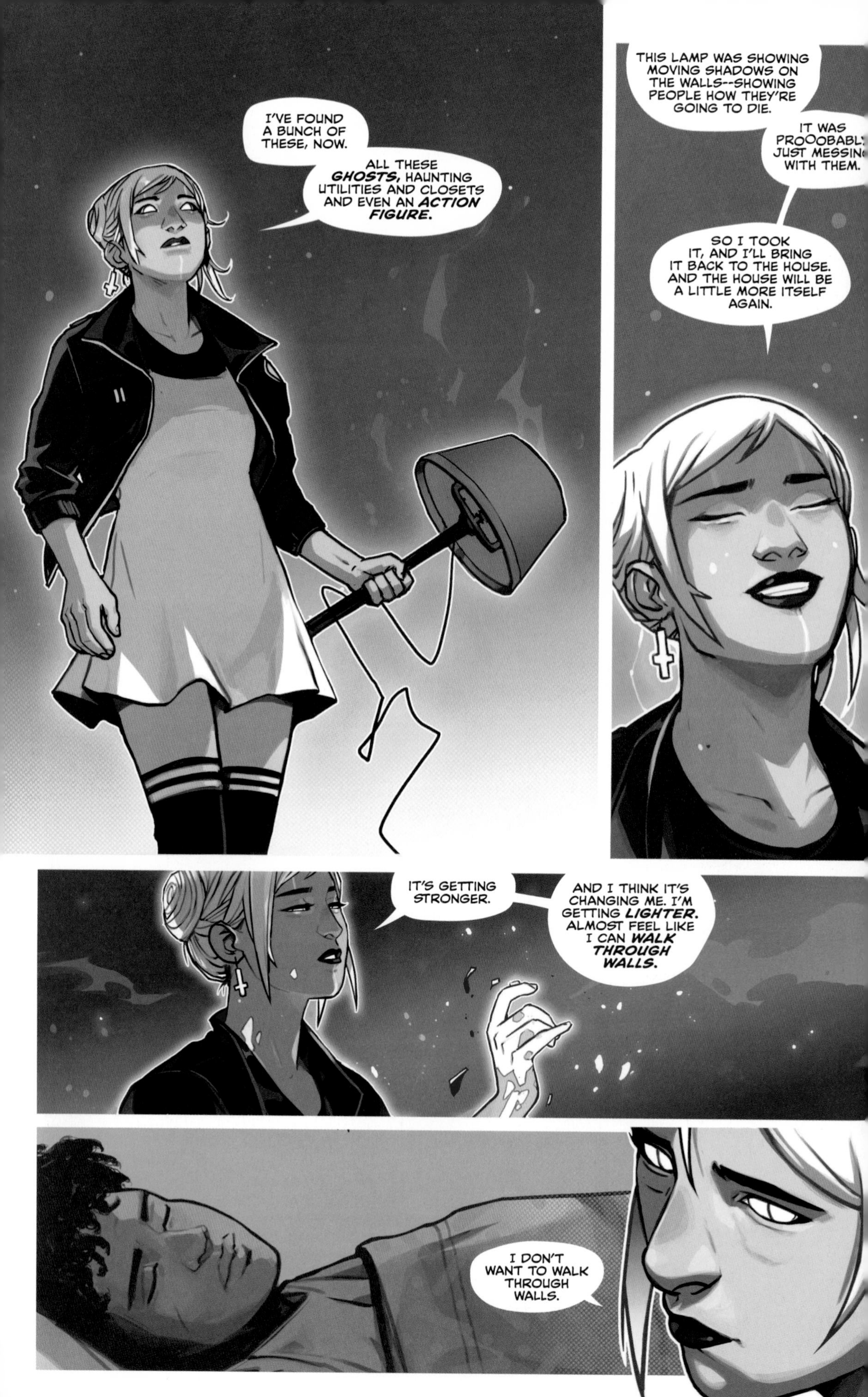
I'VE FOUND A BUNCH OF THESE, NOW.
ALL THESE GHOSTS, HAUNTING UTILITIES AND CLOSETS AND EVEN AN ACTION FIGURE.
THIS LAMP WAS SHOWING MOVING SHADOWS ON THE WALLS--SHOWING PEOPLE HOW THEY'RE GOING TO DIE.
IT WAS PROOOBABL JUST MESSIN WITH THEM.
SO I TOOK IT, AND I'LL BRING IT BACK TO THE HOUSE. AND THE HOUSE WILL BE A LITTLE MORE ITSELF AGAIN.
IT'S GETTING STRONGER.
AND I THINK IT'S CHANGING ME. I'M GETTING LIGHTER. ALMOST FEEL LIKE I CAN WALK THROUGH WALLS.
I DON'T WANT TO WALK THROUGH WALLS.

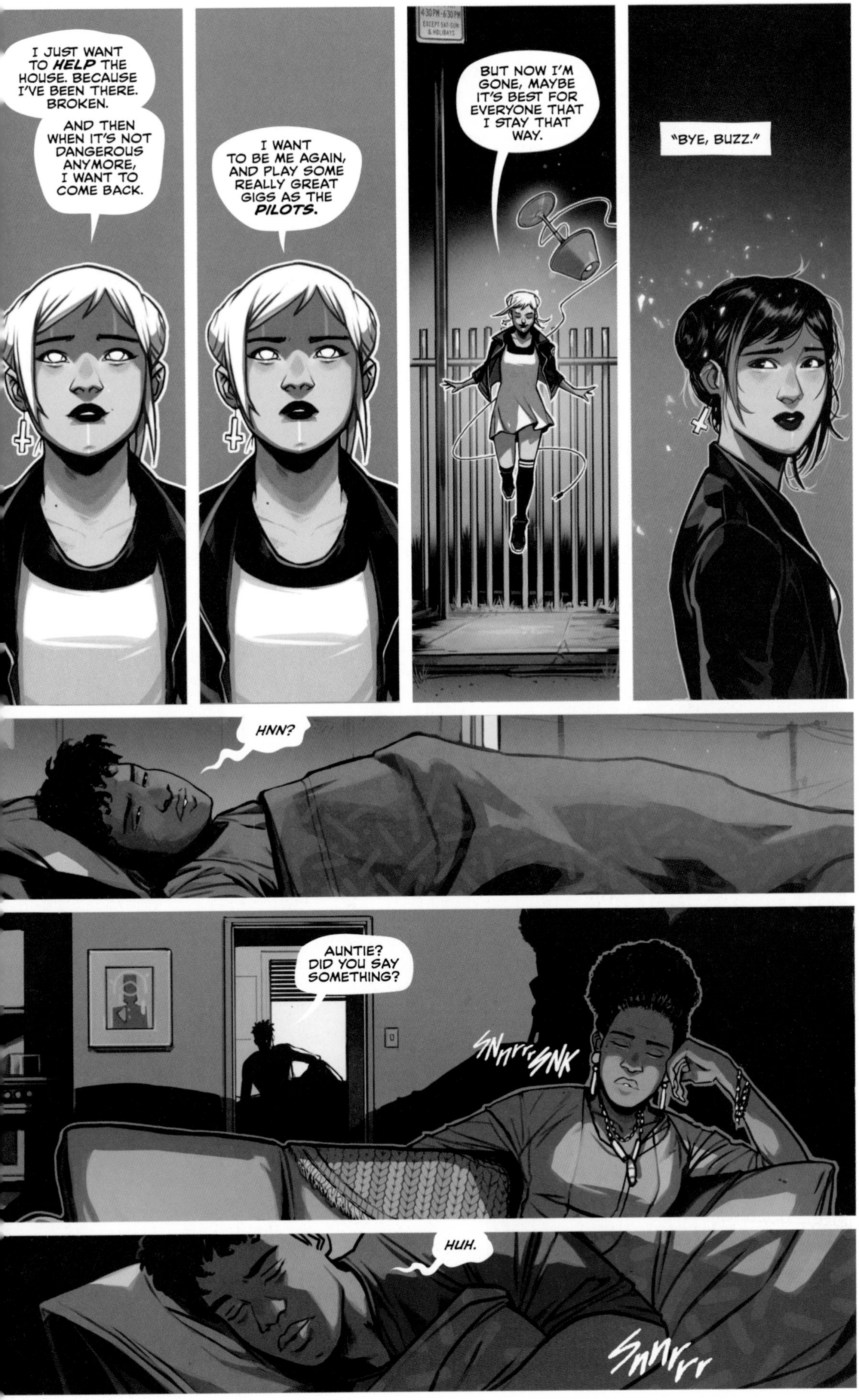
I JUST WANT TO ***HELP*** THE HOUSE. BECAUSE I'VE BEEN THERE. BROKEN.
AND THEN WHEN IT'S NOT DANGEROUS ANYMORE, I WANT TO COME BACK.
I WANT TO BE ME AGAIN, AND PLAY SOME REALLY GREAT GIGS AS THE ***PILOTS.***
4:30PM-6:30PM
EXCEPT SAT-SUN & HOLIDAYS
BUT NOW I'M GONE, MAYBE IT'S BEST FOR EVERYONE THAT I STAY THAT WAY.
"BYE, BUZZ."
HNN?
AUNTIE? DID YOU SAY SOMETHING?
SNnrrr SNK
HUH.
Snnrrr

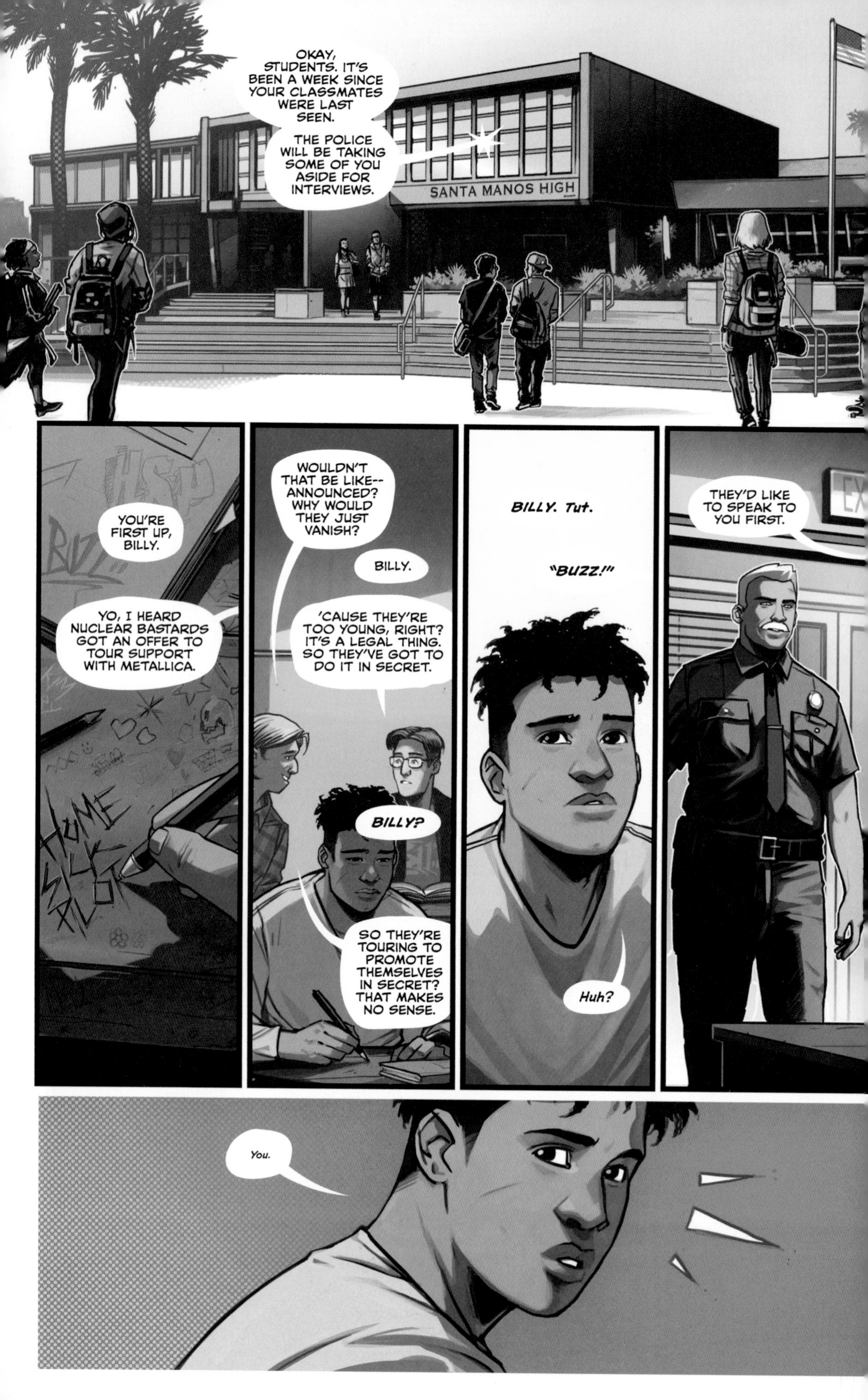
OKAY, STUDENTS. IT'S BEEN A WEEK SINCE YOUR CLASSMATES WERE LAST SEEN.
THE POLICE WILL BE TAKING SOME OF YOU ASIDE FOR INTERVIEWS.
SANTA MANOS HIGH
YOU'RE FIRST UP, BILLY.
YO, I HEARD NUCLEAR BASTARDS GOT AN OFFER TO TOUR SUPPORT WITH METALLICA.
WOULDN'T THAT BE LIKE-- ANNOUNCED? WHY WOULD THEY JUST VANISH?
BILLY.
'CAUSE THEY'RE TOO YOUNG, RIGHT? IT'S A LEGAL THING. SO THEY'VE GOT TO DO IT IN SECRET.
BILLY?
SO THEY'RE TOURING TO PROMOTE THEMSELVES IN SECRET? THAT MAKES NO SENSE.
BILLY. Tut.
"BUZZ!"
Huh?
THEY'D LIKE TO SPEAK TO YOU FIRST.
EXIT
You.

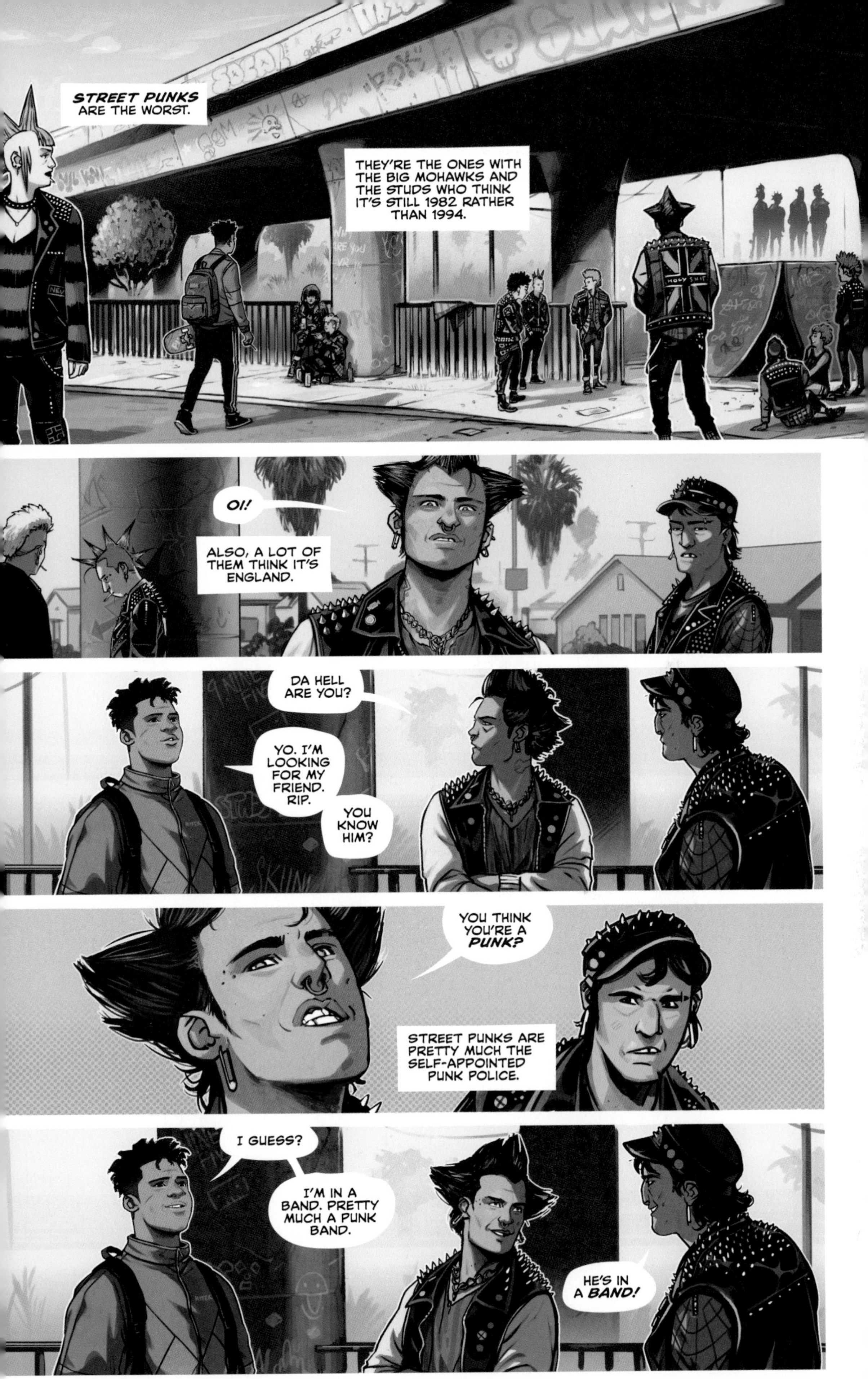
STREET PUNKS ARE THE WORST.
THEY'RE THE ONES WITH THE BIG MOHAWKS AND THE STUDS WHO THINK IT'S STILL 1982 RATHER THAN 1994.
OI!
ALSO, A LOT OF THEM THINK IT'S ENGLAND.
DA HELL ARE YOU?
YO. I'M LOOKING FOR MY FRIEND. RIP.
YOU KNOW HIM?
YOU THINK YOU'RE A PUNK?
STREET PUNKS ARE PRETTY MUCH THE SELF-APPOINTED PUNK POLICE.
I GUESS?
I'M IN A BAND. PRETTY MUCH A PUNK BAND.
HE'S IN A BAND!

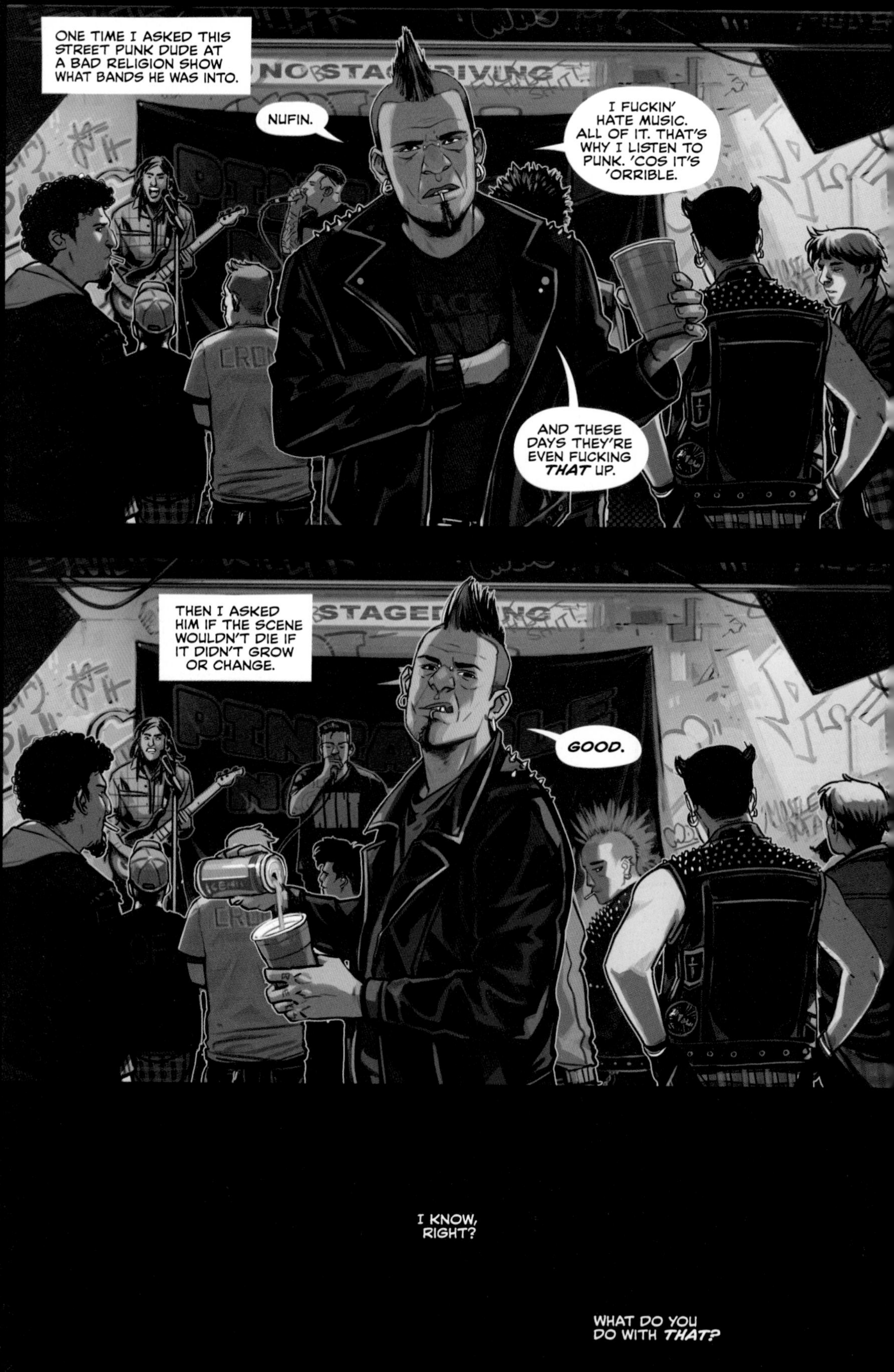
ONE TIME I ASKED THIS STREET PUNK DUDE AT A BAD RELIGION SHOW WHAT BANDS HE WAS INTO.
NUFIN.
I FUCKIN' HATE MUSIC. ALL OF IT. THAT'S WHY I LISTEN TO PUNK. 'COS IT'S 'ORRIBLE.
AND THESE DAYS THEY'RE EVEN FUCKING *THAT* UP.
THEN I ASKED HIM IF THE SCENE WOULDN'T DIE IF IT DIDN'T GROW OR CHANGE.
GOOD.
I KNOW, RIGHT?
WHAT DO YOU DO WITH *THAT?*

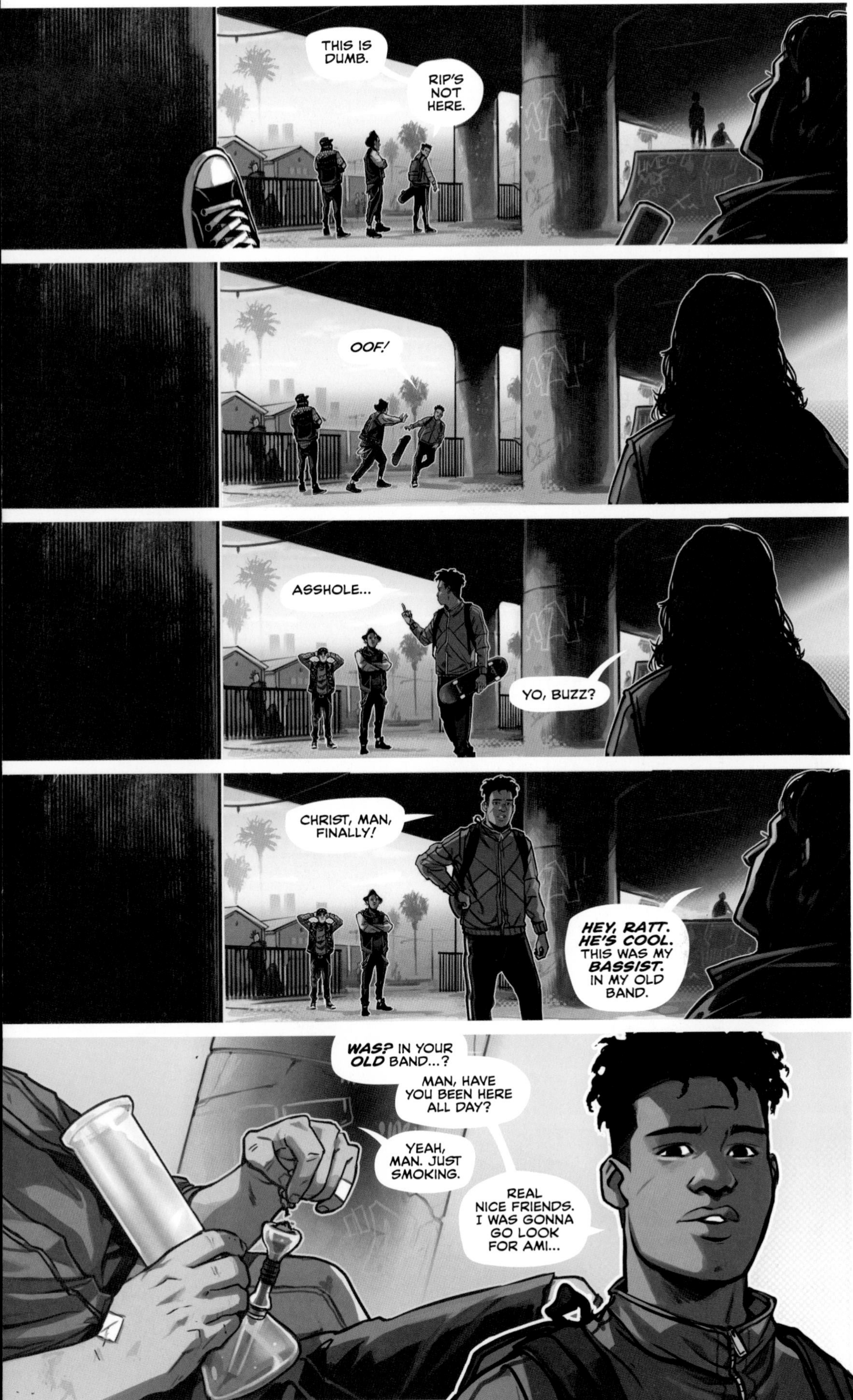
THIS IS DUMB.
RIP'S NOT HERE.
OOF!
ASSHOLE...
YO, BUZZ?
CHRIST, MAN, FINALLY!
HEY, RATT. HE'S COOL. THIS WAS MY BASSIST. IN MY OLD BAND.
WAS? IN YOUR OLD BAND...?
MAN, HAVE YOU BEEN HERE ALL DAY?
YEAH, MAN. JUST SMOKING.
REAL NICE FRIENDS. I WAS GONNA GO LOOK FOR AMI...

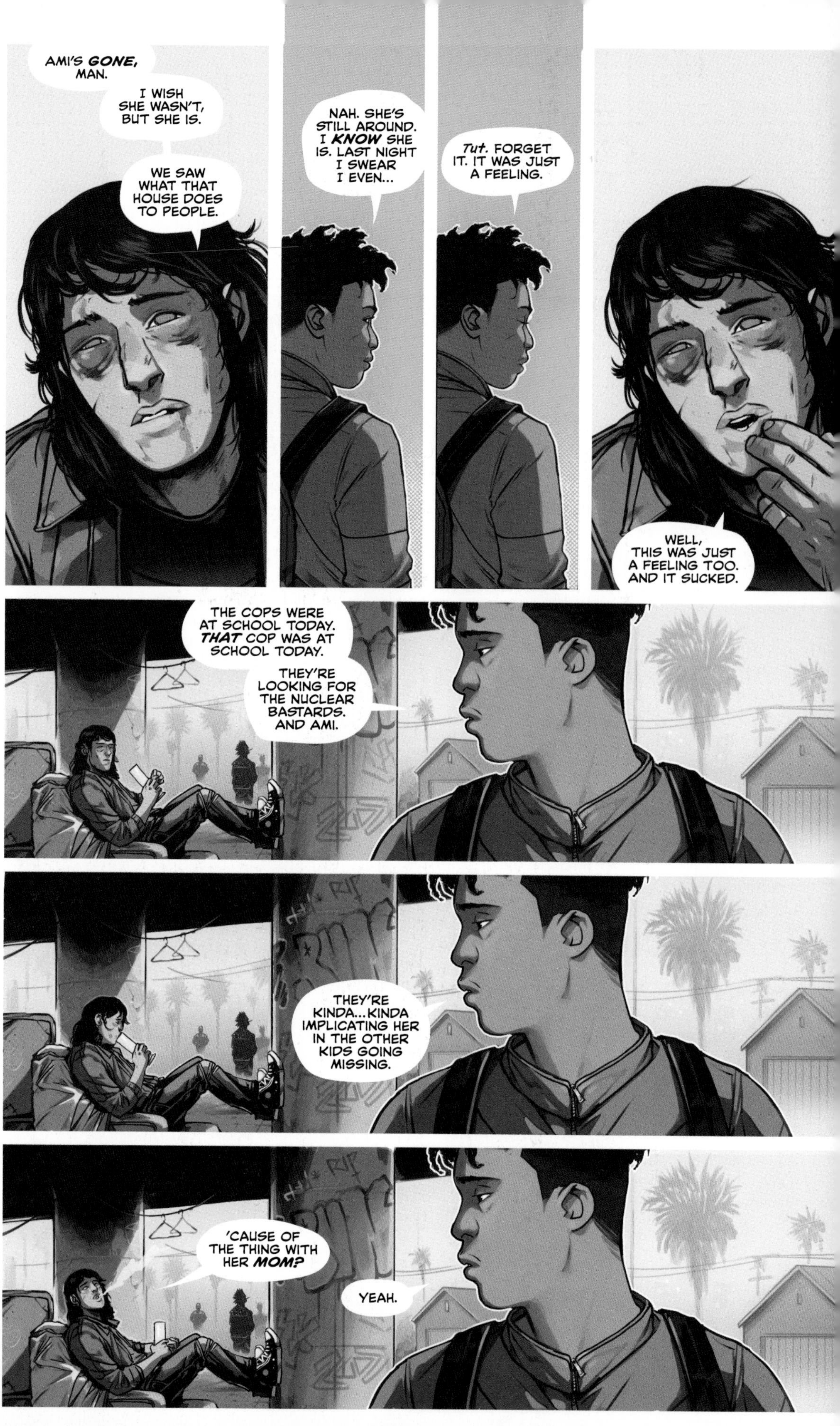
AMI'S **GONE**, MAN.
I WISH SHE WASN'T, BUT SHE IS.
WE SAW WHAT THAT HOUSE DOES TO PEOPLE.
NAH. SHE'S STILL AROUND. I **KNOW** SHE IS. LAST NIGHT I SWEAR I EVEN...
Tut. FORGET IT. IT WAS JUST A FEELING.
WELL, THIS WAS JUST A FEELING TOO. AND IT SUCKED.
THE COPS WERE AT SCHOOL TODAY. **THAT** COP WAS AT SCHOOL TODAY.
THEY'RE LOOKING FOR THE NUCLEAR BASTARDS. AND AMI.
THEY'RE KINDA...KINDA IMPLICATING HER IN THE OTHER KIDS GOING MISSING.
'CAUSE OF THE THING WITH HER **MOM?**
YEAH.

I REALLY,
REALLY, REALLY
WISH THEY'D
STOP TALKING
ABOUT THAT.

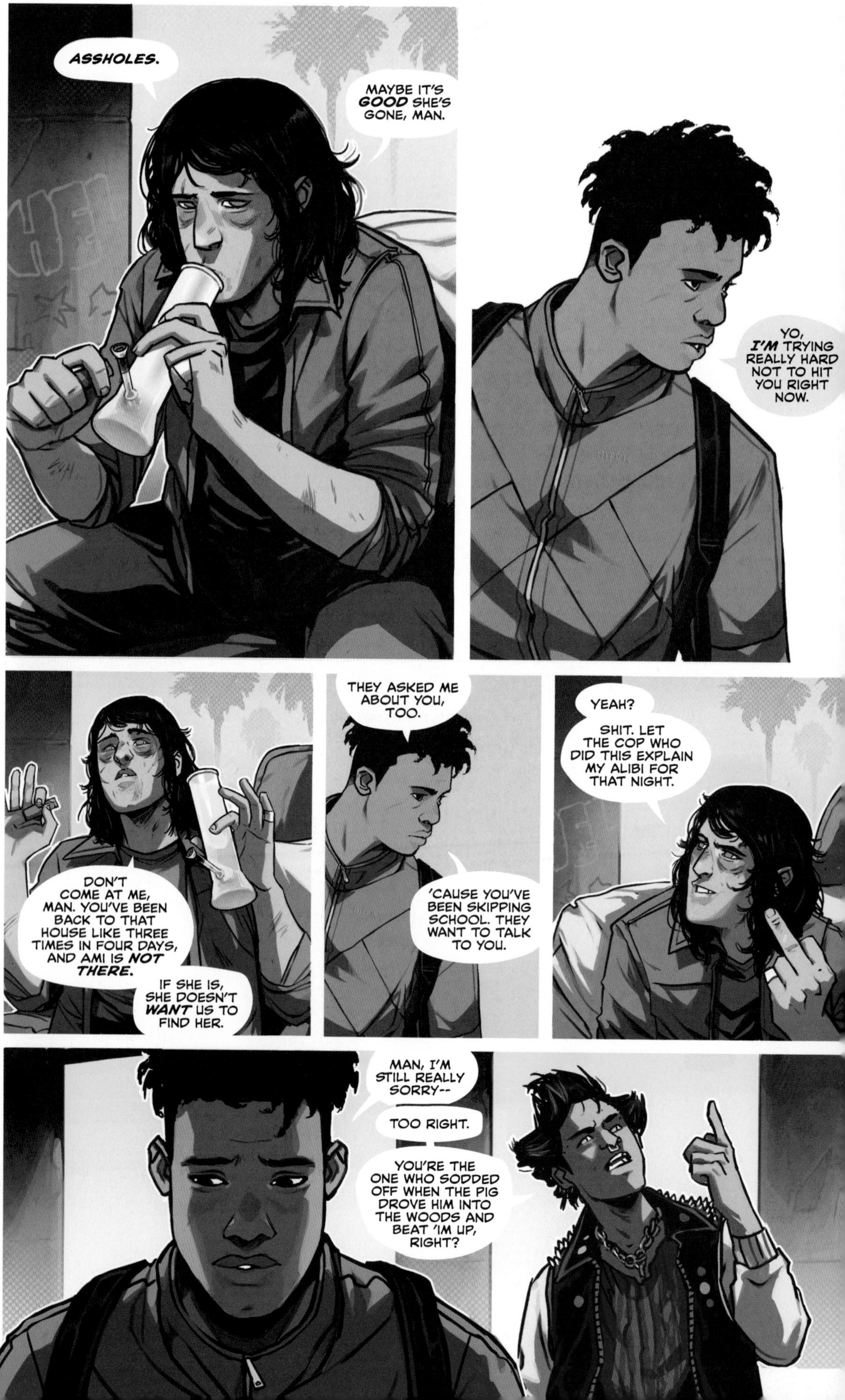
ASSHOLES.
MAYBE IT'S GOOD SHE'S GONE, MAN.
YO, I'M TRYING REALLY HARD NOT TO HIT YOU RIGHT NOW.
DON'T COME AT ME, MAN. YOU'VE BEEN BACK TO THAT HOUSE LIKE THREE TIMES IN FOUR DAYS, AND AMI IS NOT THERE.
IF SHE IS, SHE DOESN'T WANT US TO FIND HER.
THEY ASKED ME ABOUT YOU, TOO.
'CAUSE YOU'VE BEEN SKIPPING SCHOOL. THEY WANT TO TALK TO YOU.
YEAH?
SHIT. LET THE COP WHO DID THIS EXPLAIN MY ALIBI FOR THAT NIGHT.
MAN, I'M STILL REALLY SORRY--
TOO RIGHT.
YOU'RE THE ONE WHO SODDED OFF WHEN THE PIG DROVE HIM INTO THE WOODS AND BEAT 'IM UP, RIGHT?

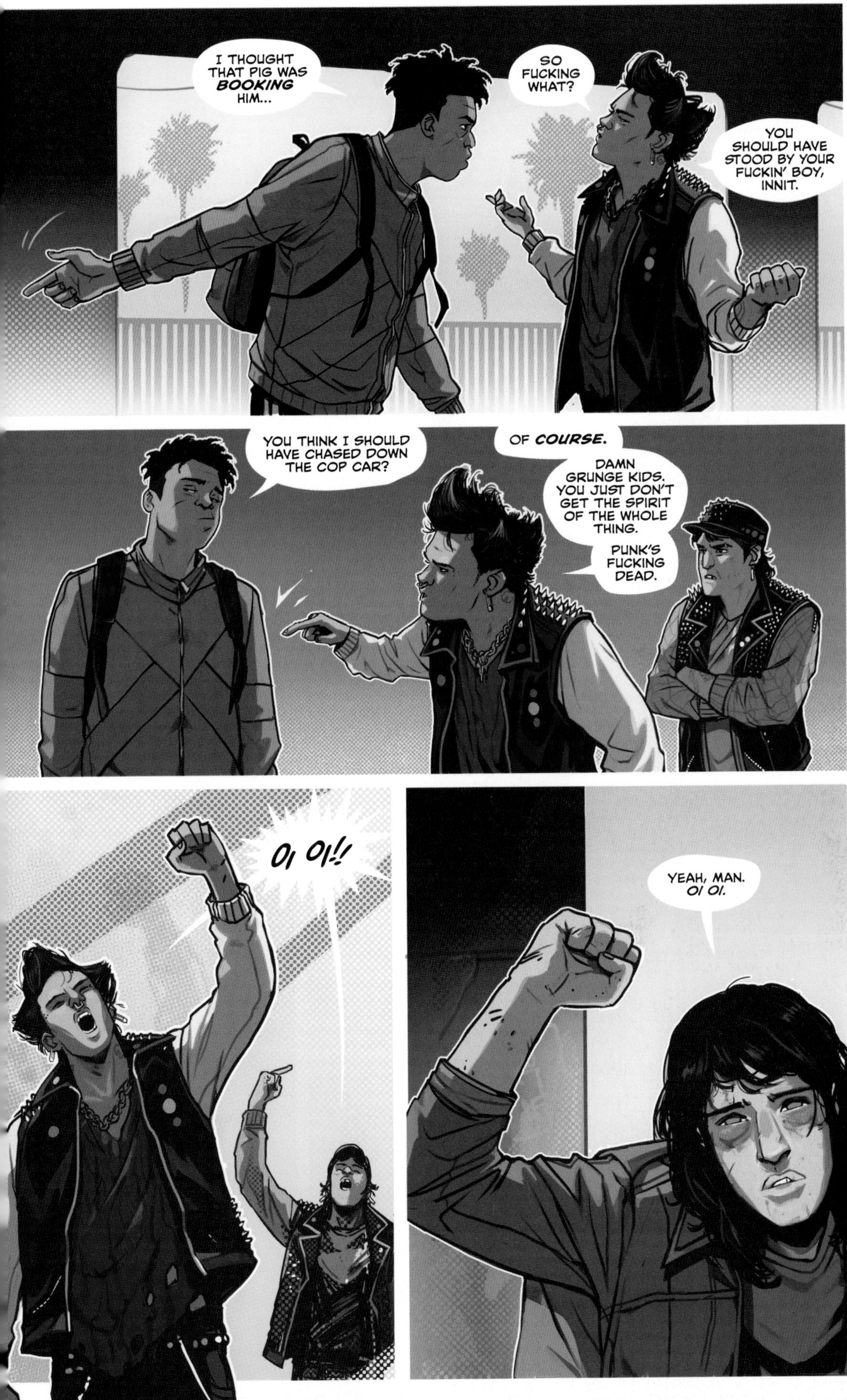
I THOUGHT THAT PIG WAS *BOOKING* HIM...
SO FUCKING WHAT?
YOU SHOULD HAVE STOOD BY YOUR FUCKIN' BOY, INNIT.
YOU THINK I SHOULD HAVE CHASED DOWN THE COP CAR?
OF *COURSE.*
DAMN GRUNGE KIDS. YOU JUST DON'T GET THE SPIRIT OF THE WHOLE THING.
PUNK'S FUCKING DEAD.
OI OI!!
YEAH, MAN. *OI OI.*

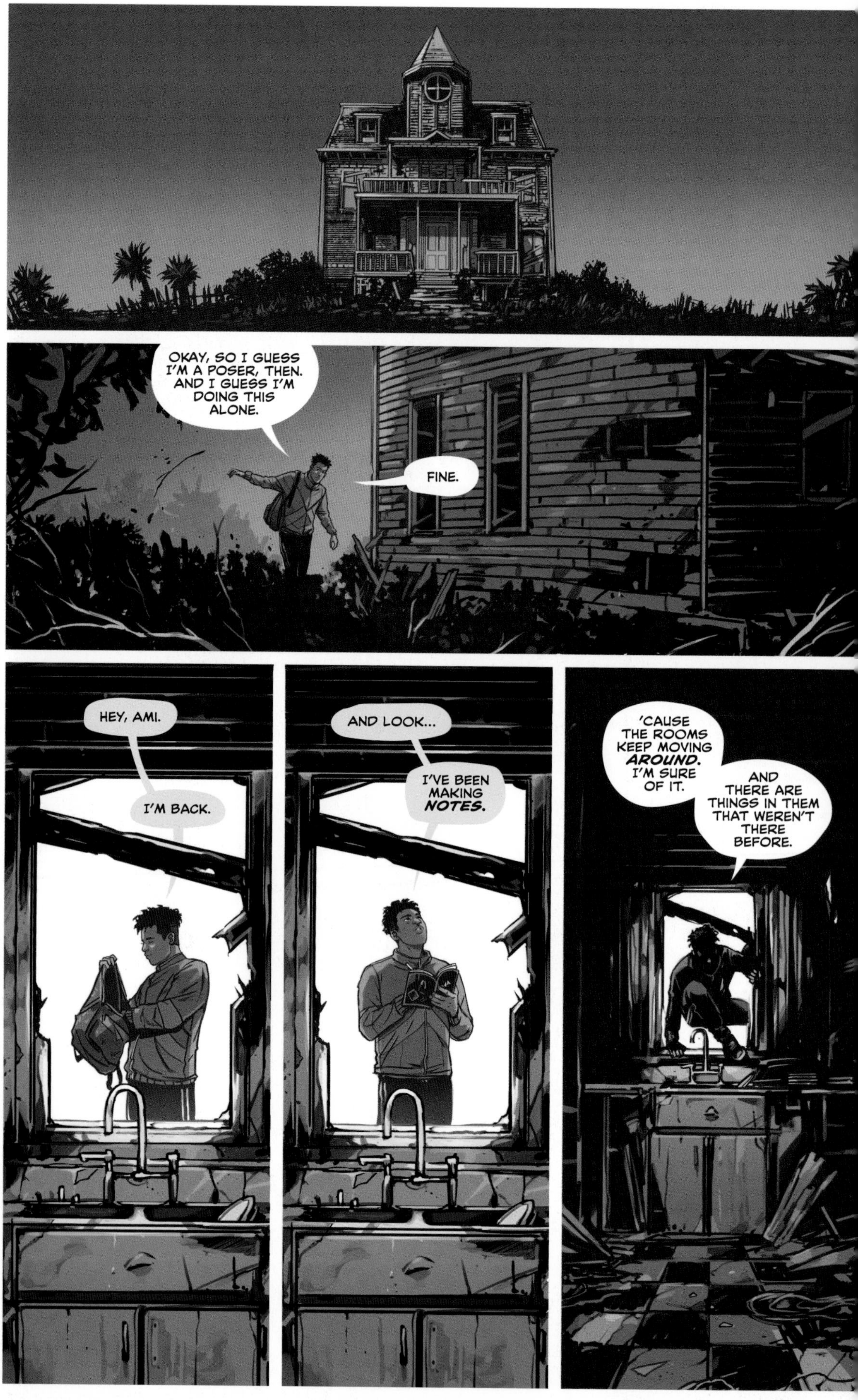
OKAY, SO I GUESS I'M A POSER, THEN. AND I GUESS I'M DOING THIS ALONE.
FINE.
HEY, AMI.
I'M BACK.
AND LOOK...
I'VE BEEN MAKING *NOTES.*
'CAUSE THE ROOMS KEEP MOVING *AROUND.* I'M SURE OF IT.
AND THERE ARE THINGS IN THEM THAT WEREN'T THERE BEFORE.

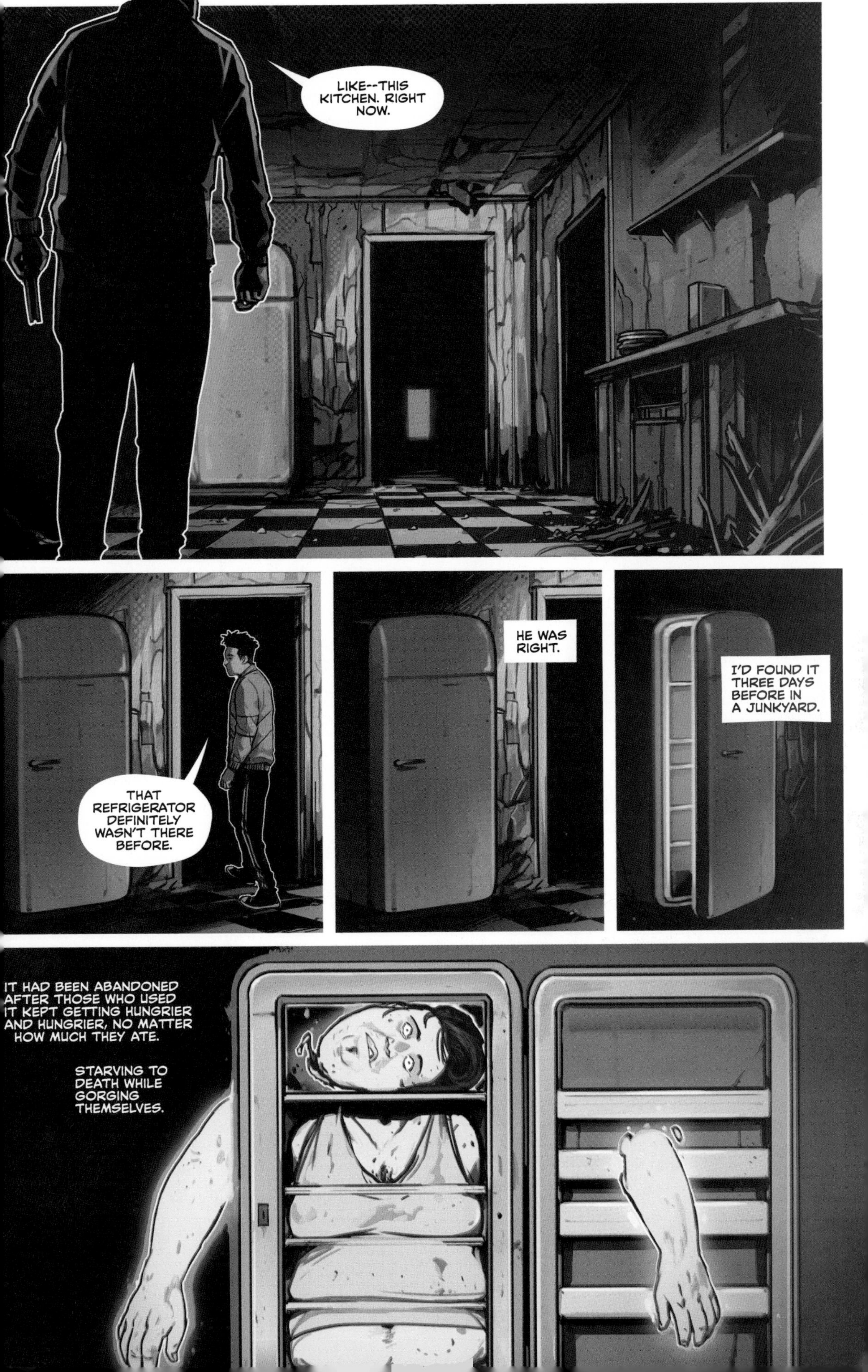
LIKE--THIS KITCHEN. RIGHT NOW.
THAT REFRIGERATOR DEFINITELY WASN'T THERE BEFORE.
HE WAS RIGHT.
I'D FOUND IT THREE DAYS BEFORE IN A JUNKYARD.
IT HAD BEEN ABANDONED AFTER THOSE WHO USED IT KEPT GETTING HUNGRIER AND HUNGRIER, NO MATTER HOW MUCH THEY ATE.
STARVING TO DEATH WHILE GORGING THEMSELVES.

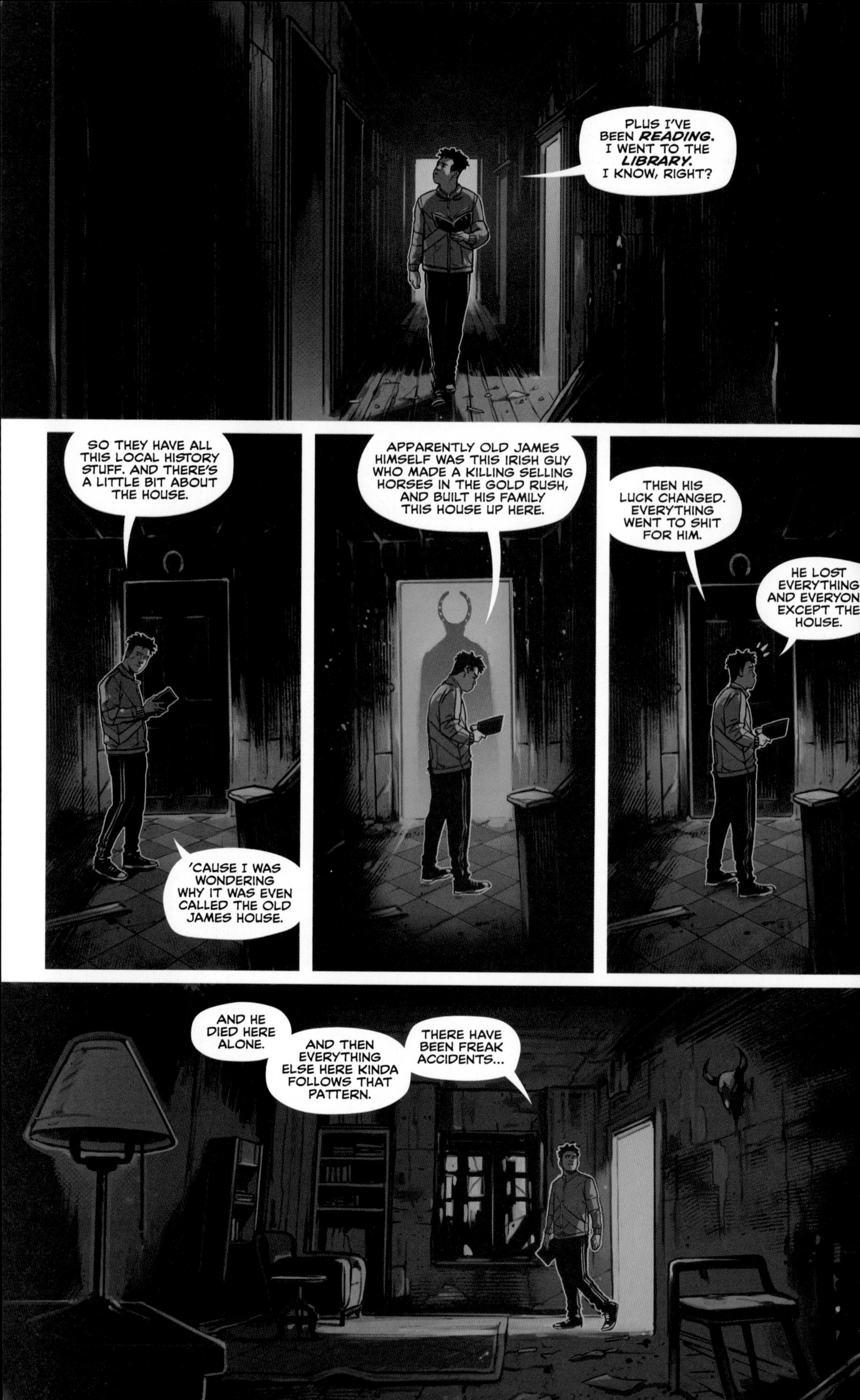
PLUS I'VE BEEN ***READING.*** I WENT TO THE ***LIBRARY.*** I KNOW, RIGHT?
SO THEY HAVE ALL THIS LOCAL HISTORY STUFF. AND THERE'S A LITTLE BIT ABOUT THE HOUSE.
'CAUSE I WAS WONDERING WHY IT WAS EVEN CALLED THE OLD JAMES HOUSE.
APPARENTLY OLD JAMES HIMSELF WAS THIS IRISH GUY WHO MADE A KILLING SELLING HORSES IN THE GOLD RUSH, AND BUILT HIS FAMILY THIS HOUSE UP HERE.
THEN HIS LUCK CHANGED. EVERYTHING WENT TO SHIT FOR HIM.
HE LOST EVERYTHING AND EVERYON EXCEPT THE HOUSE.
AND HE DIED HERE ALONE.
AND THEN EVERYTHING ELSE HERE KINDA FOLLOWS THAT PATTERN.
THERE HAVE BEEN FREAK ACCIDENTS...

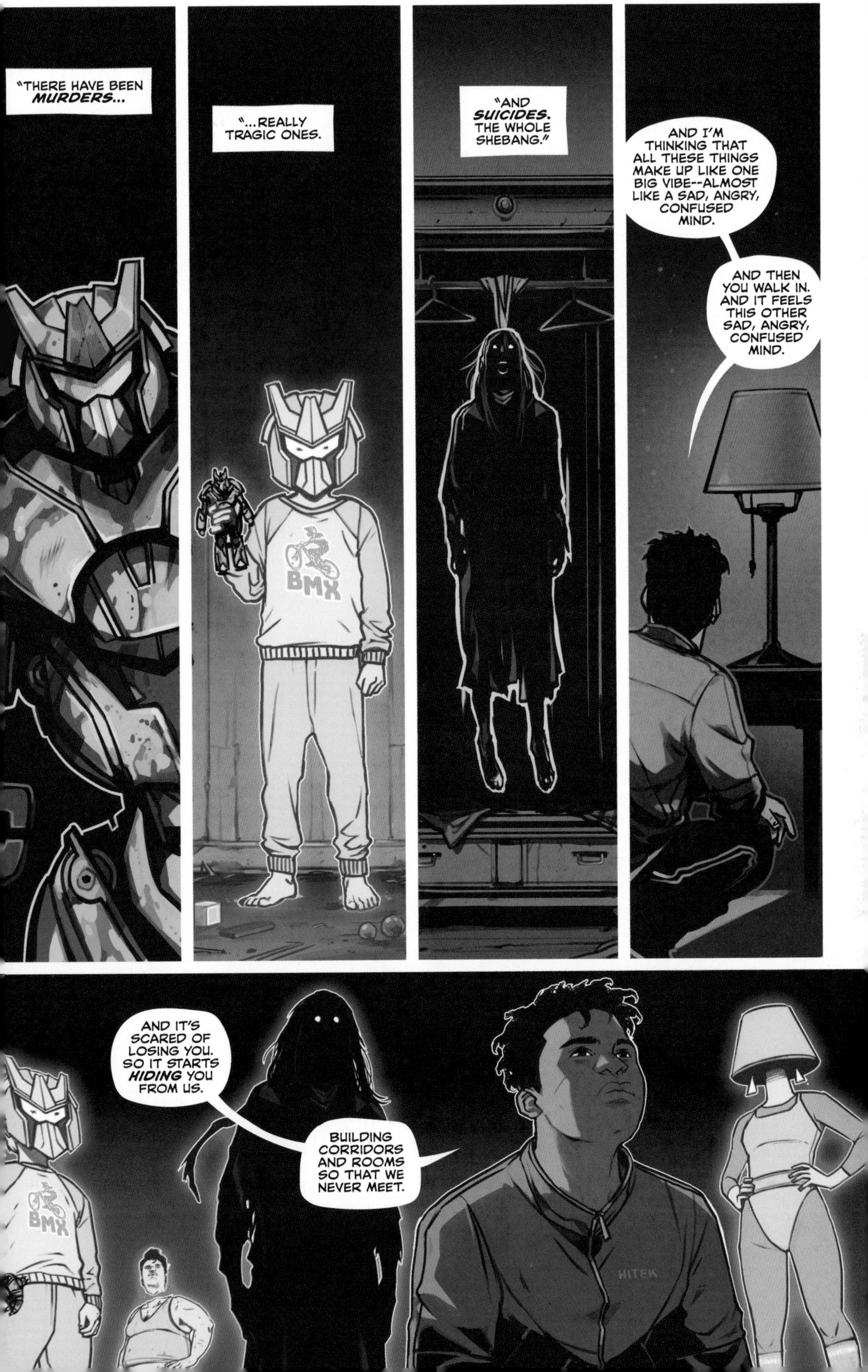
"THERE HAVE BEEN MURDERS...
"...REALLY TRAGIC ONES.
BMX
"AND SUICIDES. THE WHOLE SHEBANG."
AND I'M THINKING THAT ALL THESE THINGS MAKE UP LIKE ONE BIG VIBE--ALMOST LIKE A SAD, ANGRY, CONFUSED MIND.
AND THEN YOU WALK IN. AND IT FEELS THIS OTHER SAD, ANGRY, CONFUSED MIND.
AND IT'S SCARED OF LOSING YOU. SO IT STARTS HIDING YOU FROM US.
BUILDING CORRIDORS AND ROOMS SO THAT WE NEVER MEET.
BMX
HITEK

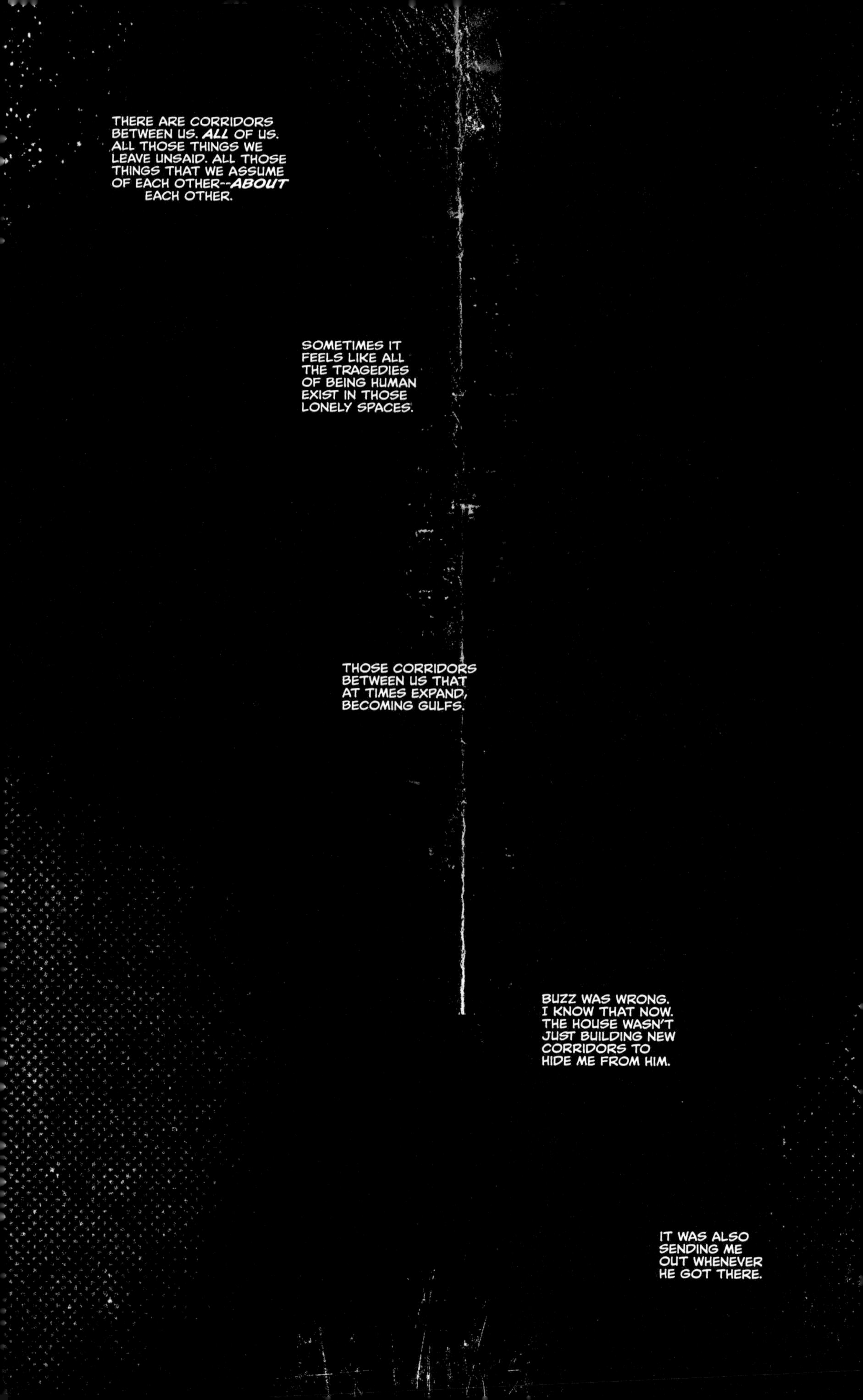
THERE ARE CORRIDORS BETWEEN US. ALL OF US. ALL THOSE THINGS WE LEAVE UNSAID. ALL THOSE THINGS THAT WE ASSUME OF EACH OTHER--ABOUT EACH OTHER.
SOMETIMES IT FEELS LIKE ALL THE TRAGEDIES OF BEING HUMAN EXIST IN THOSE LONELY SPACES.
THOSE CORRIDORS BETWEEN US THAT AT TIMES EXPAND, BECOMING GULFS.
BUZZ WAS WRONG. I KNOW THAT NOW. THE HOUSE WASN'T JUST BUILDING NEW CORRIDORS TO HIDE ME FROM HIM.
IT WAS ALSO SENDING ME OUT WHENEVER HE GOT THERE.

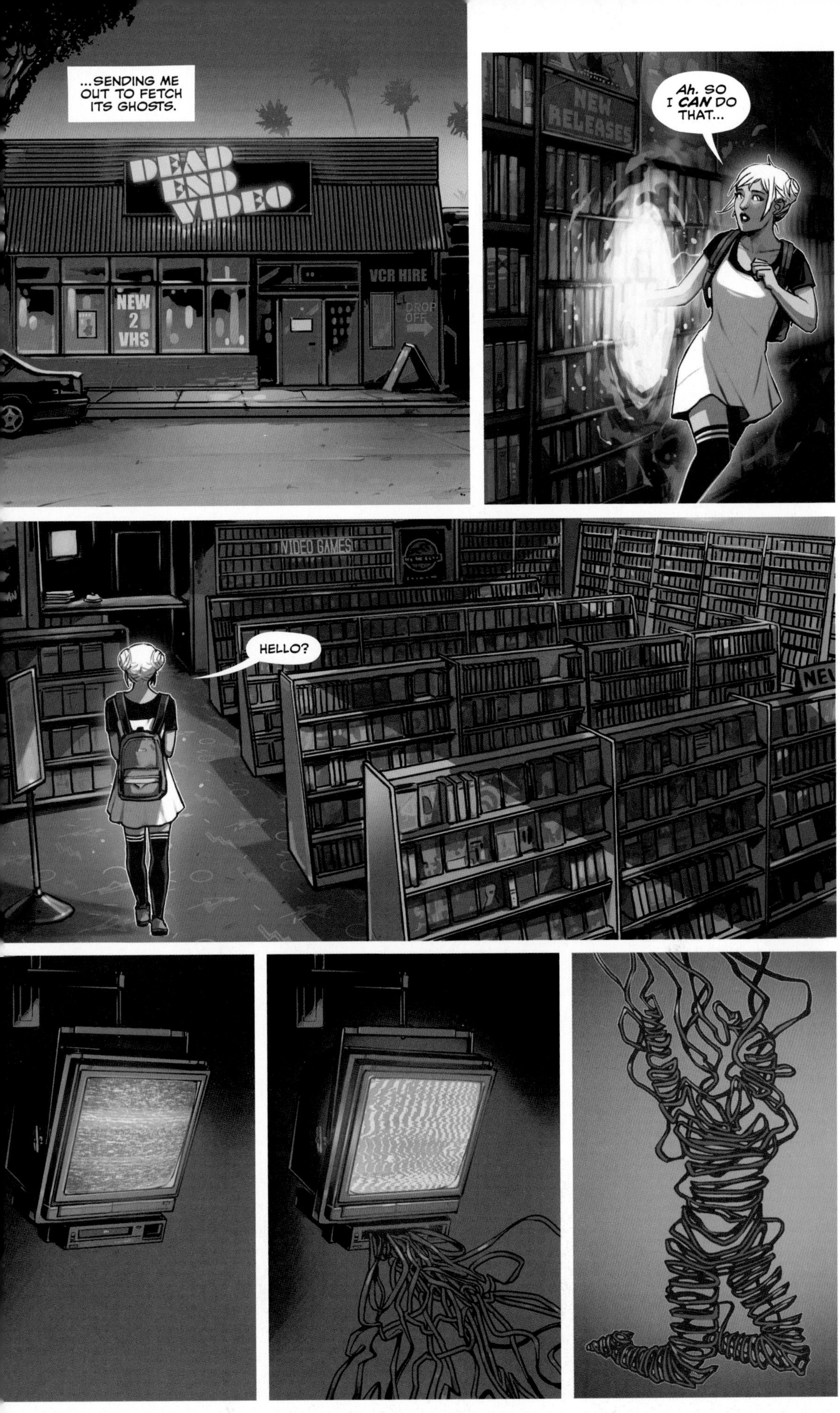
...SENDING ME OUT TO FETCH ITS GHOSTS.
DEAD END VIDEO
NEW 2 VHS
VCR HIRE
DROP OFF
Ah. SO I CAN DO THAT...
NEW RELEASES
VIDEO GAMES
HELLO?

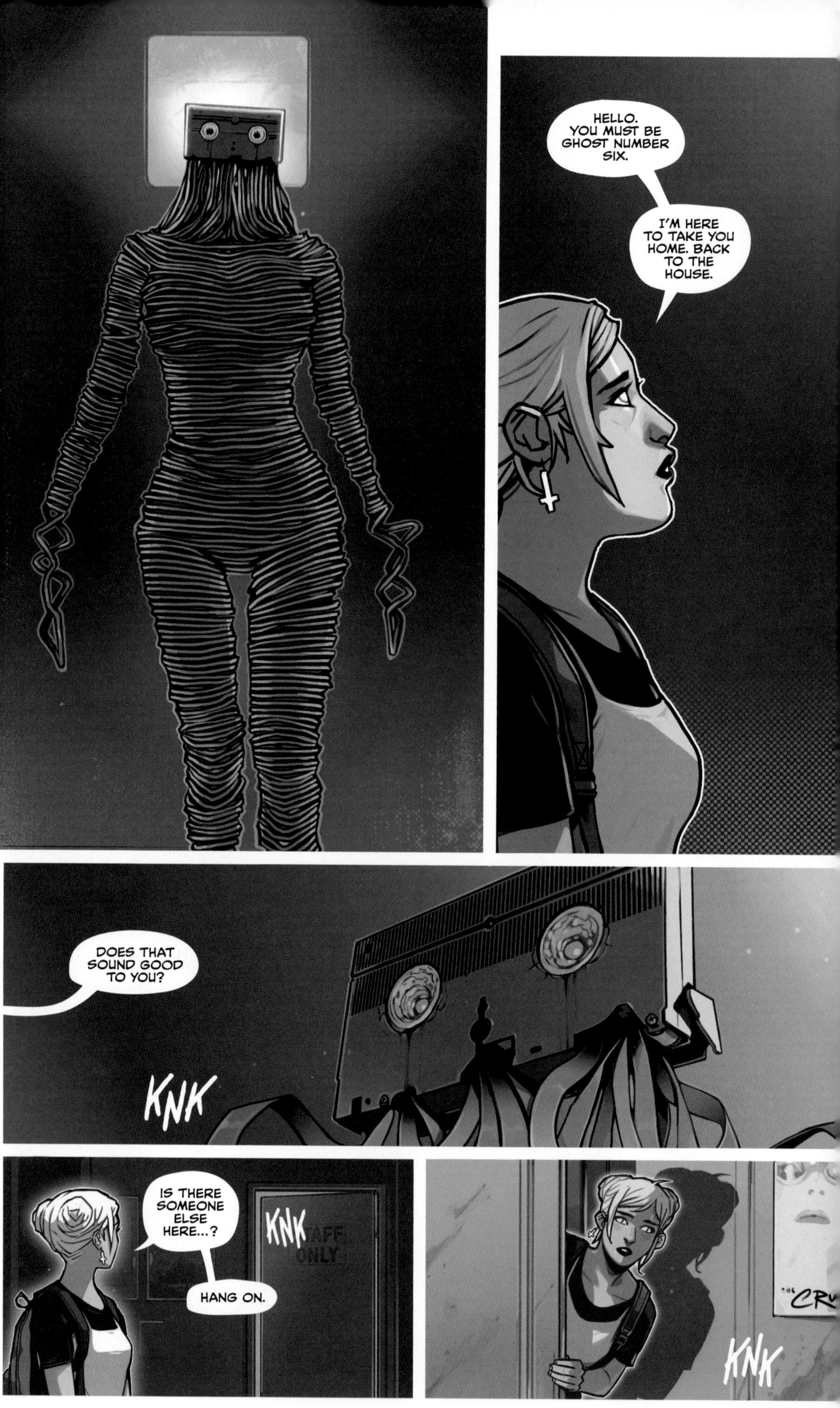
HELLO. YOU MUST BE GHOST NUMBER SIX.
I'M HERE TO TAKE YOU HOME. BACK TO THE HOUSE.
DOES THAT SOUND GOOD TO YOU?
KNK
IS THERE SOMEONE ELSE HERE...?
HANG ON.
KNK
STAFF ONLY
KNK

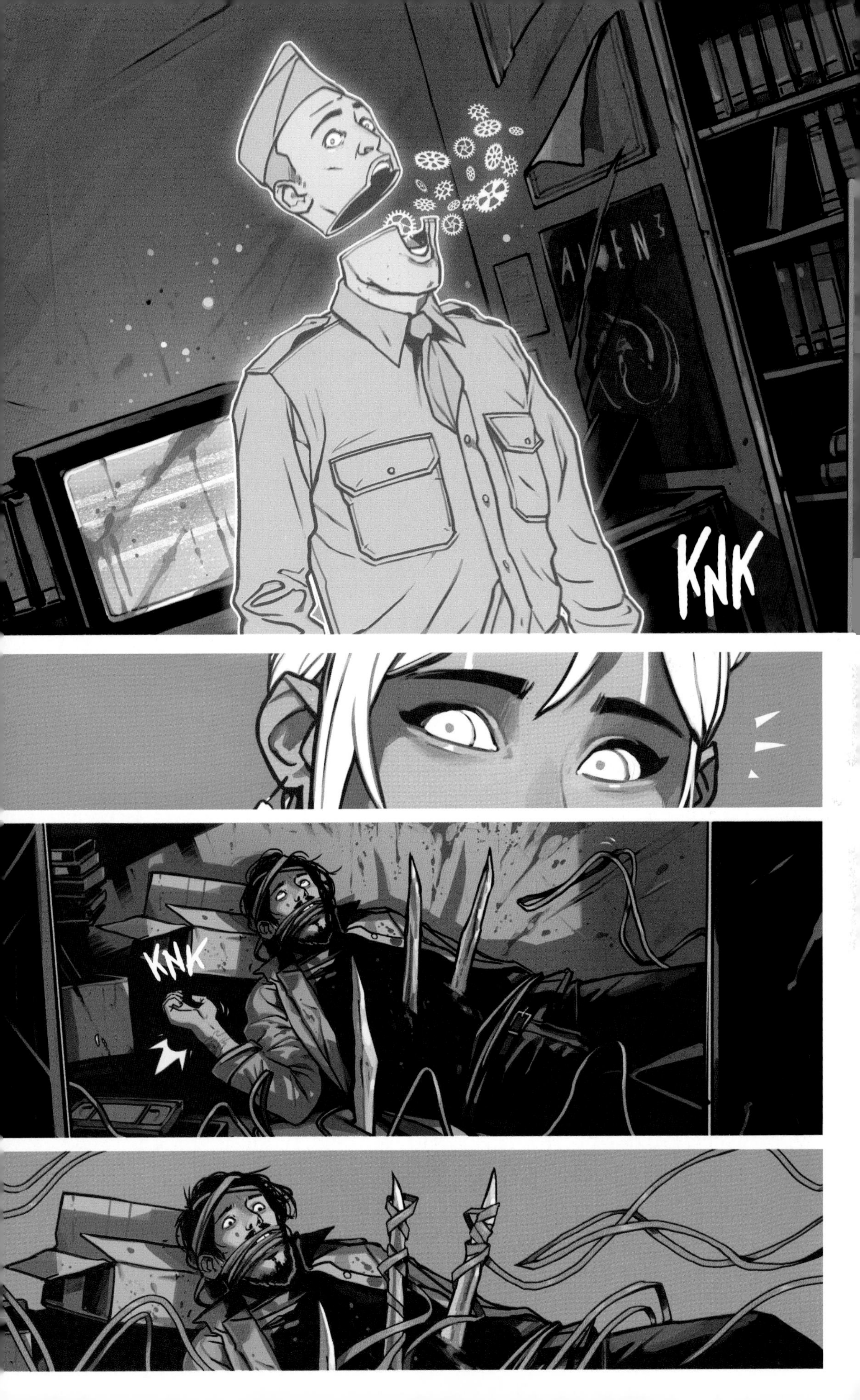
ALIEN3
KNK
KNK

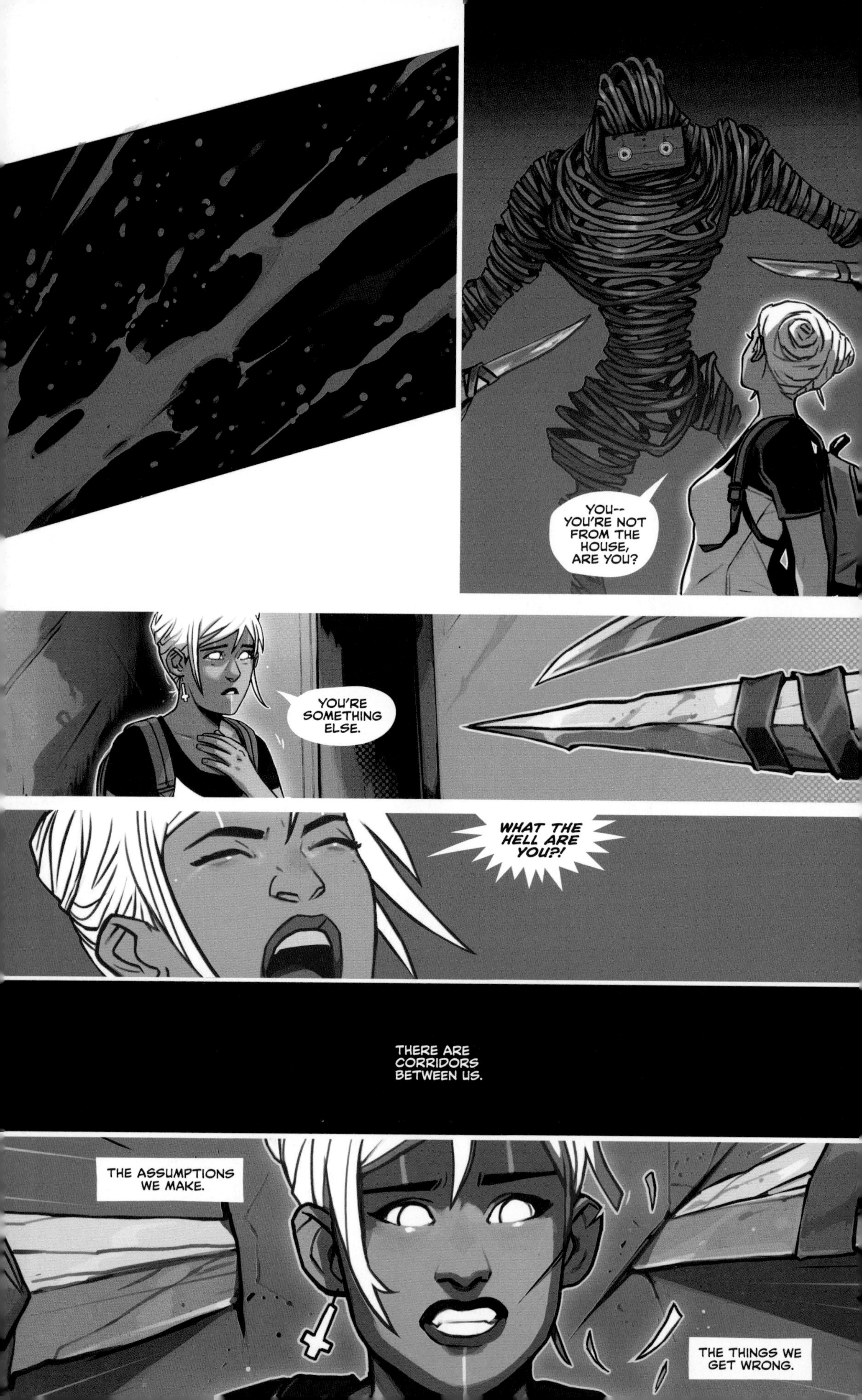
YOU--
YOU'RE NOT FROM THE HOUSE, ARE YOU?
YOU'RE SOMETHING ELSE.
WHAT THE HELL ARE YOU?!
THERE ARE CORRIDORS BETWEEN US.
THE ASSUMPTIONS WE MAKE.
THE THINGS WE GET WRONG.

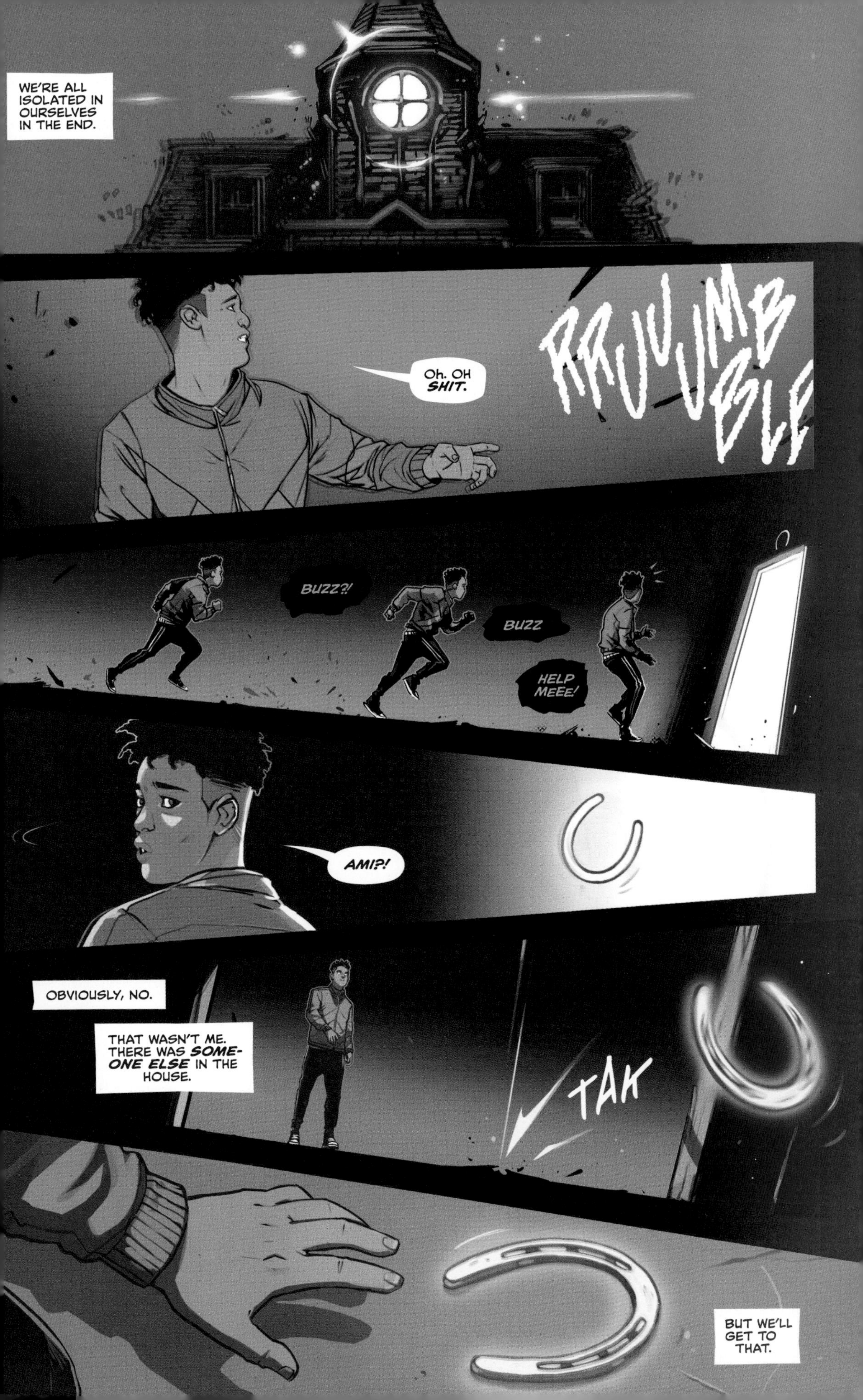
WE'RE ALL ISOLATED IN OURSELVES IN THE END.
Oh. OH SHIT.
RRUUMBBLE
BUZZ?!
BUZZ
HELP MEEE!
AMI?!
OBVIOUSLY, NO.
THAT WASN'T ME. THERE WAS SOME-ONE ELSE IN THE HOUSE.
TAK
BUT WE'LL GET TO THAT.

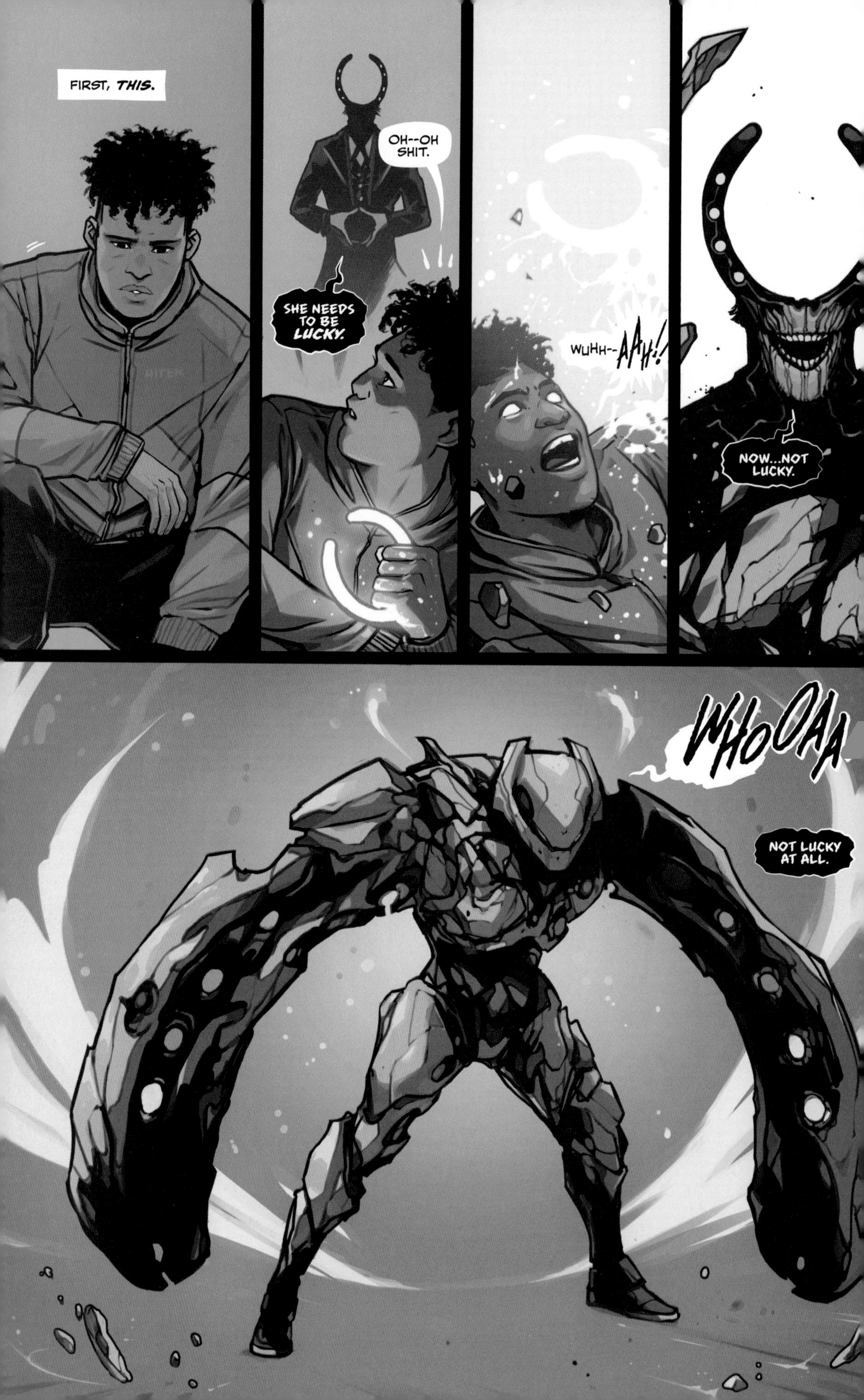
FIRST, THIS.
OH--OH SHIT.
SHE NEEDS TO BE LUCKY.
WUHH--AAH!!
NOW...NOT LUCKY.
WHOOAA
NOT LUCKY AT ALL.

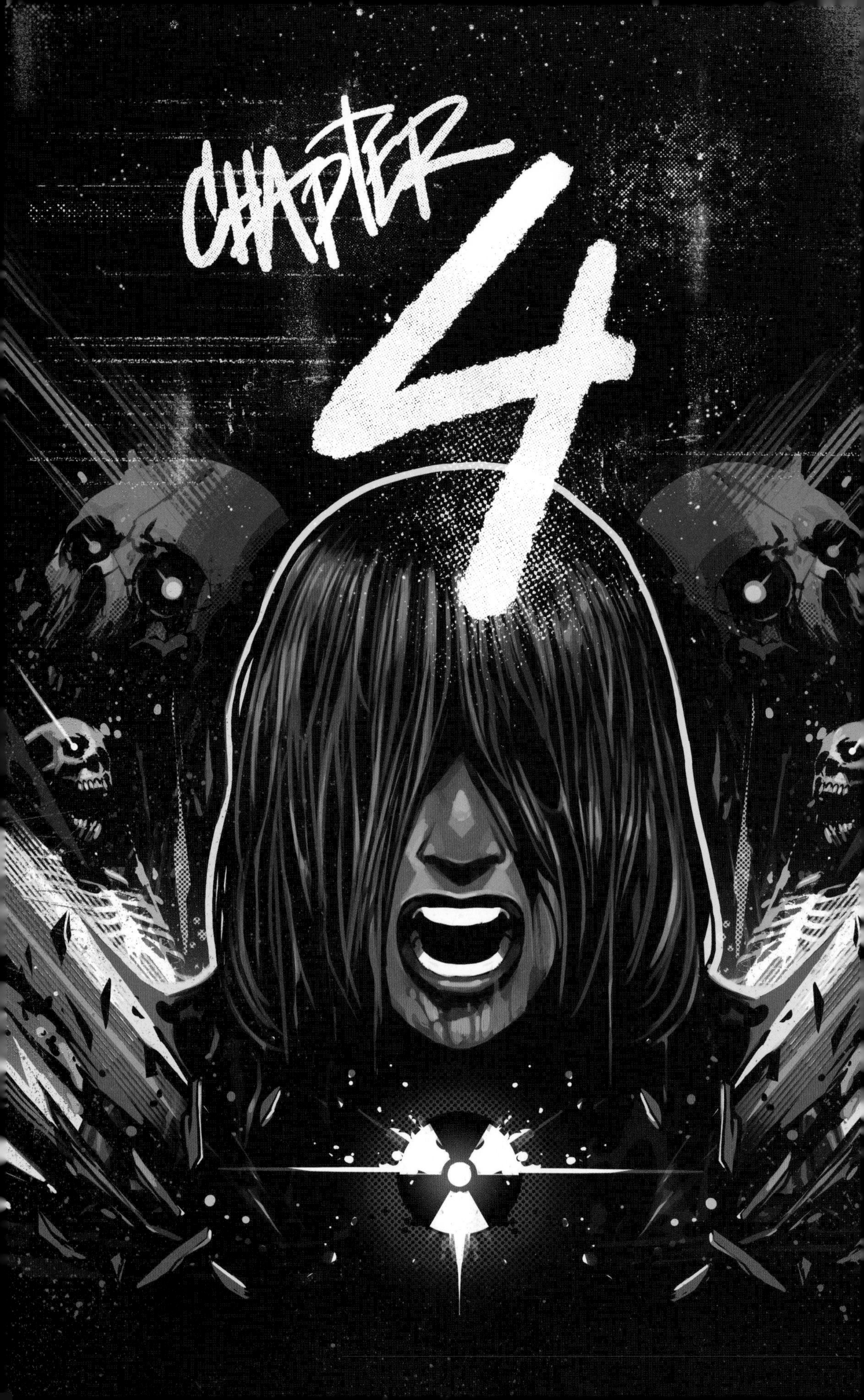
CHAPTER
4

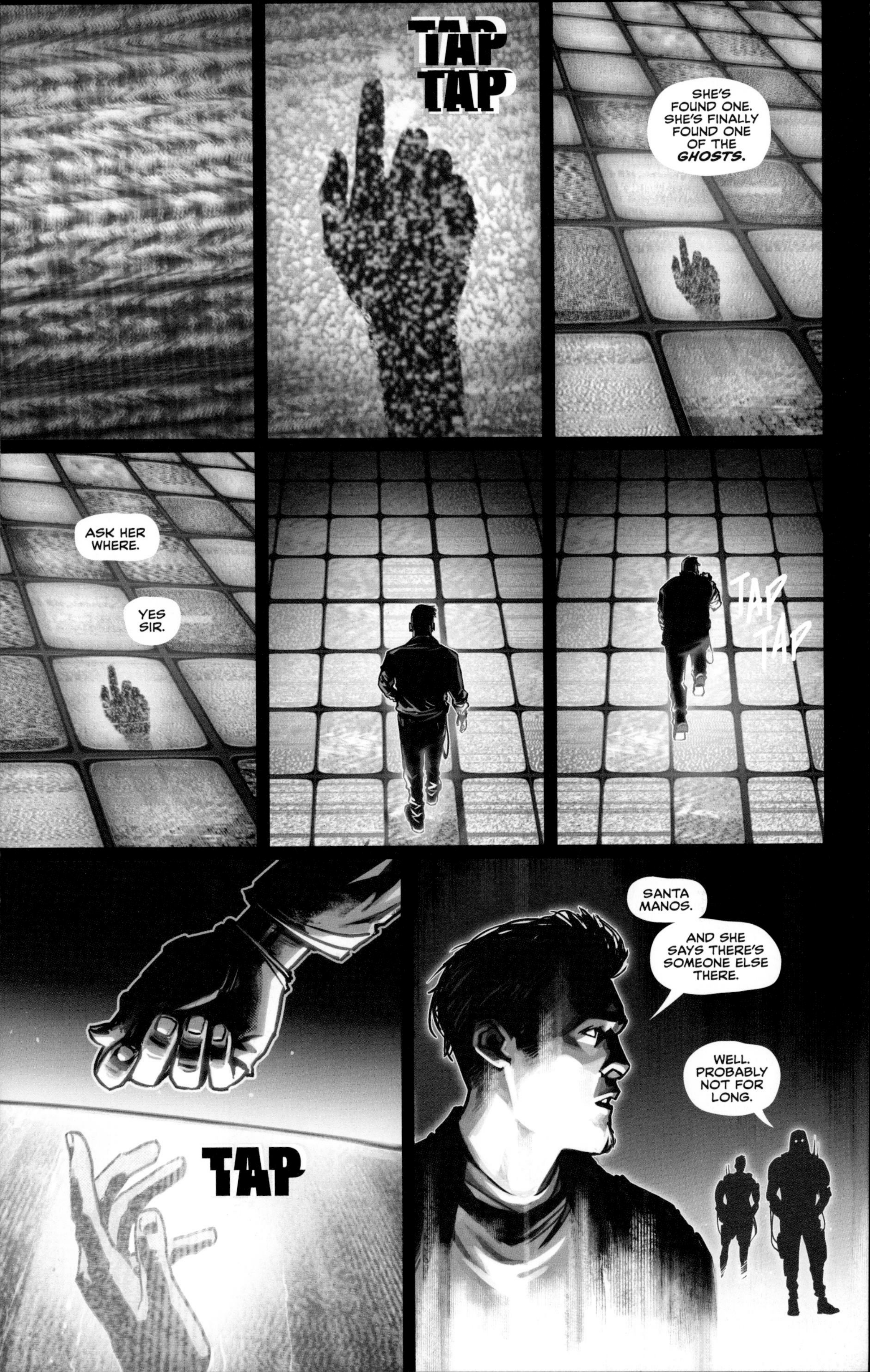
TAP TAP
SHE'S FOUND ONE. SHE'S FINALLY FOUND ONE OF THE *GHOSTS*.
ASK HER WHERE.
YES SIR.
TAP TAP
TAP
SANTA MANOS.
AND SHE SAYS THERE'S SOMEONE ELSE THERE.
WELL. PROBABLY NOT FOR LONG.

SANTA MANOS.

THE AFORE-MENTIONED GHOST.

THE "SOMEONE ELSE THERE."

WHO IS ME.

ANHH!

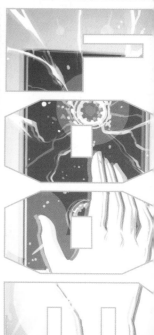

SO, I WON. THEN I STOOD UP AND SAID SOMETHING WITTY. I WENT IN TO CHECK ON THE CLOCK GHOST IN ALL ITS HACKED-UP BITS.

I SAVED IT, AND I TOOK IT BACK TO THE HOUSE. ALL SAFE.

THAT'S WHAT HAPPENED NEXT, RIGHT?

I WISH THAT WAS WHAT HAPPENED NEXT.

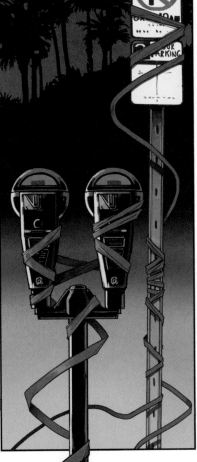

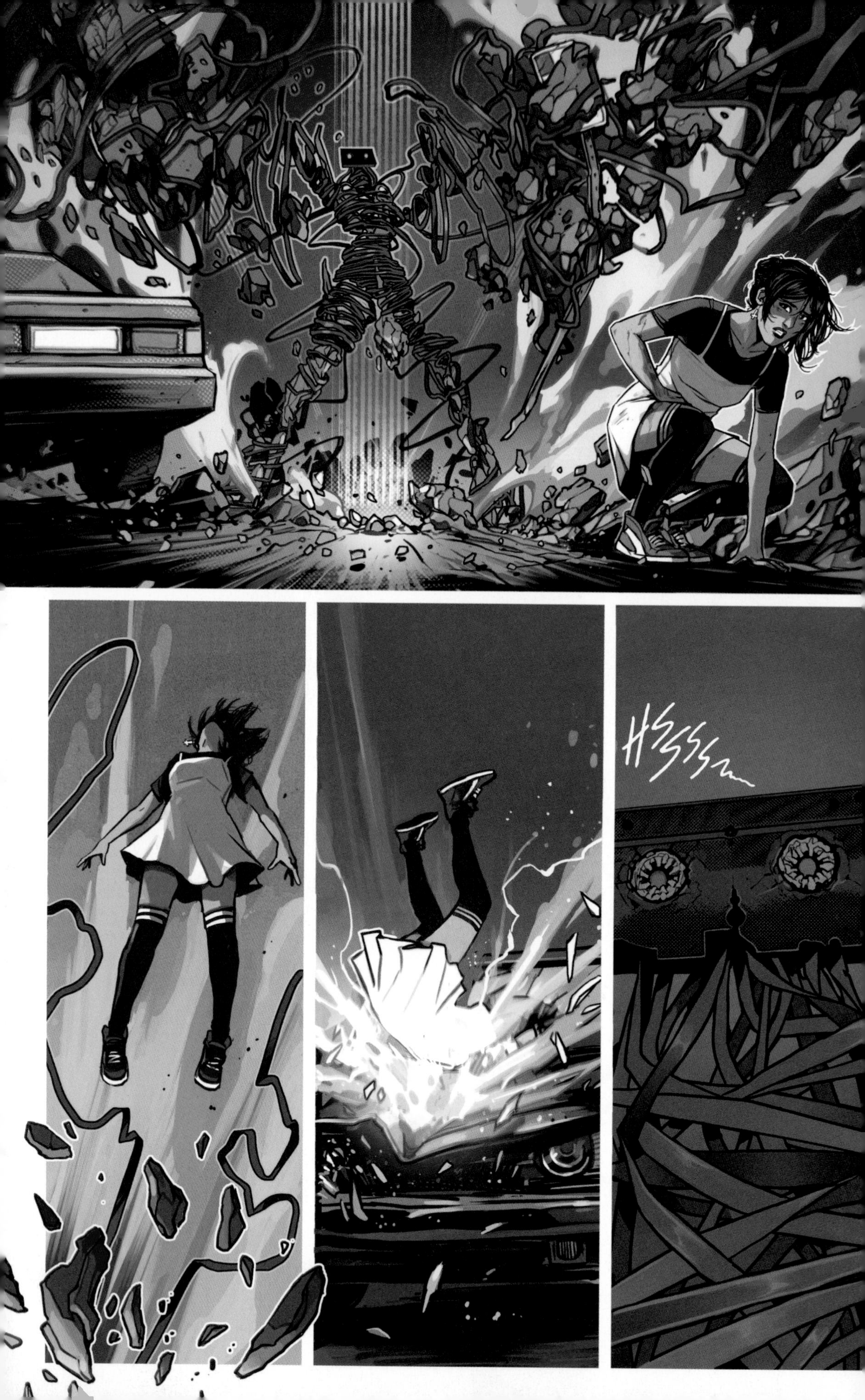
HSSSS

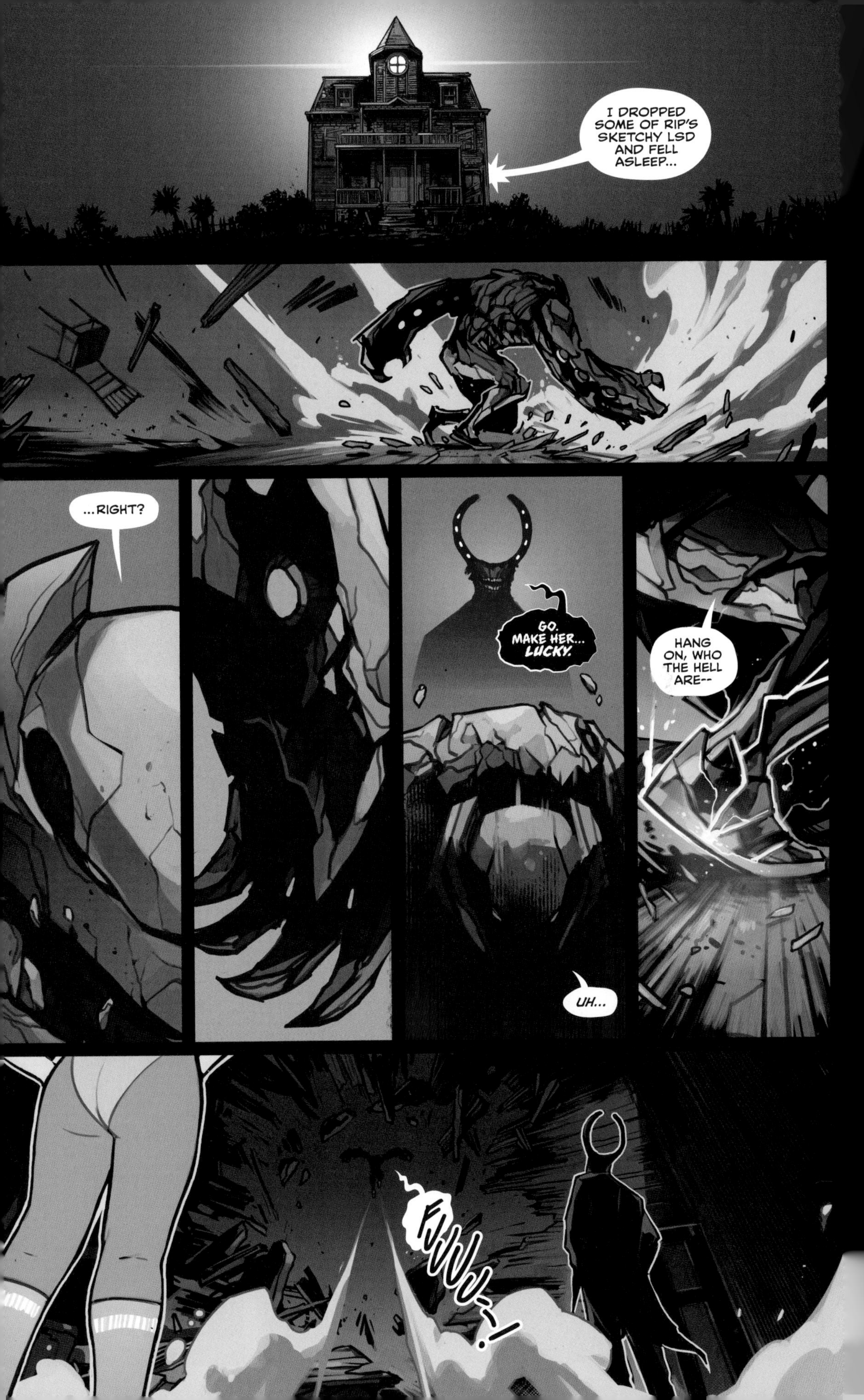
I DROPPED SOME OF RIP'S SKETCHY LSD AND FELL ASLEEP...
...RIGHT?
GO. MAKE HER... LUCKY.
UH...
HANG ON, WHO THE HELL ARE--
FUUUU--!

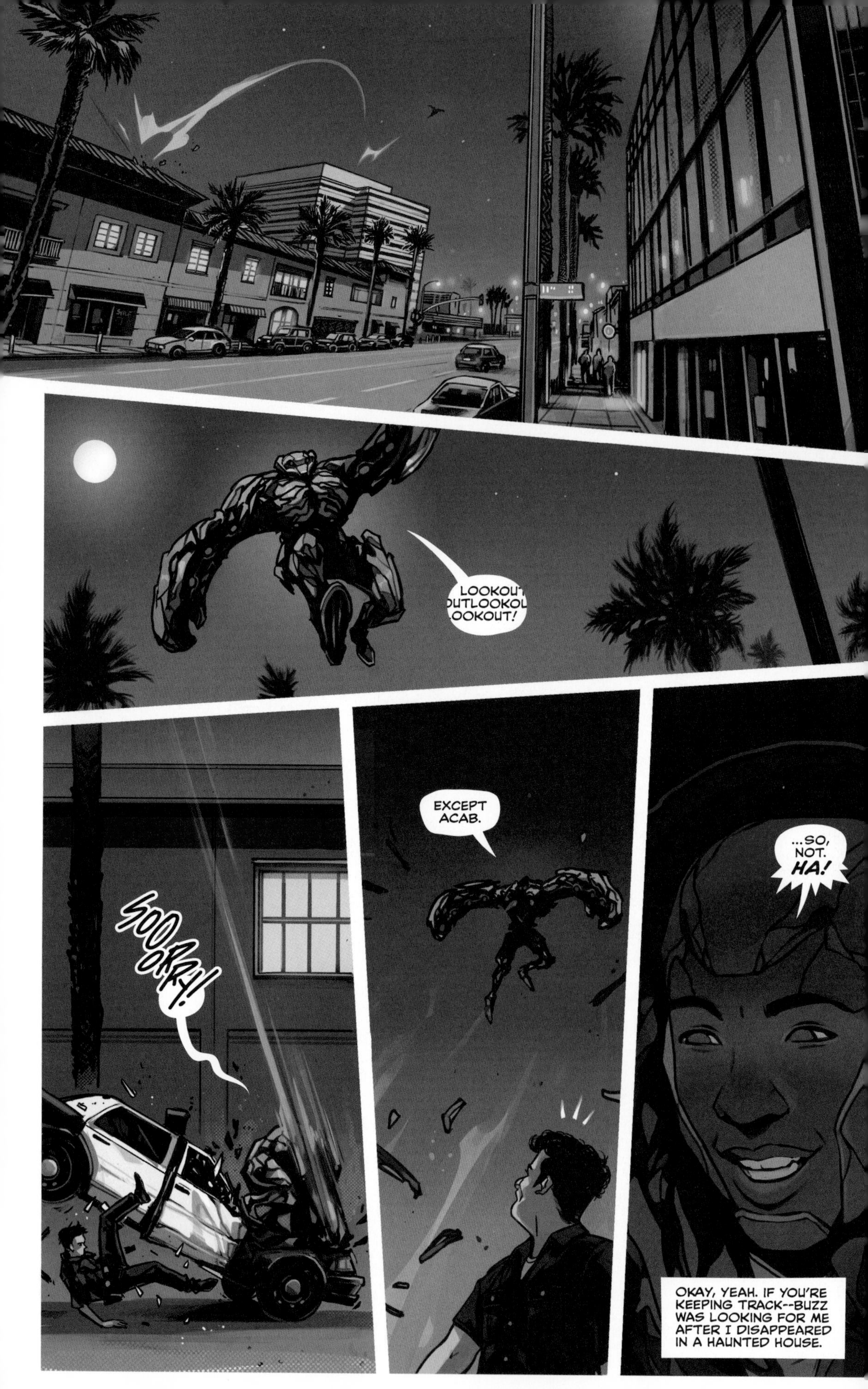
LOOKOUT
OUTLOOKOU
LOOKOUT!
SOOORRY!
EXCEPT ACAB.
...SO, NOT. HA!
OKAY, YEAH. IF YOU'RE KEEPING TRACK--BUZZ WAS LOOKING FOR ME AFTER I DISAPPEARED IN A HAUNTED HOUSE.

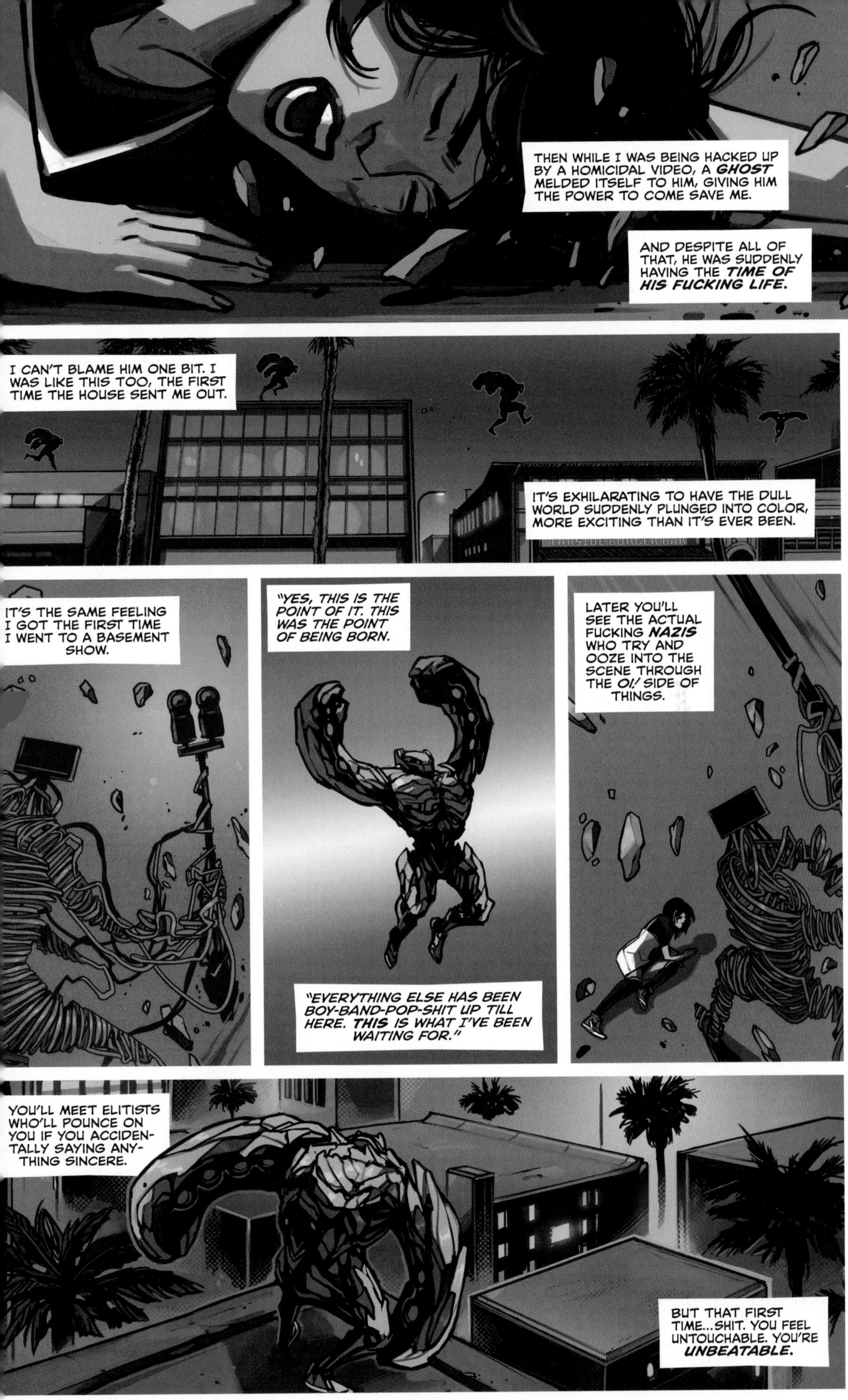
THEN WHILE I WAS BEING HACKED UP BY A HOMICIDAL VIDEO, A GHOST MELDED ITSELF TO HIM, GIVING HIM THE POWER TO COME SAVE ME.
AND DESPITE ALL OF THAT, HE WAS SUDDENLY HAVING THE TIME OF HIS FUCKING LIFE.
I CAN'T BLAME HIM ONE BIT. I WAS LIKE THIS TOO, THE FIRST TIME THE HOUSE SENT ME OUT.
IT'S EXHILARATING TO HAVE THE DULL WORLD SUDDENLY PLUNGED INTO COLOR, MORE EXCITING THAN IT'S EVER BEEN.
IT'S THE SAME FEELING I GOT THE FIRST TIME I WENT TO A BASEMENT SHOW.
"YES, THIS IS THE POINT OF IT. THIS WAS THE POINT OF BEING BORN.
"EVERYTHING ELSE HAS BEEN BOY-BAND-POP-SHIT UP TILL HERE. THIS IS WHAT I'VE BEEN WAITING FOR."
LATER YOU'LL SEE THE ACTUAL FUCKING NAZIS WHO TRY AND OOZE INTO THE SCENE THROUGH THE OI! SIDE OF THINGS.
YOU'LL MEET ELITISTS WHO'LL POUNCE ON YOU IF YOU ACCIDENTALLY SAYING ANYTHING SINCERE.
BUT THAT FIRST TIME...SHIT. YOU FEEL UNTOUCHABLE. YOU'RE UNBEATABLE.

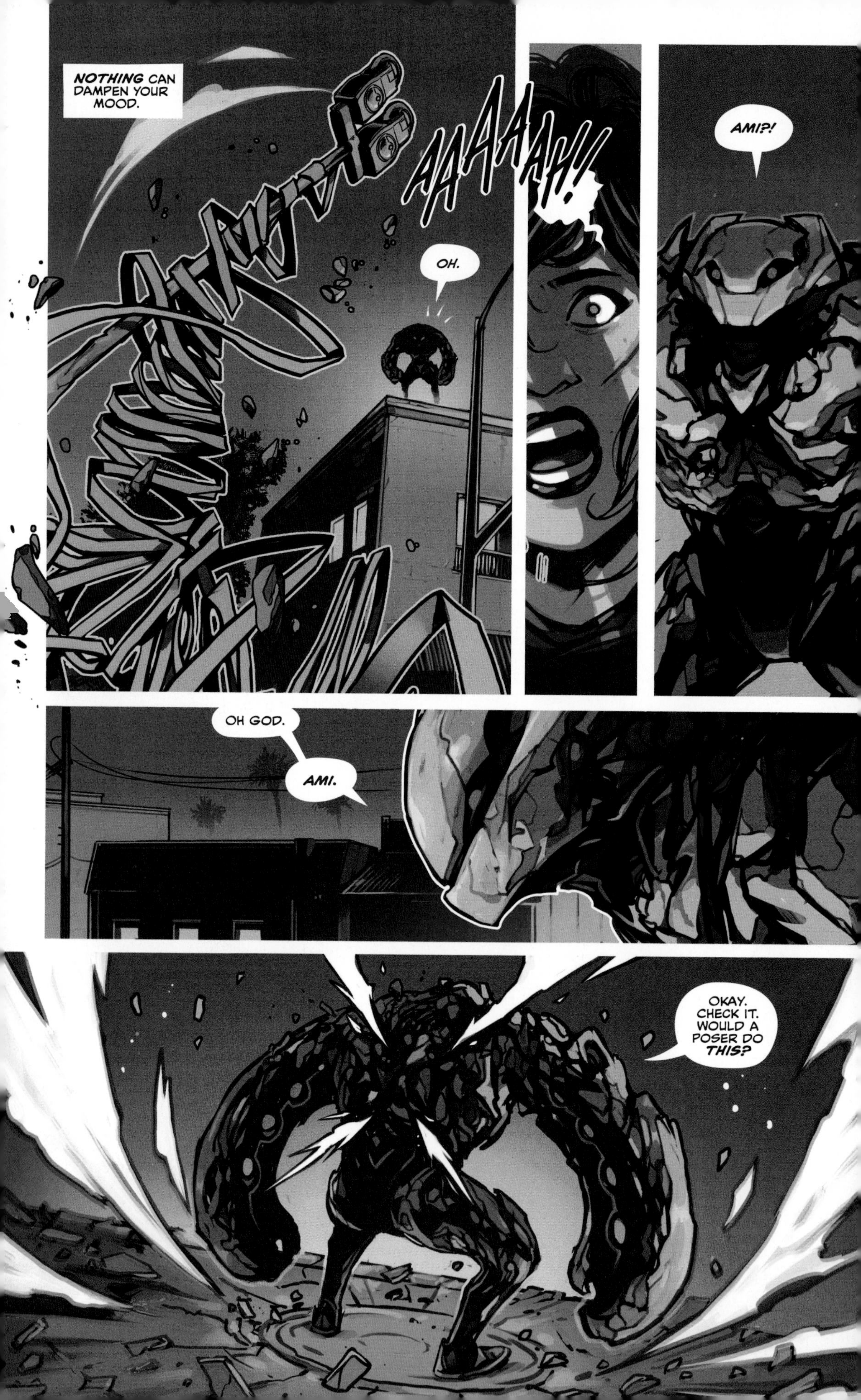
NOTHING CAN DAMPEN YOUR MOOD.
AAAAAH!!
OH.
AMI?!
OH GOD.
AMI.
OKAY. CHECK IT. WOULD A POSER DO THIS?

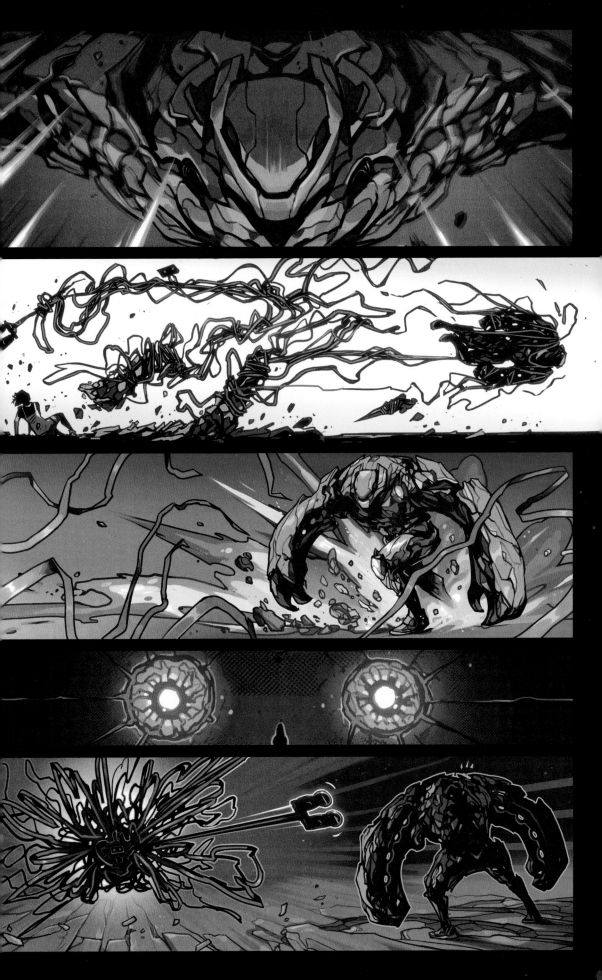

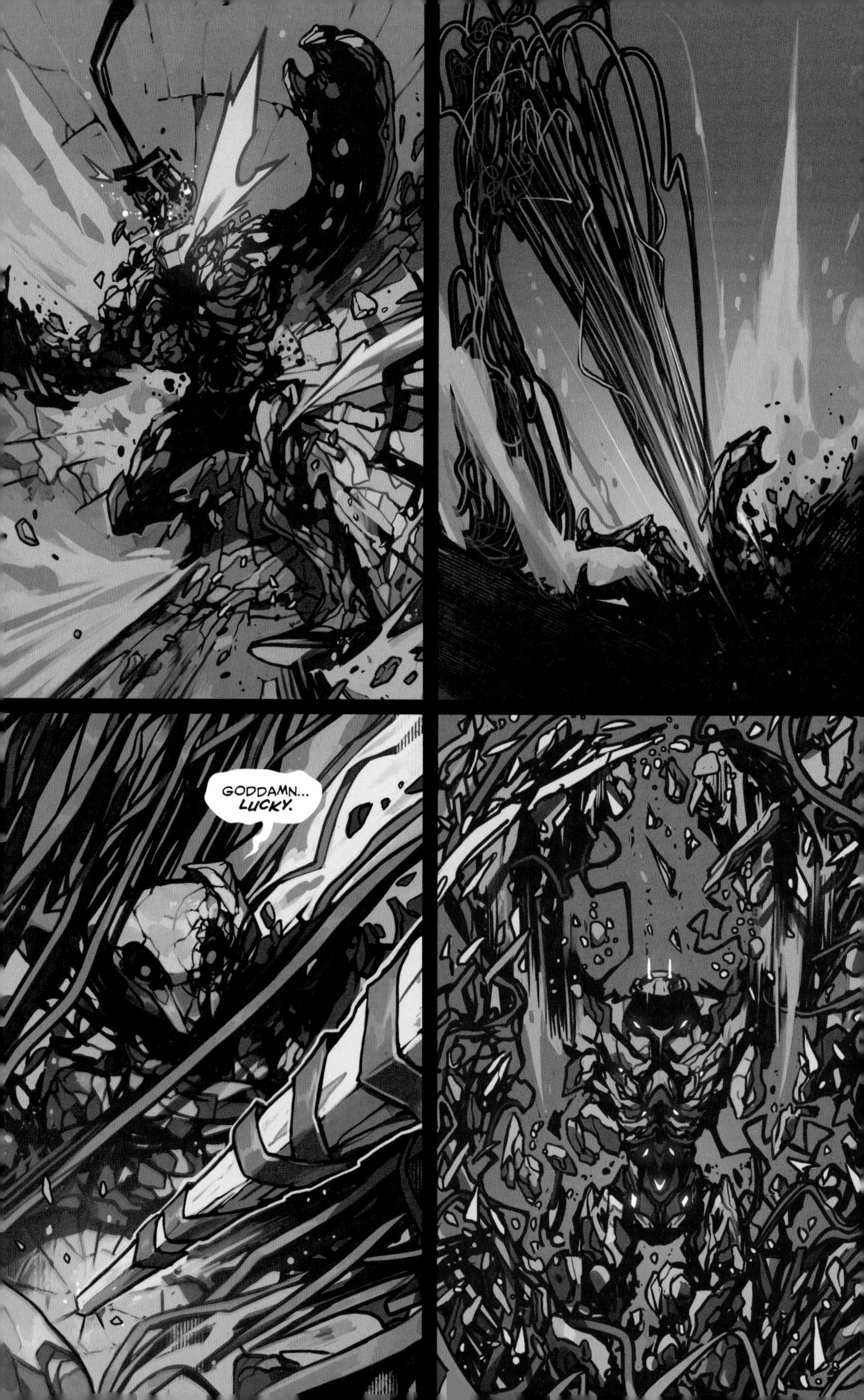
GODDAMN... LUCKY.

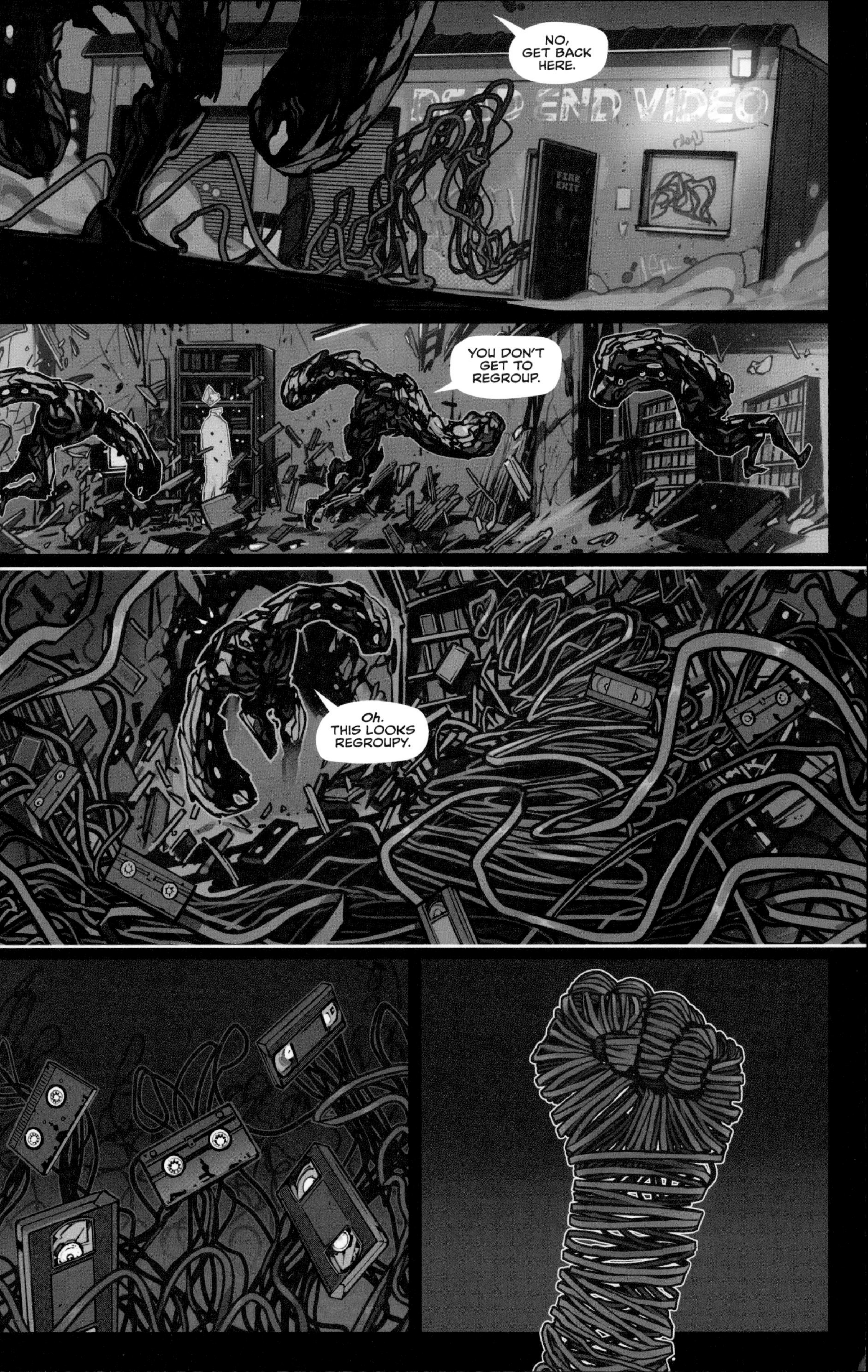
NO, GET BACK HERE.
DEAD END VIDEO
FIRE EXIT
YOU DON'T GET TO REGROUP.
Oh. THIS LOOKS REGROUPY.

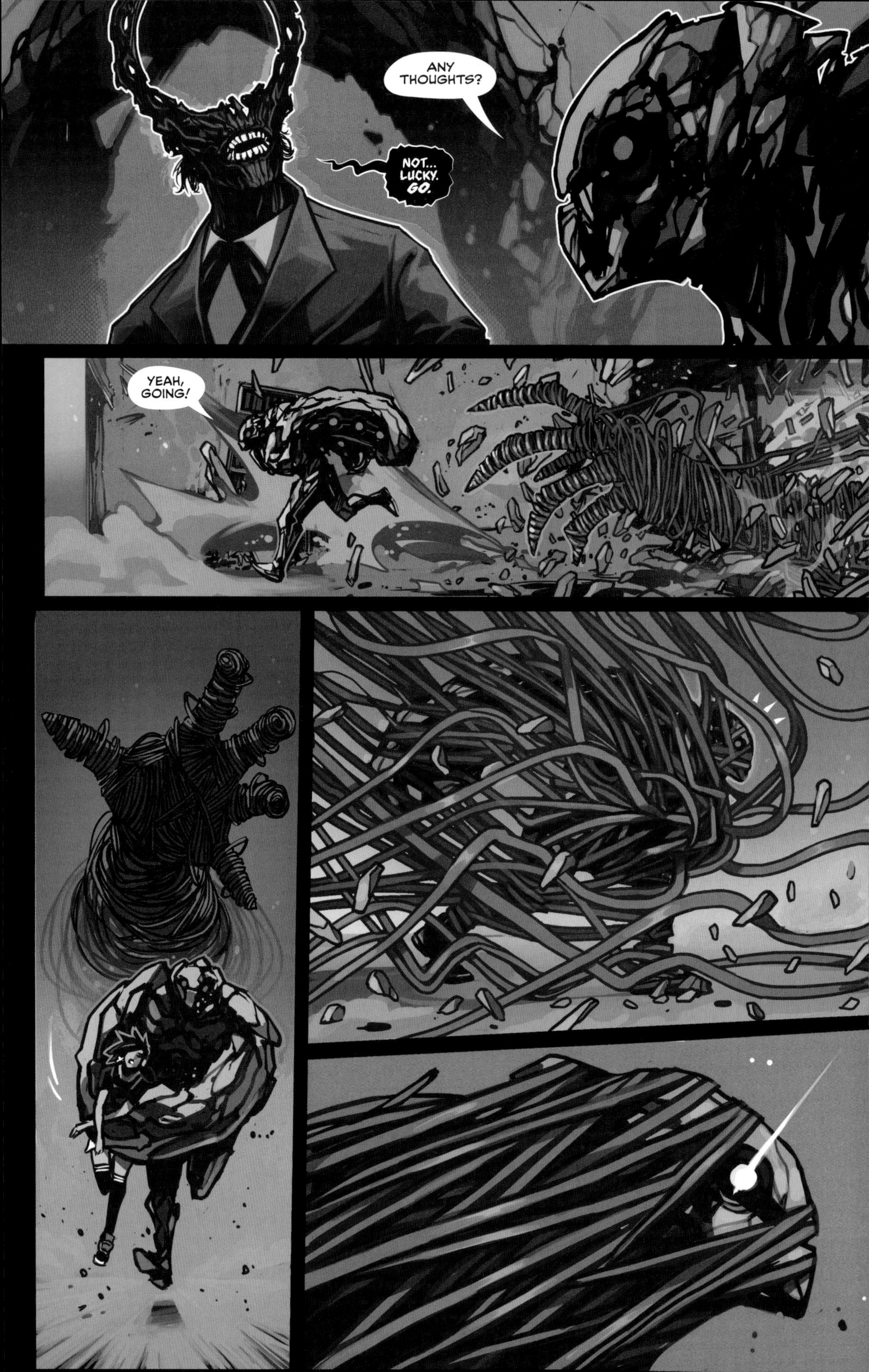
ANY THOUGHTS?
NOT... LUCKY. GO.
YEAH, GOING!

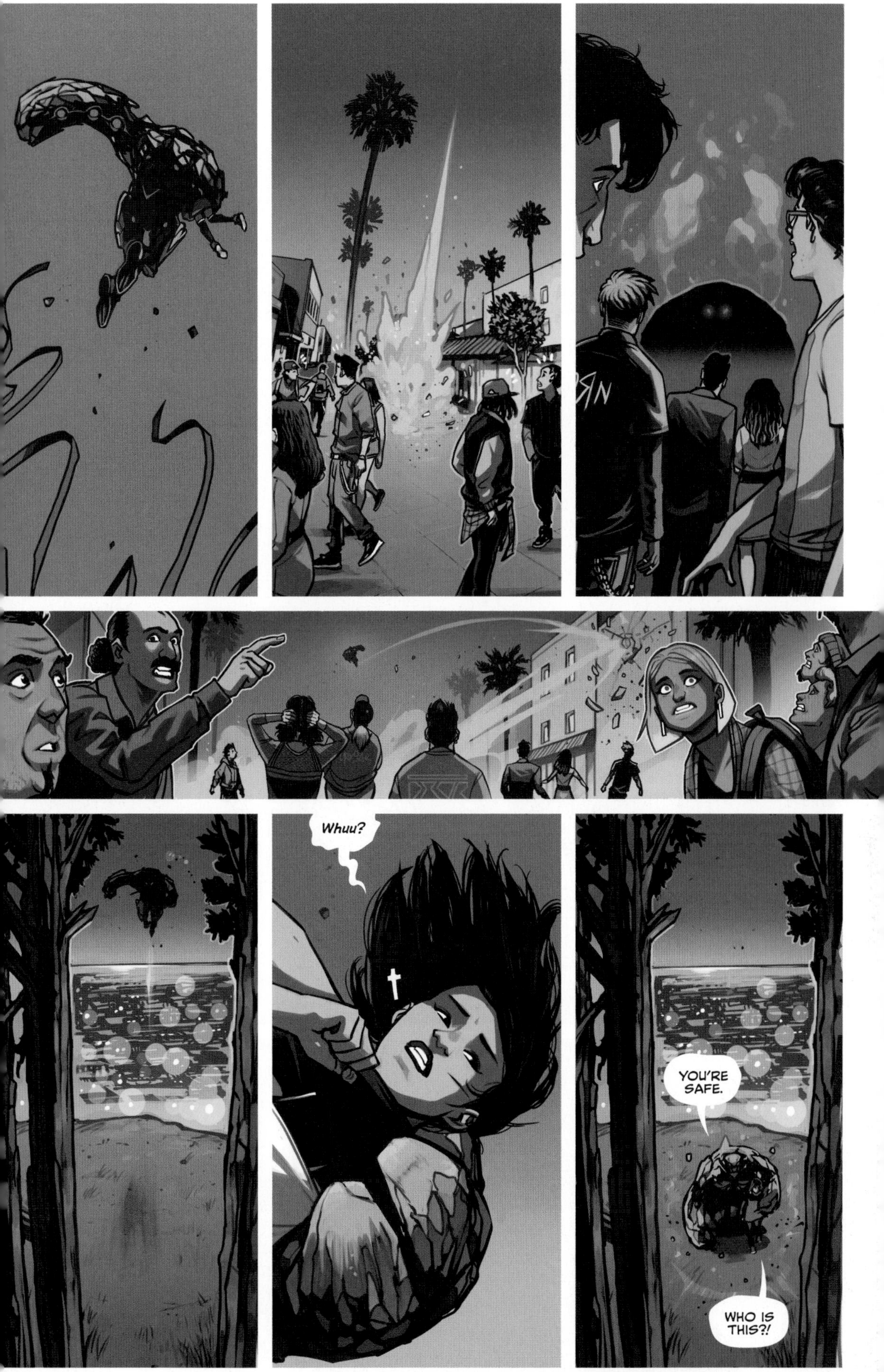
Whuu?
YOU'RE SAFE.
WHO IS THIS?!

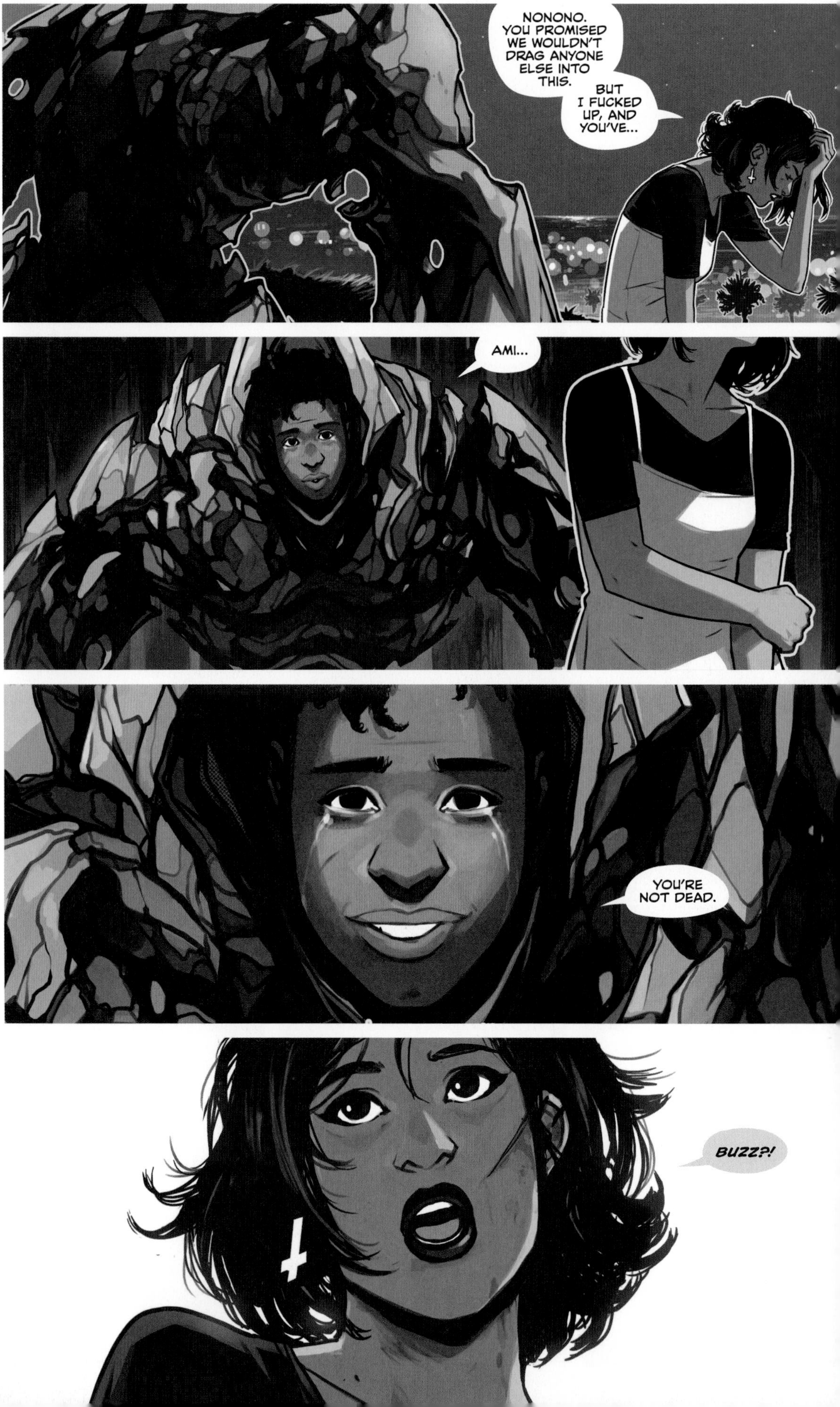
NONONO. YOU PROMISED WE WOULDN'T DRAG ANYONE ELSE INTO THIS.
BUT I FUCKED UP, AND YOU'VE...
AMI...
YOU'RE NOT DEAD.
BUZZ?!

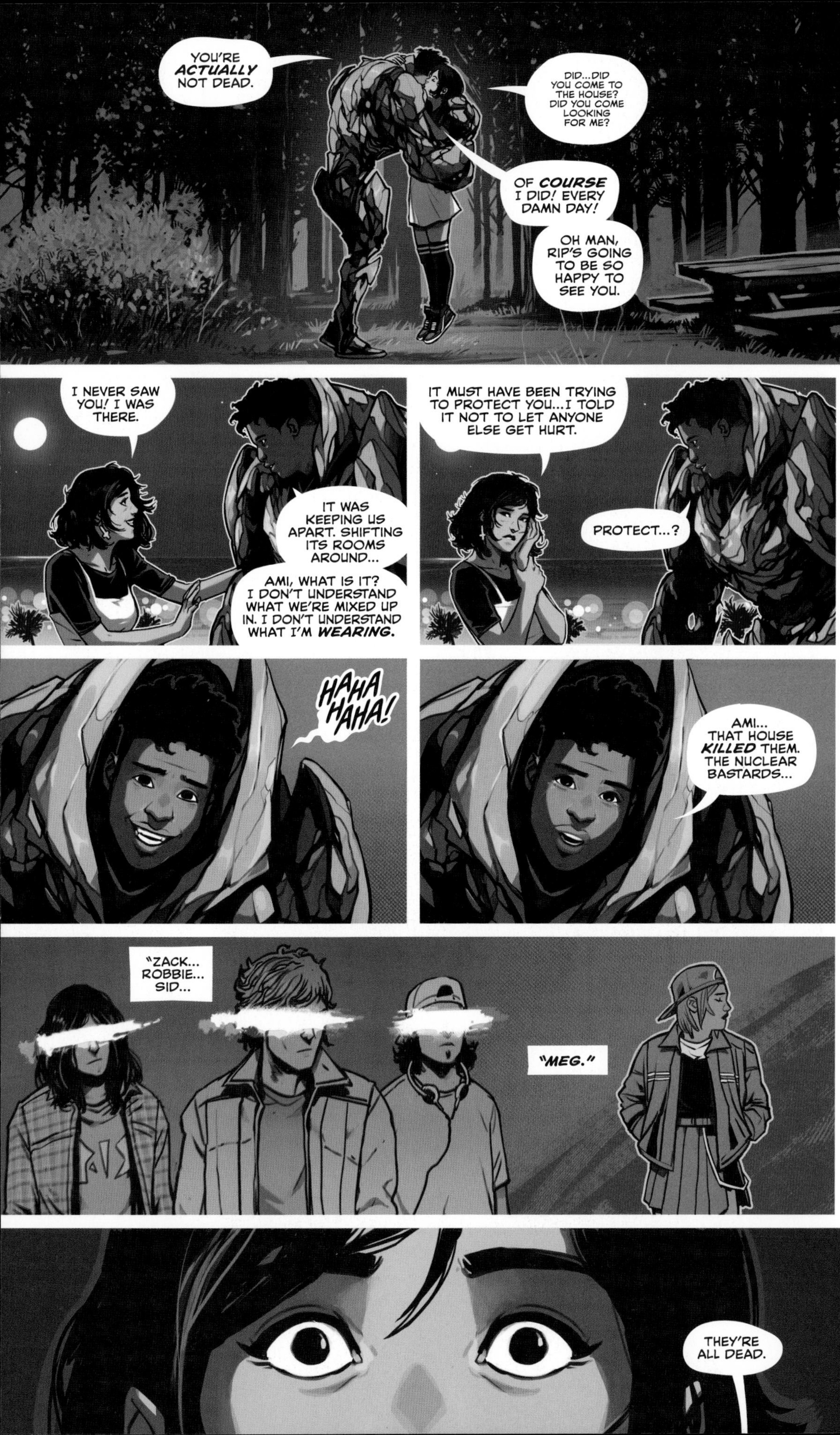
YOU'RE ACTUALLY NOT DEAD.
DID...DID YOU COME TO THE HOUSE? DID YOU COME LOOKING FOR ME?
OF COURSE I DID! EVERY DAMN DAY!
OH MAN, RIP'S GOING TO BE SO HAPPY TO SEE YOU.
I NEVER SAW YOU! I WAS THERE.
IT WAS KEEPING US APART. SHIFTING ITS ROOMS AROUND...
AMI, WHAT IS IT? I DON'T UNDERSTAND WHAT WE'RE MIXED UP IN. I DON'T UNDERSTAND WHAT I'M WEARING.
IT MUST HAVE BEEN TRYING TO PROTECT YOU...I TOLD IT NOT TO LET ANYONE ELSE GET HURT.
PROTECT...?
HAHA HAHA!
AMI... THAT HOUSE KILLED THEM. THE NUCLEAR BASTARDS...
"ZACK... ROBBIE... SID...
"MEG."
THEY'RE ALL DEAD.

THAT PROBABLY MARKS
THE POINT WHERE THE
HONEYMOON PERIOD
ENDED BETWEEN ME AND
THE OLD JAMES HOUSE.
WHEN THE SHINE CAME
OFF THE FIRST FLUSH
OF THE RELATIONSHIP.

EVEN THEN,
I STILL TRIED
TO DEFEND IT.

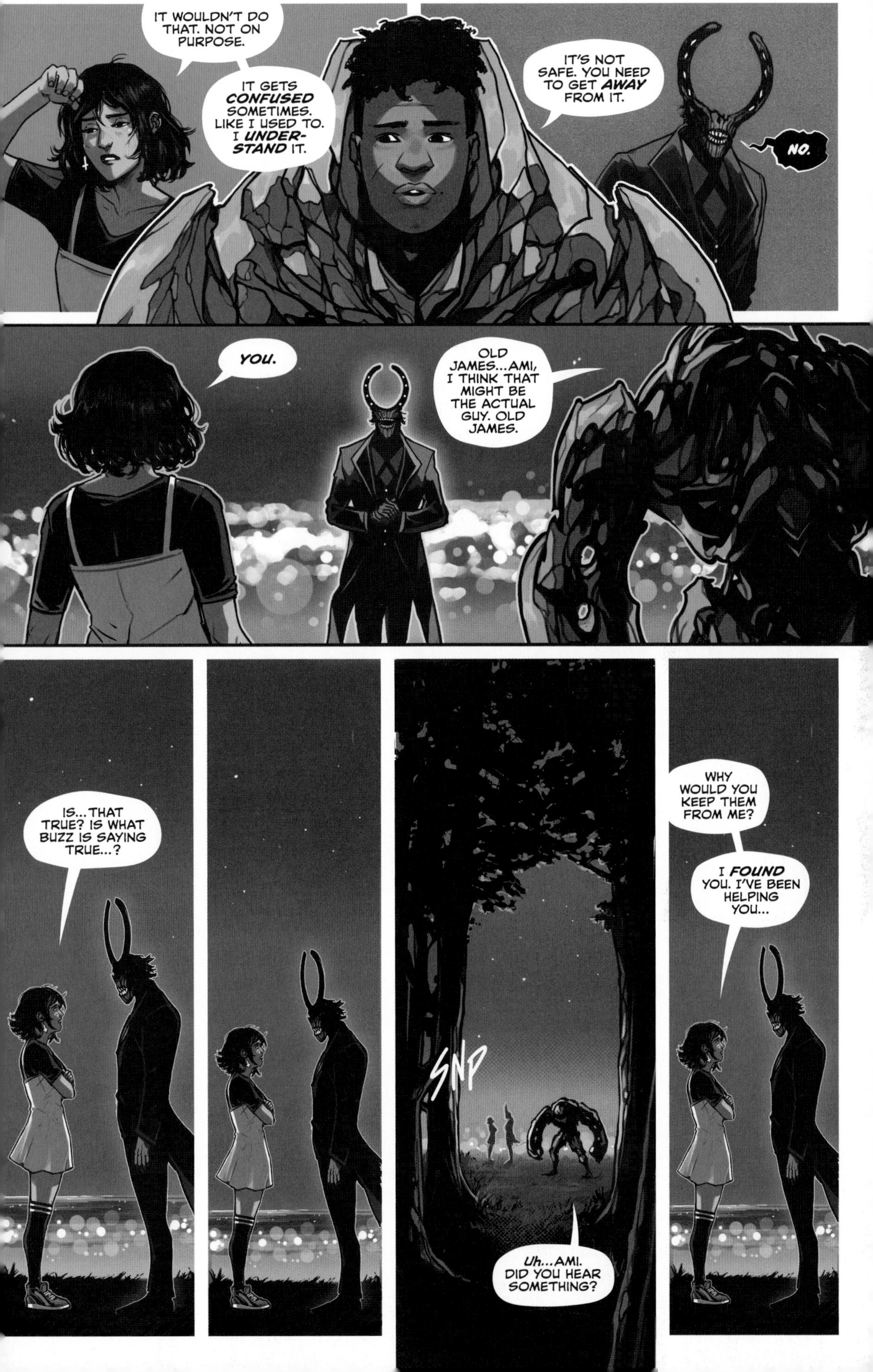
IT WOULDN'T DO THAT. NOT ON PURPOSE.
IT GETS CONFUSED SOMETIMES. LIKE I USED TO. I UNDER-STAND IT.
IT'S NOT SAFE. YOU NEED TO GET AWAY FROM IT.
NO.
YOU.
OLD JAMES...AMI, I THINK THAT MIGHT BE THE ACTUAL GUY. OLD JAMES.
IS...THAT TRUE? IS WHAT BUZZ IS SAYING TRUE...?
SNP
Uh...AMI. DID YOU HEAR SOMETHING?
WHY WOULD YOU KEEP THEM FROM ME?
I FOUND YOU. I'VE BEEN HELPING YOU...

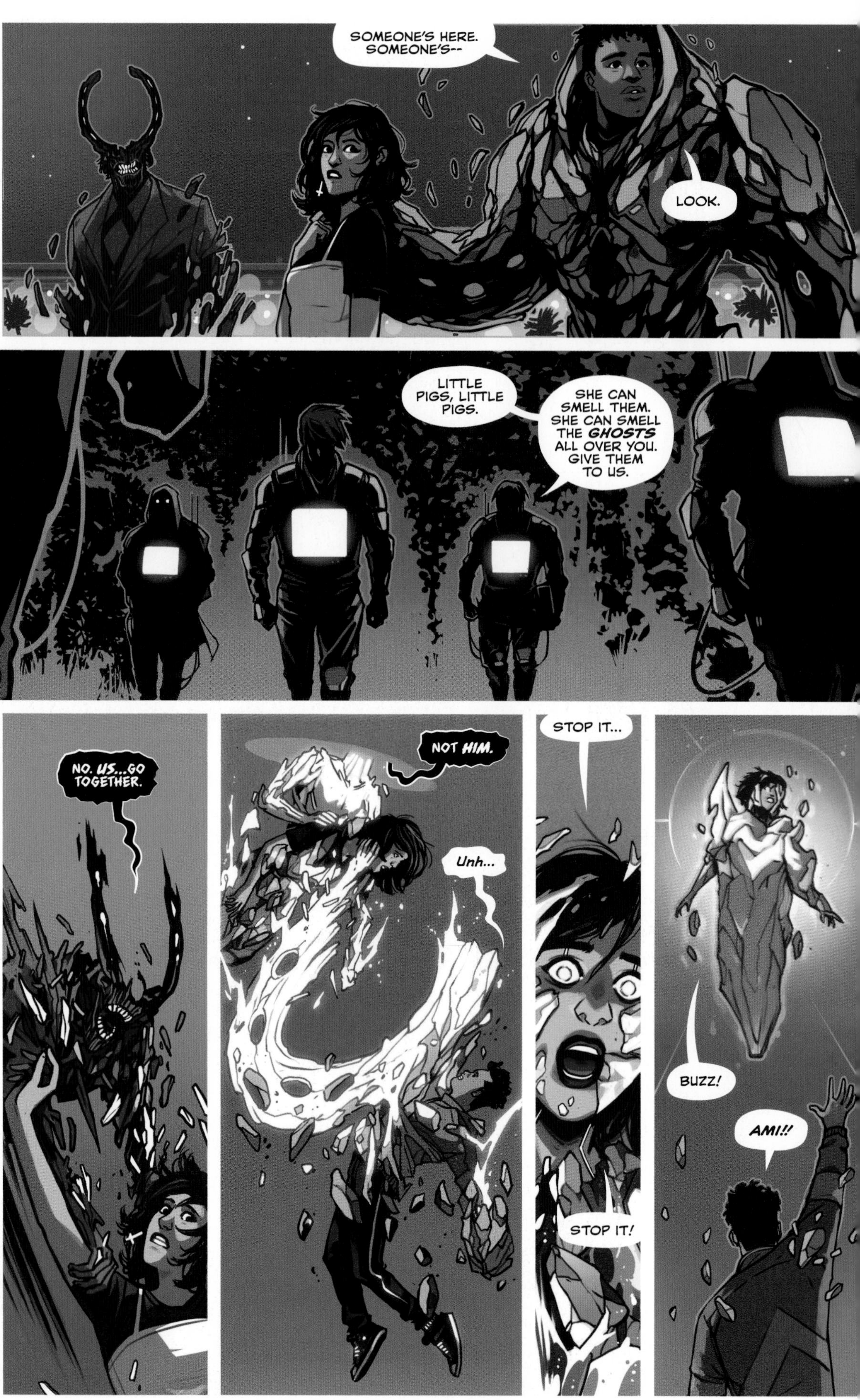
SOMEONE'S HERE. SOMEONE'S--
LOOK.
LITTLE PIGS, LITTLE PIGS.
SHE CAN SMELL THEM. SHE CAN SMELL THE *GHOSTS* ALL OVER YOU. GIVE THEM TO US.
NO. *US*...GO TOGETHER.
NOT *HIM.*
Unh...
STOP IT...
STOP IT!
BUZZ!
AMI!!

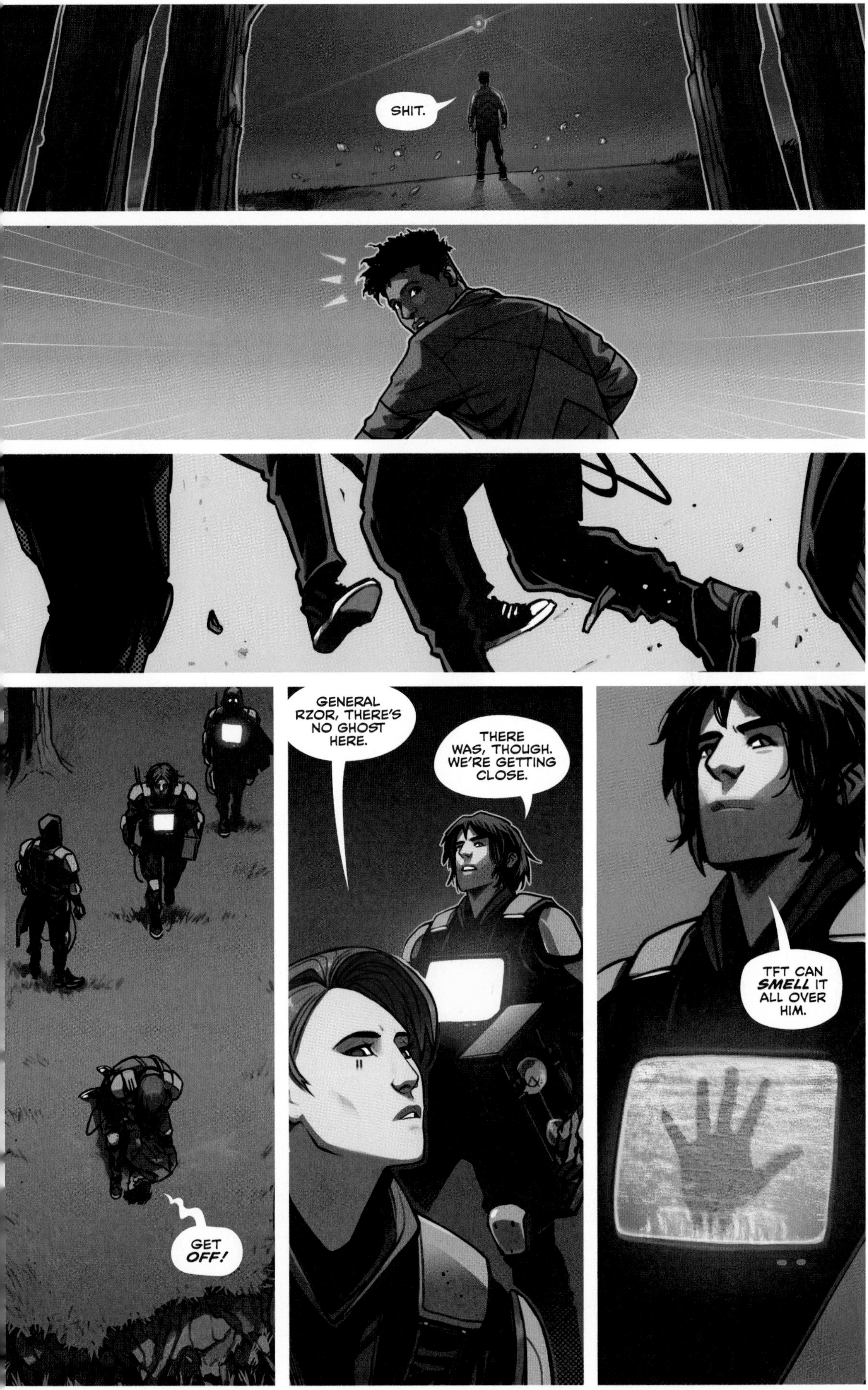
SHIT.
GET OFF!
GENERAL RZOR, THERE'S NO GHOST HERE.
THERE WAS, THOUGH. WE'RE GETTING CLOSE.
THEY CAN SMELL IT ALL OVER HIM.

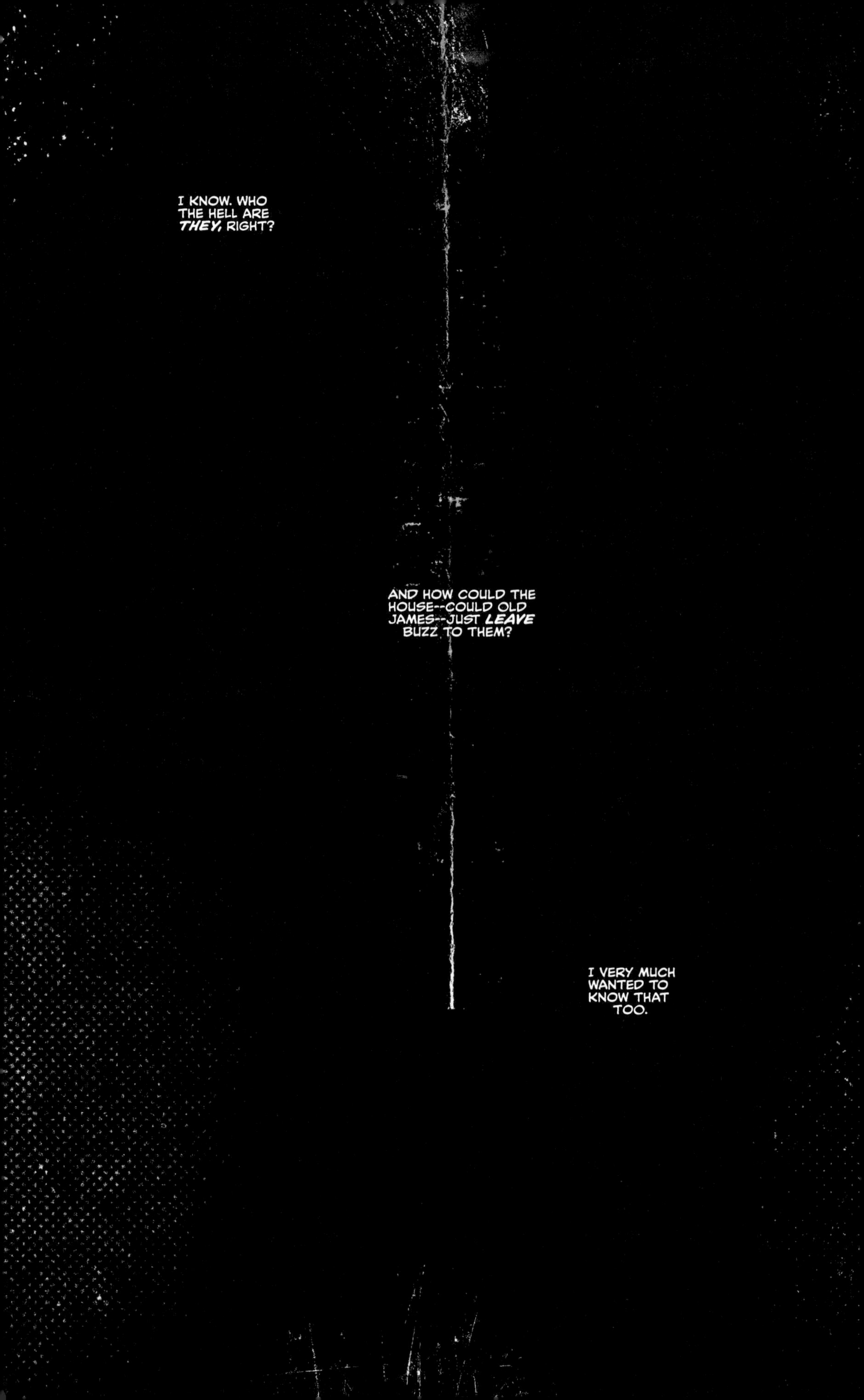
I KNOW. WHO THE HELL ARE *THEY,* RIGHT?
AND HOW COULD THE HOUSE--COULD OLD JAMES--JUST *LEAVE* BUZZ TO THEM?
I VERY MUCH WANTED TO KNOW THAT TOO.

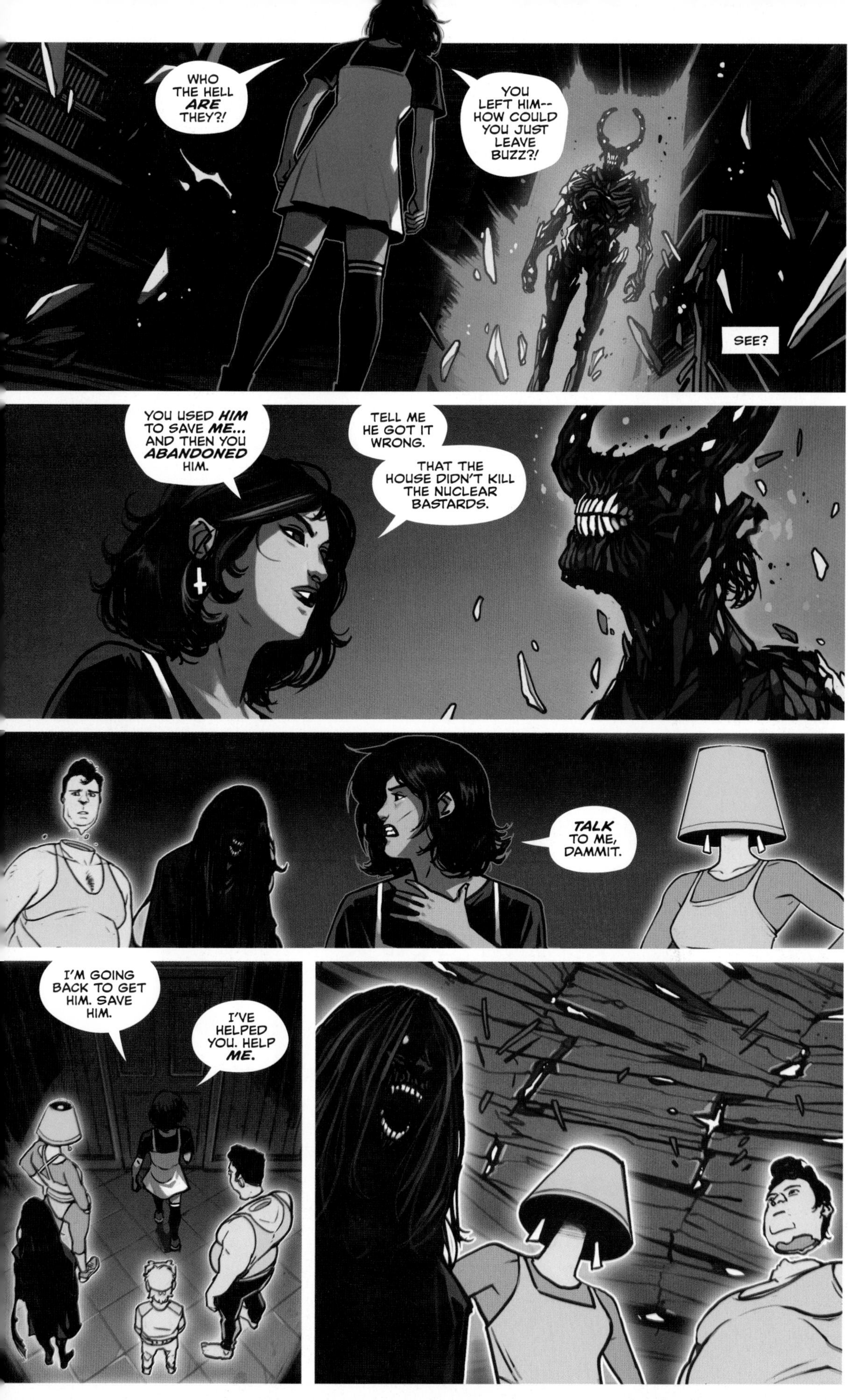
WHO THE HELL ARE THEY?!
YOU LEFT HIM-- HOW COULD YOU JUST LEAVE BUZZ?!
SEE?
YOU USED HIM TO SAVE ME... AND THEN YOU ABANDONED HIM.
TELL ME HE GOT IT WRONG.
THAT THE HOUSE DIDN'T KILL THE NUCLEAR BASTARDS.
TALK TO ME, DAMMIT.
I'M GOING BACK TO GET HIM. SAVE HIM.
I'VE HELPED YOU. HELP ME.

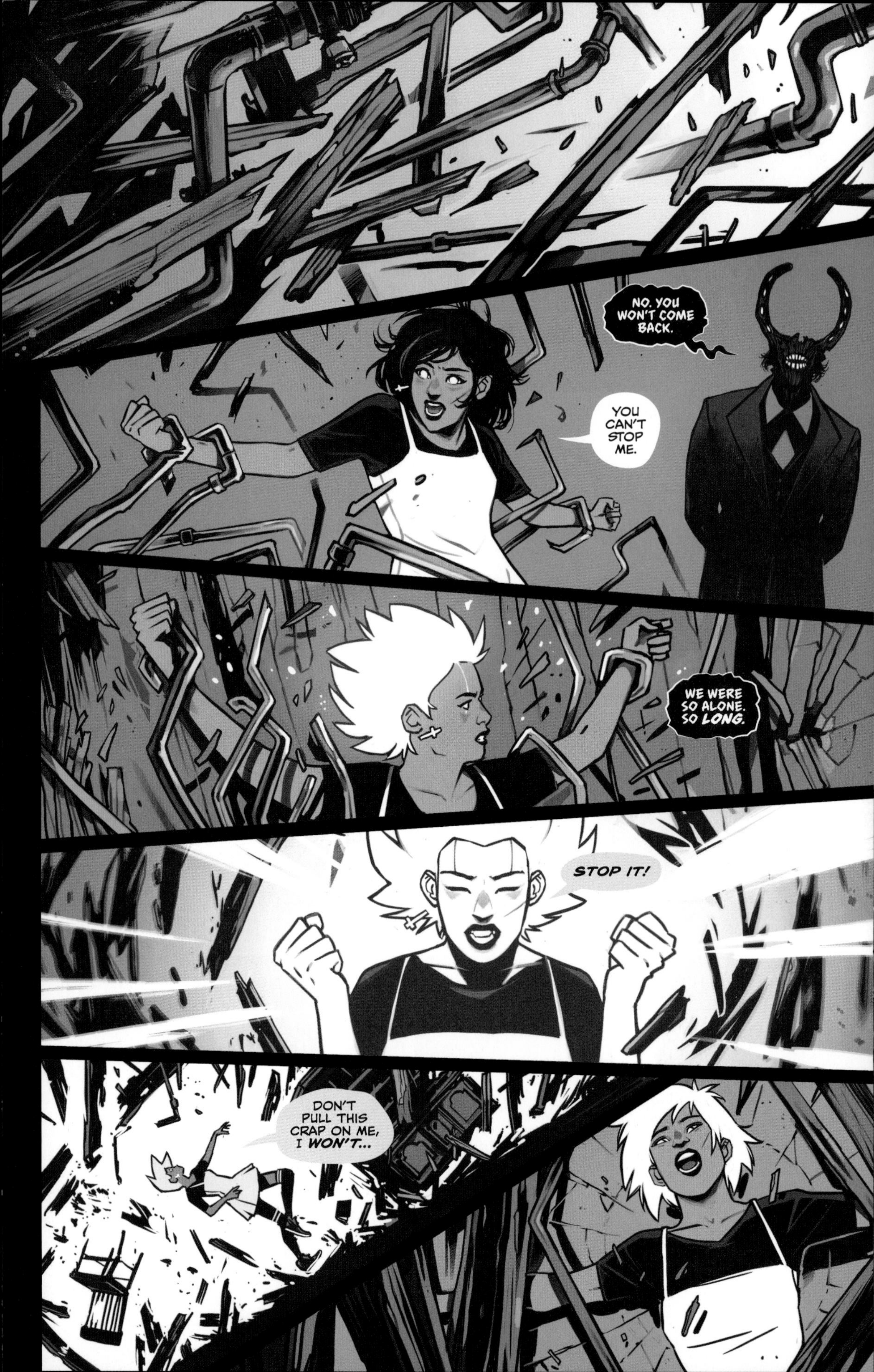

NO. YOU WON'T COME BACK.
YOU CAN'T STOP ME.
WE WERE SO ALONE. SO LONG.
STOP IT!
DON'T PULL THIS CRAP ON ME, I WON'T...

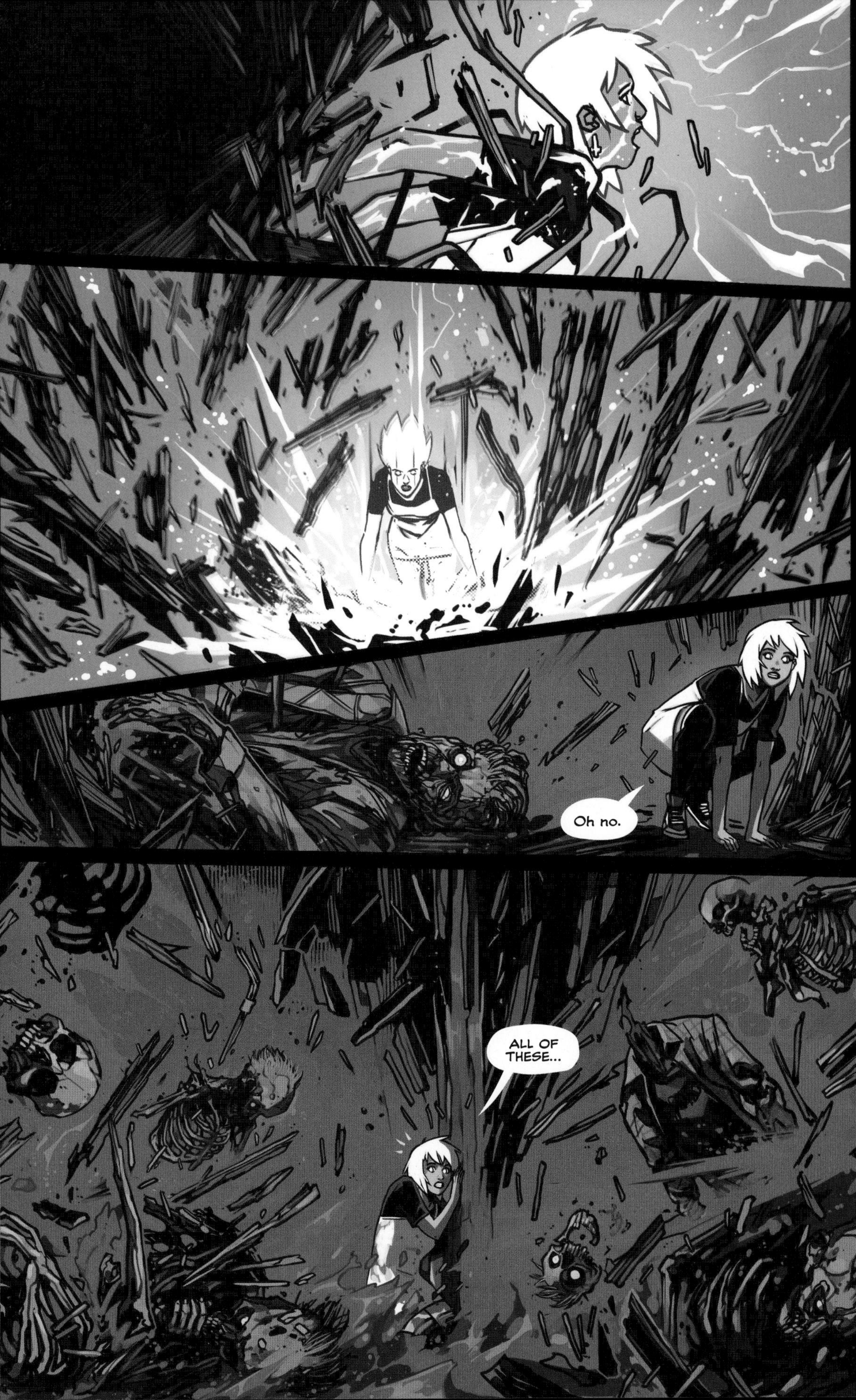
Oh no.
ALL OF THESE...

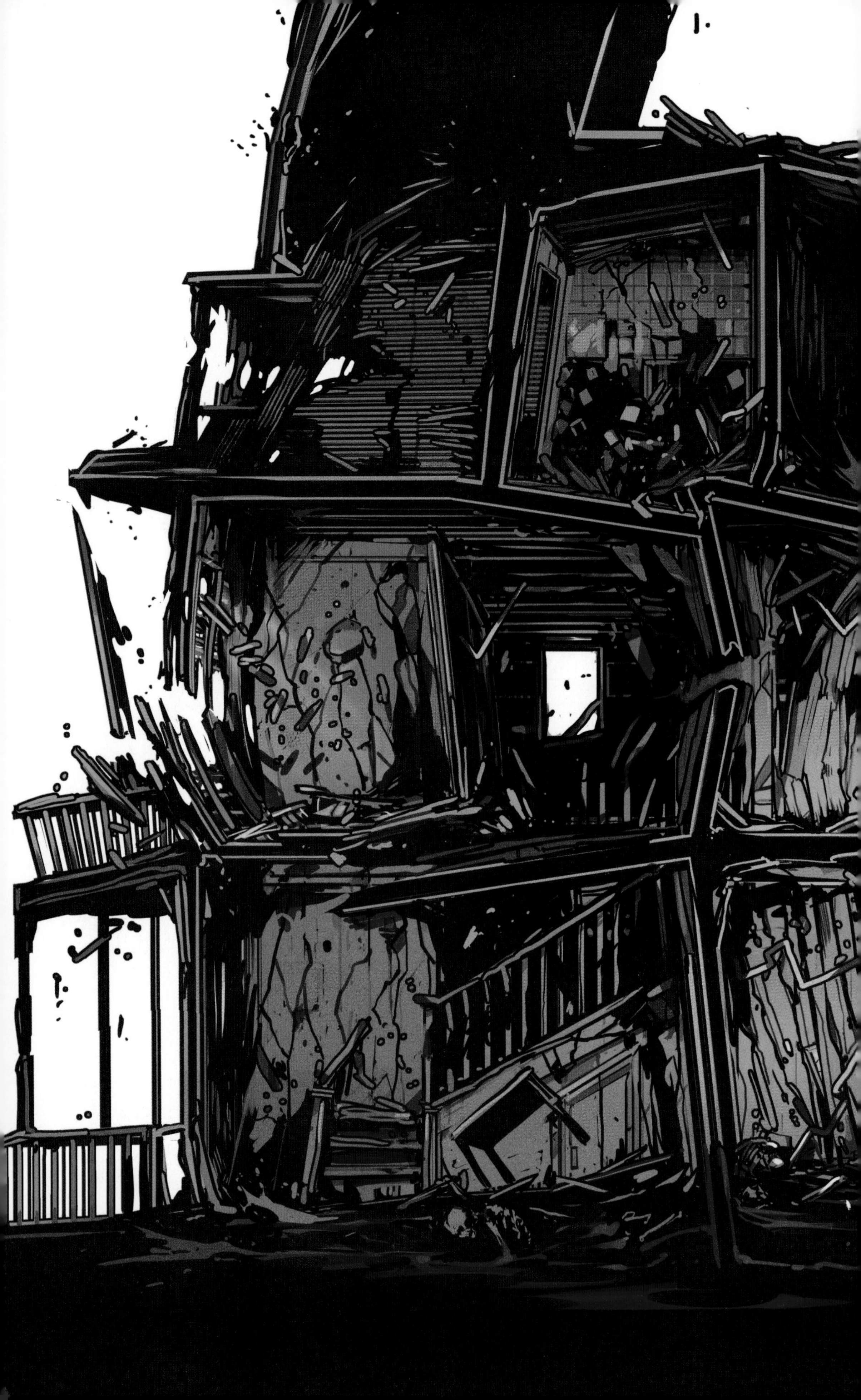

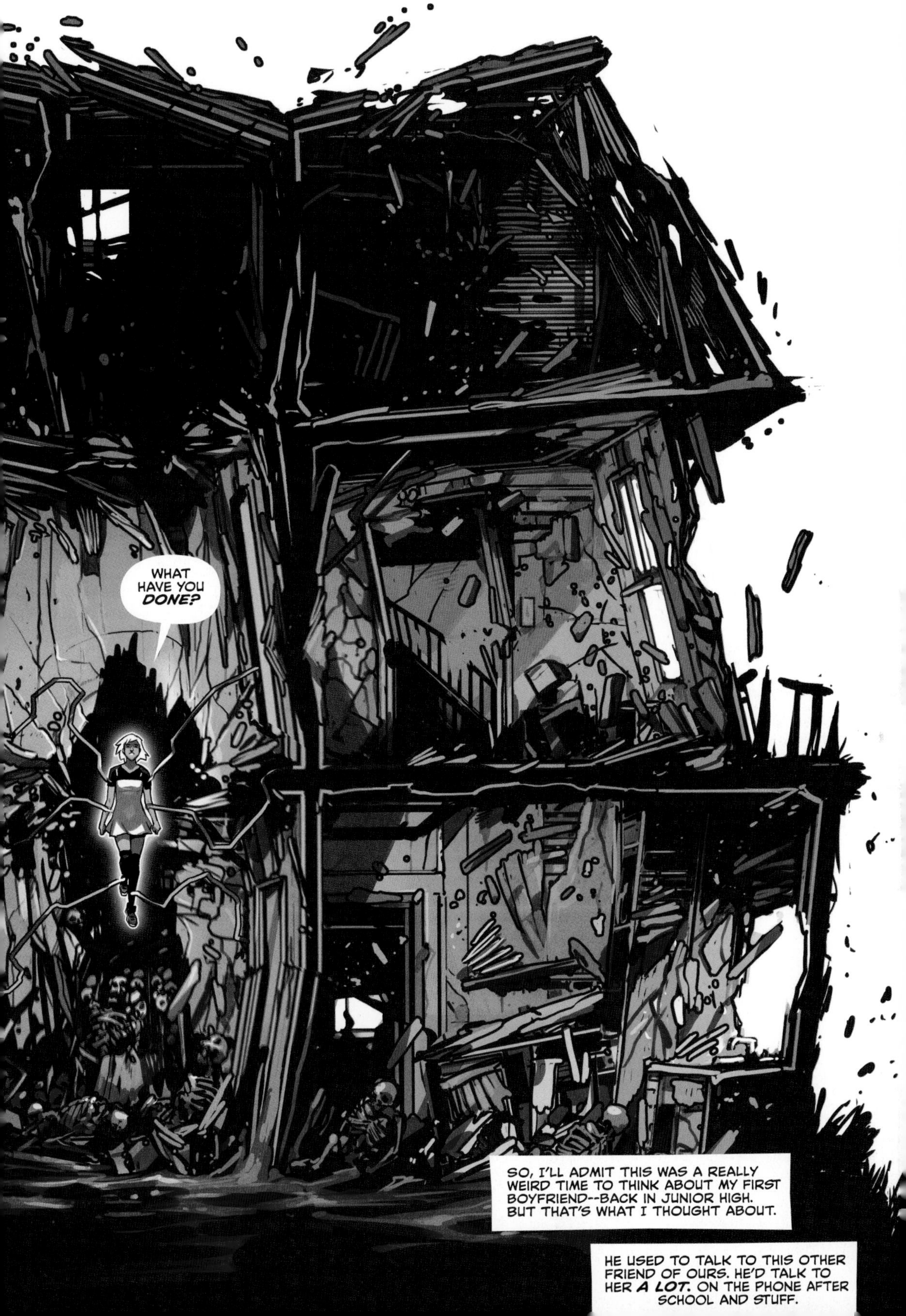
WHAT HAVE YOU *DONE?*
SO, I'LL ADMIT THIS WAS A REALLY WEIRD TIME TO THINK ABOUT MY FIRST BOYFRIEND--BACK IN JUNIOR HIGH. BUT THAT'S WHAT I THOUGHT ABOUT.
HE USED TO TALK TO THIS OTHER FRIEND OF OURS. HE'D TALK TO HER *A LOT.* ON THE PHONE AFTER SCHOOL AND STUFF.

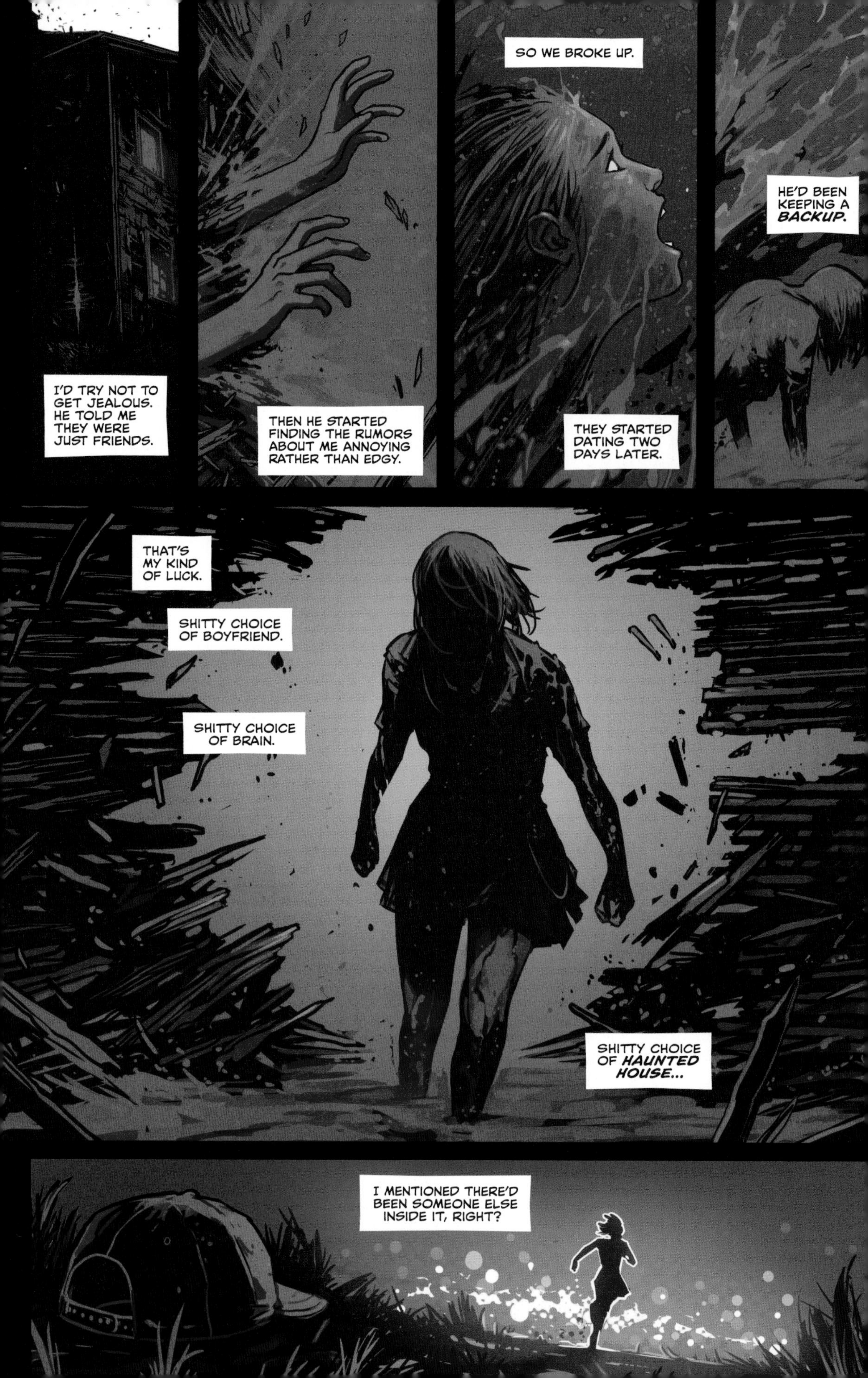
I'D TRY NOT TO GET JEALOUS. HE TOLD ME THEY WERE JUST FRIENDS.
THEN HE STARTED FINDING THE RUMORS ABOUT ME ANNOYING RATHER THAN EDGY.
SO WE BROKE UP.
THEY STARTED DATING TWO DAYS LATER.
HE'D BEEN KEEPING A ***BACKUP.***
THAT'S MY KIND OF LUCK.
SHITTY CHOICE OF BOYFRIEND.
SHITTY CHOICE OF BRAIN.
SHITTY CHOICE OF ***HAUNTED HOUSE...***
I MENTIONED THERE'D BEEN SOMEONE ELSE INSIDE IT, RIGHT?

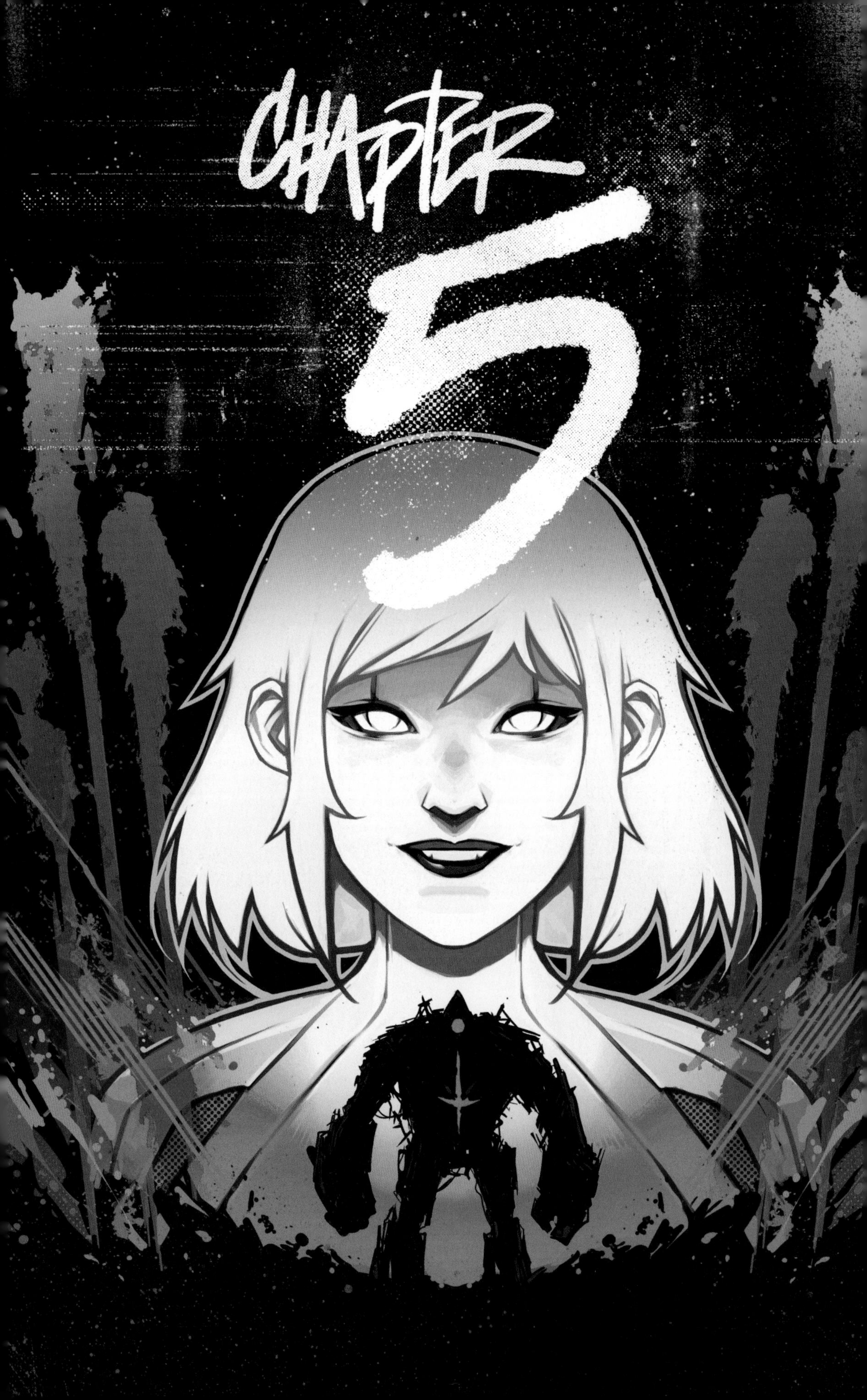
CHAPTER
5

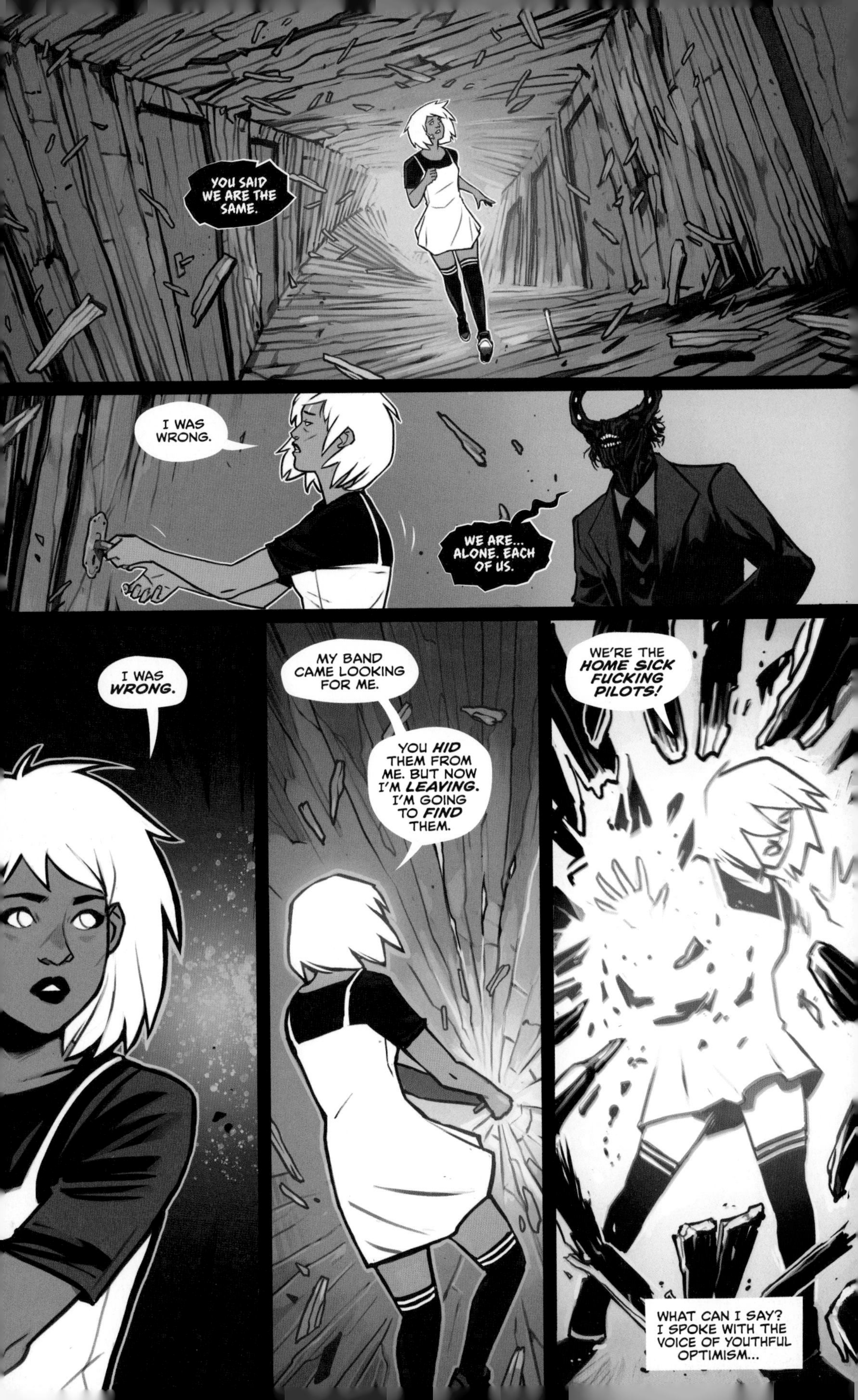
YOU SAID WE ARE THE SAME.
I WAS WRONG.
WE ARE... ALONE. EACH OF US.
I WAS *WRONG.*
MY BAND CAME LOOKING FOR ME.
YOU *HID* THEM FROM ME. BUT NOW I'M *LEAVING.* I'M GOING TO *FIND* THEM.
WE'RE THE *HOME SICK FUCKING PILOTS!*
WHAT CAN I SAY? I SPOKE WITH THE VOICE OF YOUTHFUL OPTIMISM...

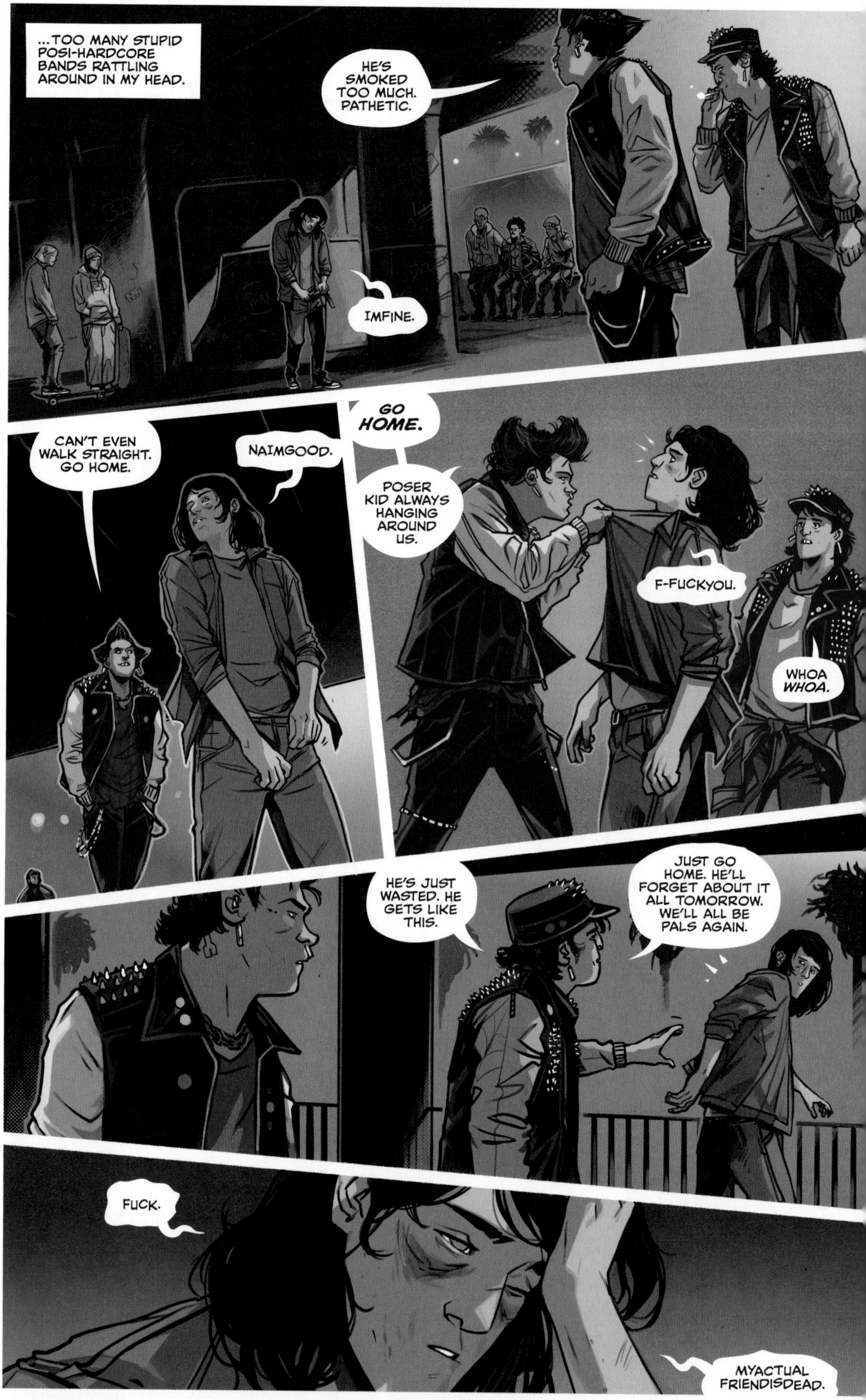
...TOO MANY STUPID POSI-HARDCORE BANDS RATTLING AROUND IN MY HEAD.
HE'S SMOKED TOO MUCH. PATHETIC.
IMFINE.
CAN'T EVEN WALK STRAIGHT. GO HOME.
NAIMGOOD.
GO HOME.
POSER KID ALWAYS HANGING AROUND US.
F-FUCKYOU.
WHOA WHOA.
HE'S JUST WASTED. HE GETS LIKE THIS.
JUST GO HOME. HE'LL FORGET ABOUT IT ALL TOMORROW. WE'LL ALL BE PALS AGAIN.
FUCK.
MYACTUAL FRIENDISDEAD.

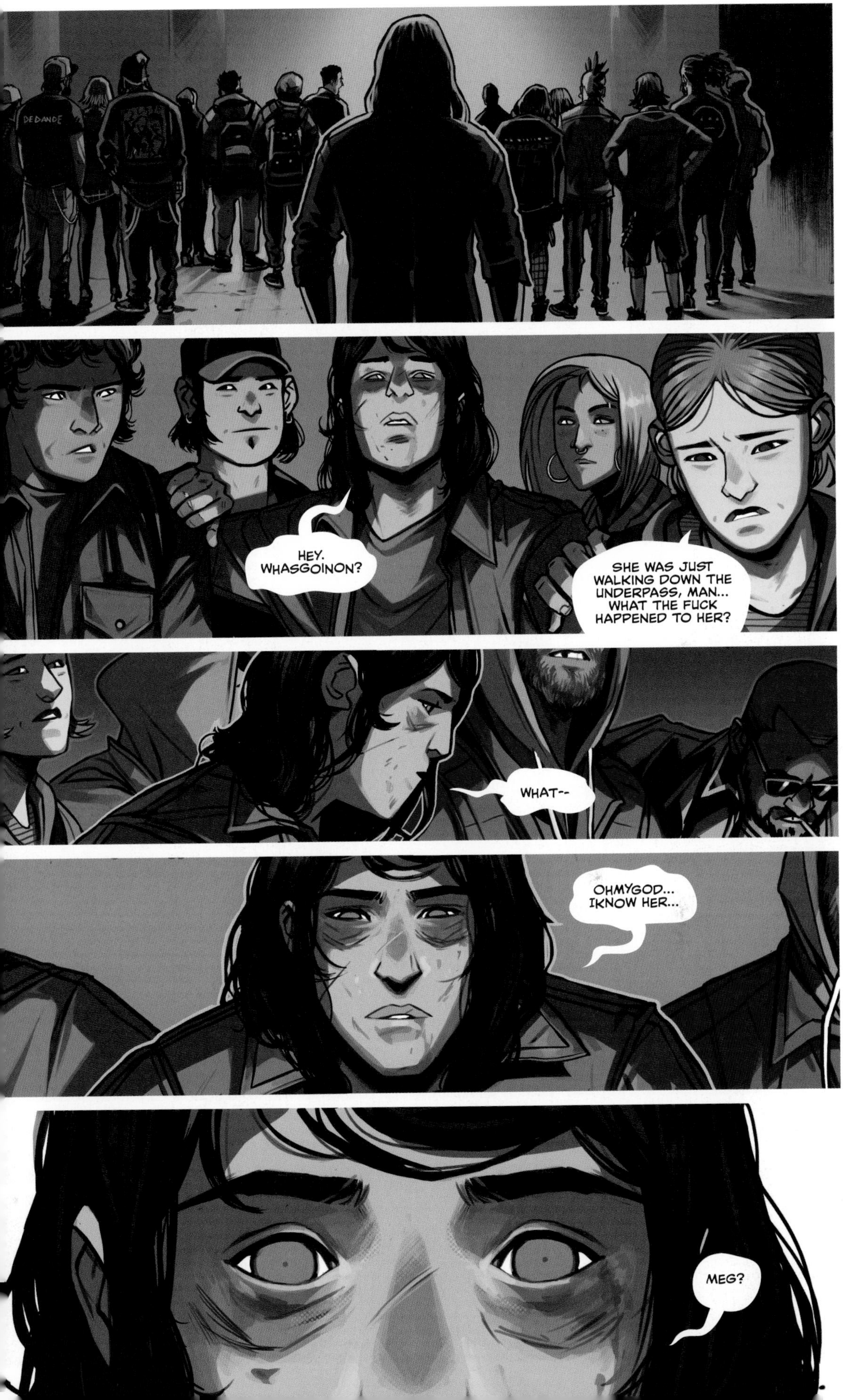
DEDANCE
HEY. WHASGOINON?
SHE WAS JUST WALKING DOWN THE UNDERPASS, MAN... WHAT THE FUCK HAPPENED TO HER?
WHAT--
OHMYGOD... IKNOW HER...
MEG?

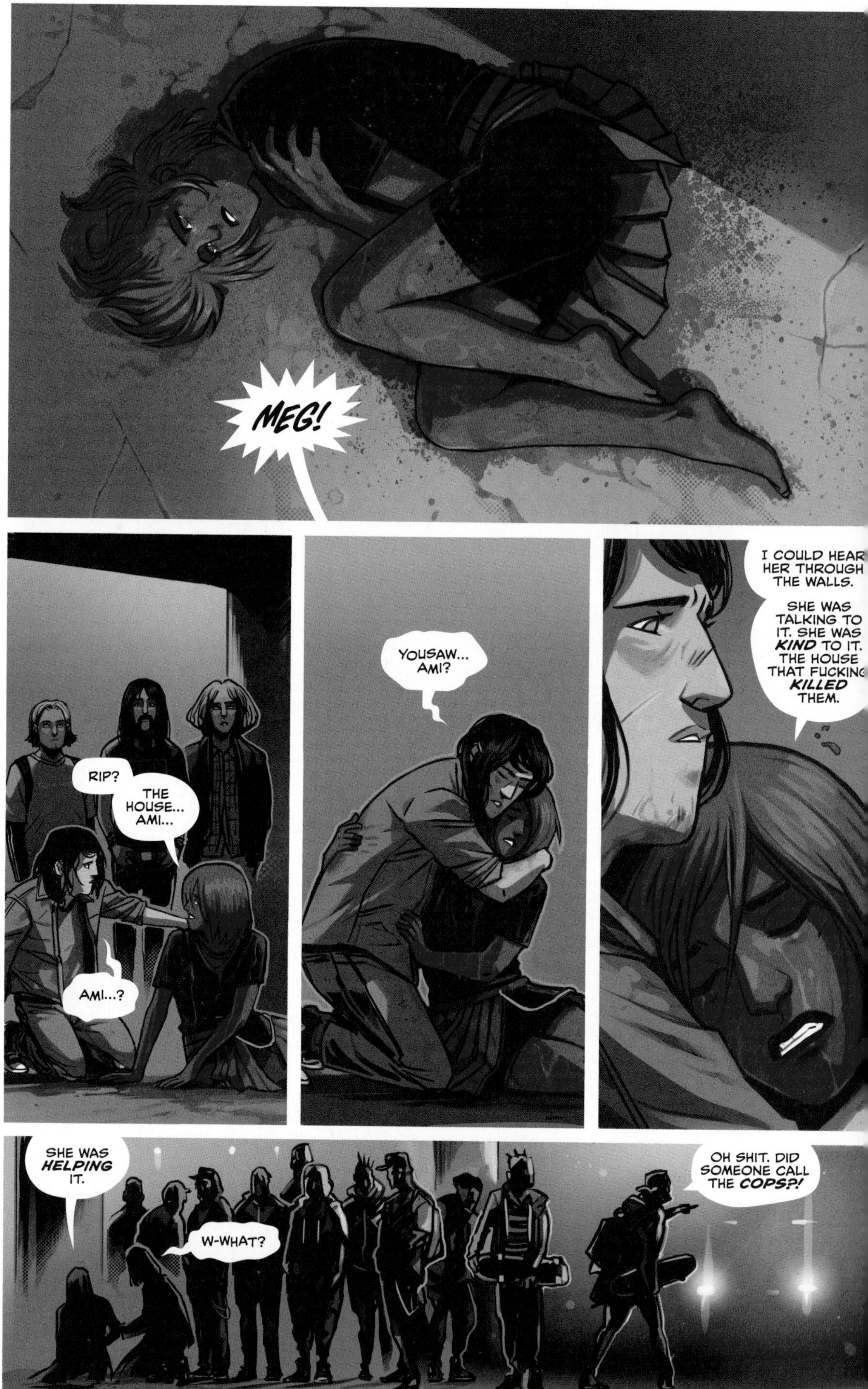
MEG!
RIP?
THE HOUSE... AMI...
AMI...?
YOUSAW... AMI?
I COULD HEAR HER THROUGH THE WALLS.
SHE WAS TALKING TO IT. SHE WAS KIND TO IT. THE HOUSE THAT FUCKING KILLED THEM.
SHE WAS HELPING IT.
W-WHAT?
OH SHIT. DID SOMEONE CALL THE COPS?!

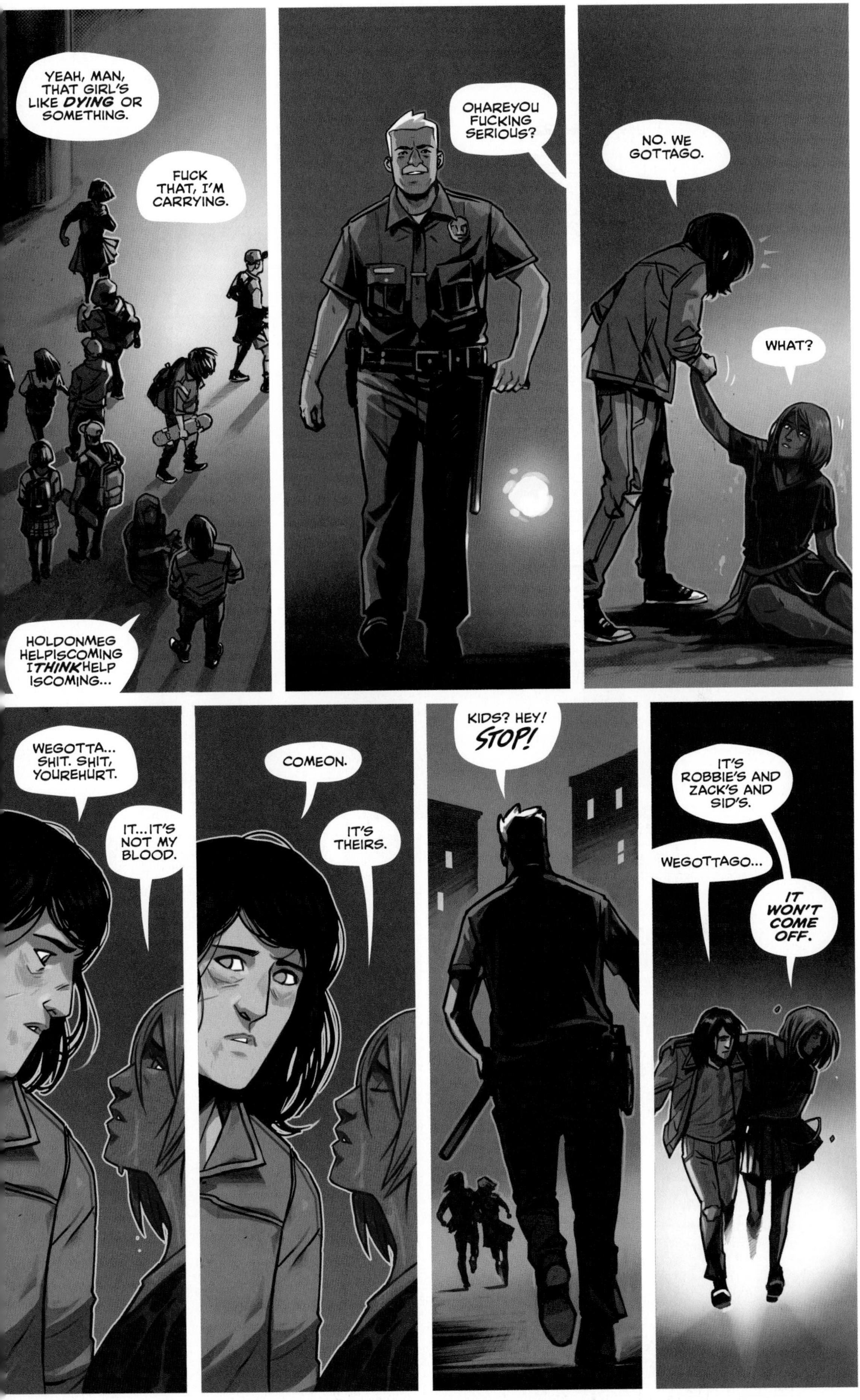
YEAH, MAN, THAT GIRL'S LIKE *DYING* OR SOMETHING.
FUCK THAT, I'M CARRYING.
HOLDONMEG HELPISCOMING I*THINK*HELP ISCOMING...
OHAREYOU FUCKING SERIOUS?
NO. WE GOTTAGO.
WHAT?
WEGOTTA... SHIT. SHIT, YOUREHURT.
IT...IT'S NOT MY BLOOD.
COMEON.
IT'S THEIRS.
KIDS? HEY! *STOP!*
IT'S ROBBIE'S AND ZACK'S AND SID'S.
WEGOTTAGO...
IT WON'T COME OFF.

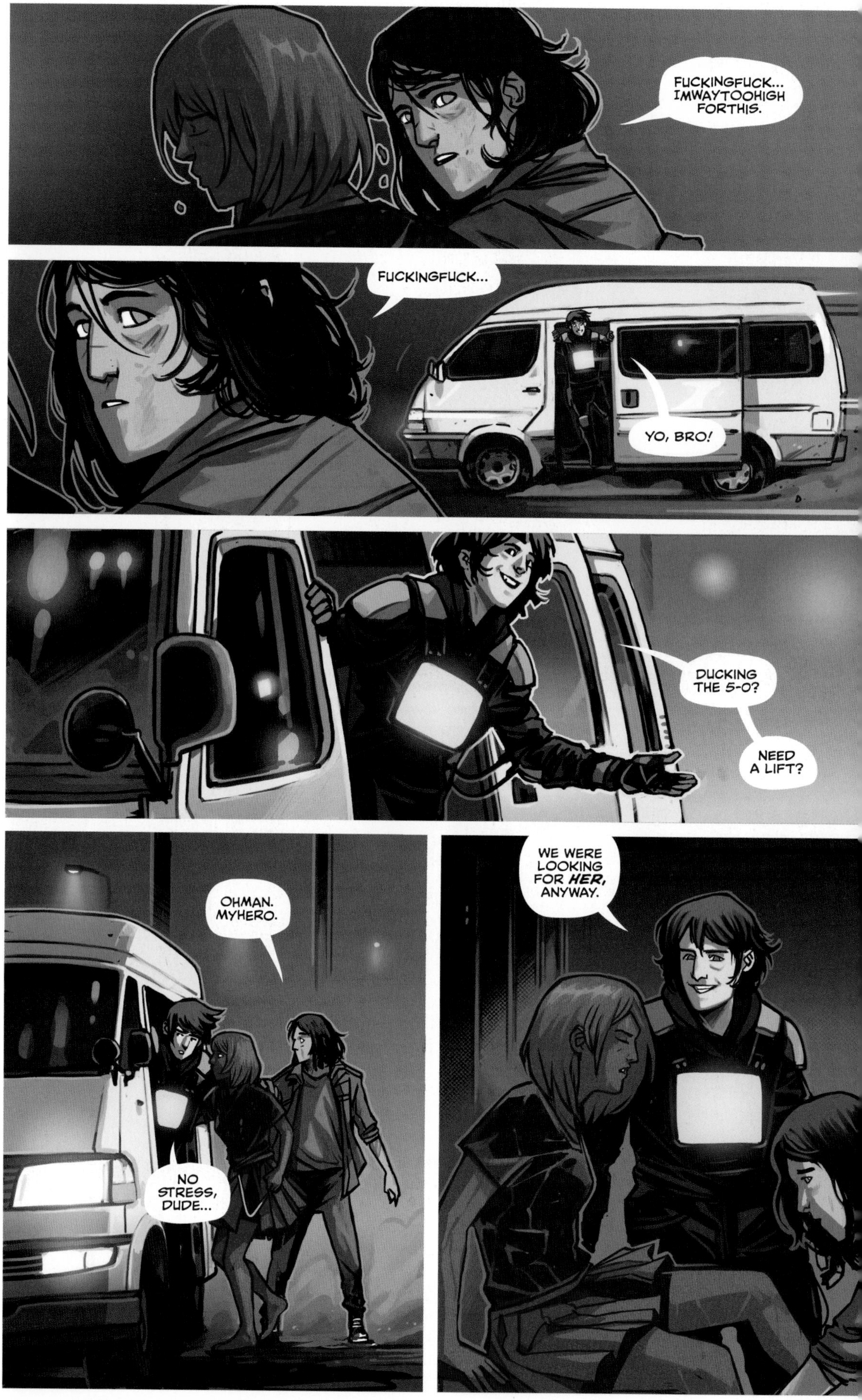
FUCKINGFUCK... IMWAYTOOHIGH FORTHIS.
FUCKINGFUCK...
YO, BRO!
DUCKING THE 5-0?
NEED A LIFT?
OHMAN. MYHERO.
NO STRESS, DUDE...
WE WERE LOOKING FOR HER, ANYWAY.

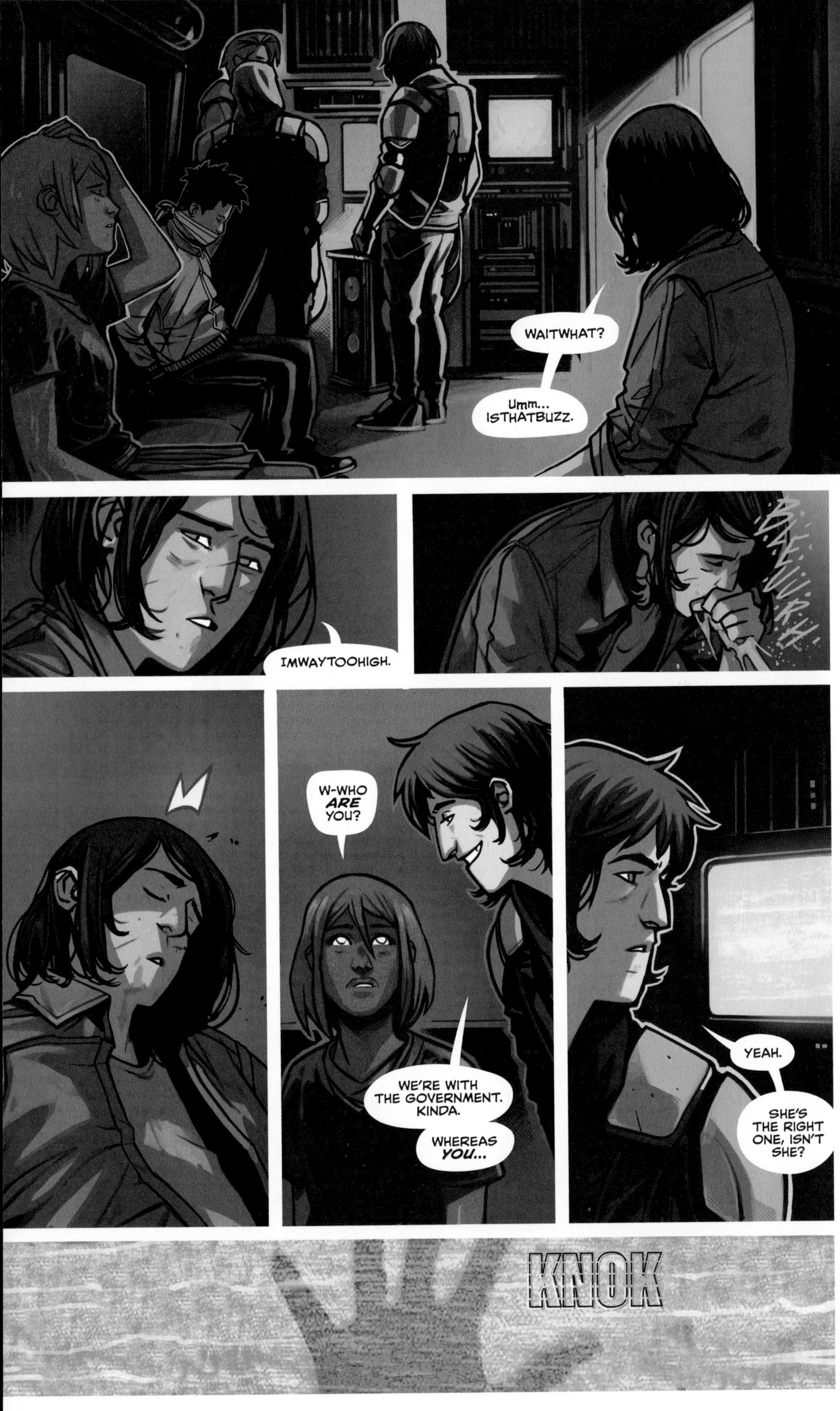
WAITWHAT?
Umm... ISTHATBUZZ.
IMWAYTOOHIGH.
W-WHO ARE YOU?
WE'RE WITH THE GOVERNMENT. KINDA.
WHEREAS YOU...
YEAH.
SHE'S THE RIGHT ONE, ISN'T SHE?
KNOK

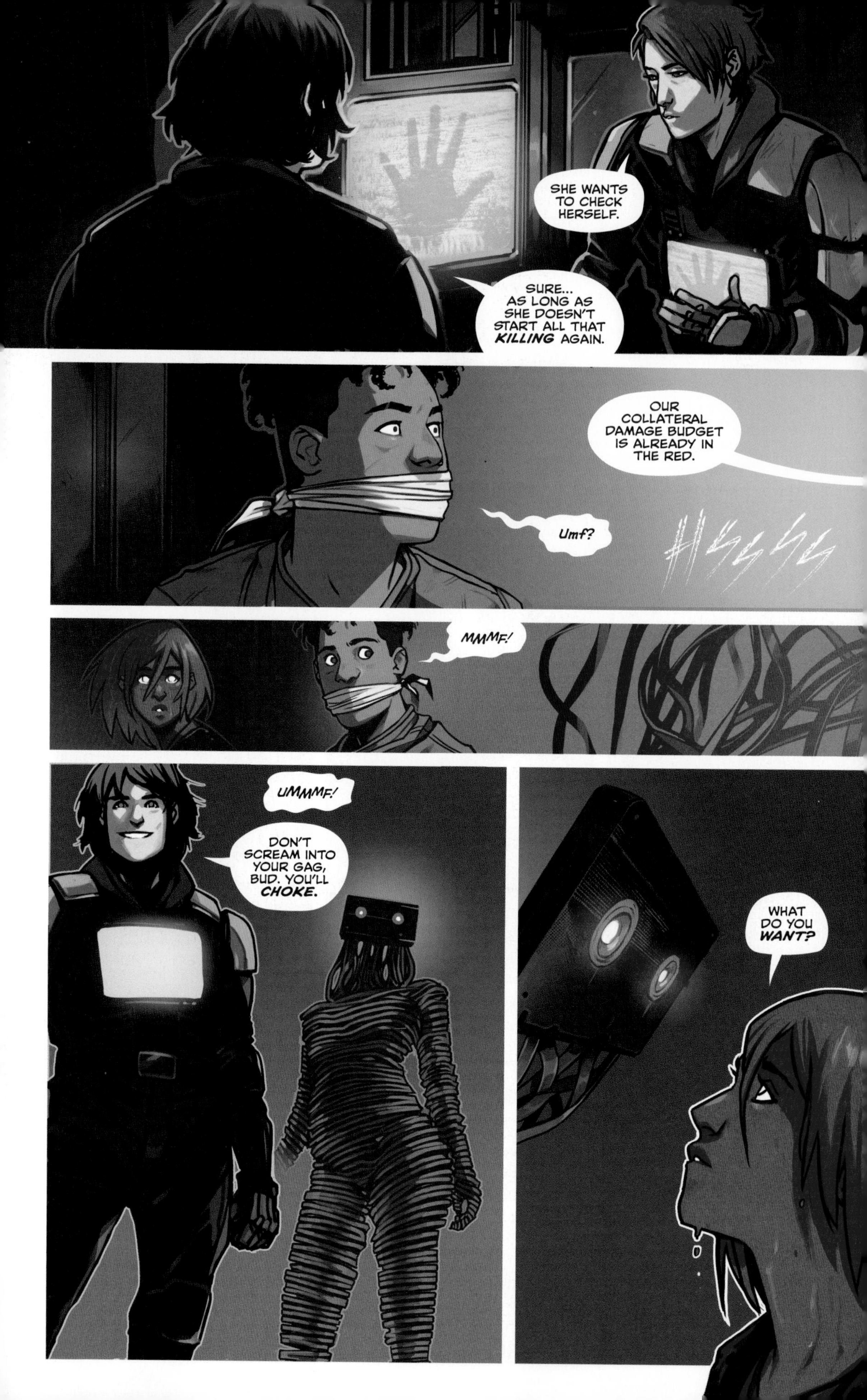
SHE WANTS TO CHECK HERSELF.
SURE... AS LONG AS SHE DOESN'T START ALL THAT KILLING AGAIN.
OUR COLLATERAL DAMAGE BUDGET IS ALREADY IN THE RED.
Umf?
MMMF!
UMMMF!
DON'T SCREAM INTO YOUR GAG, BUD. YOU'LL CHOKE.
WHAT DO YOU WANT?

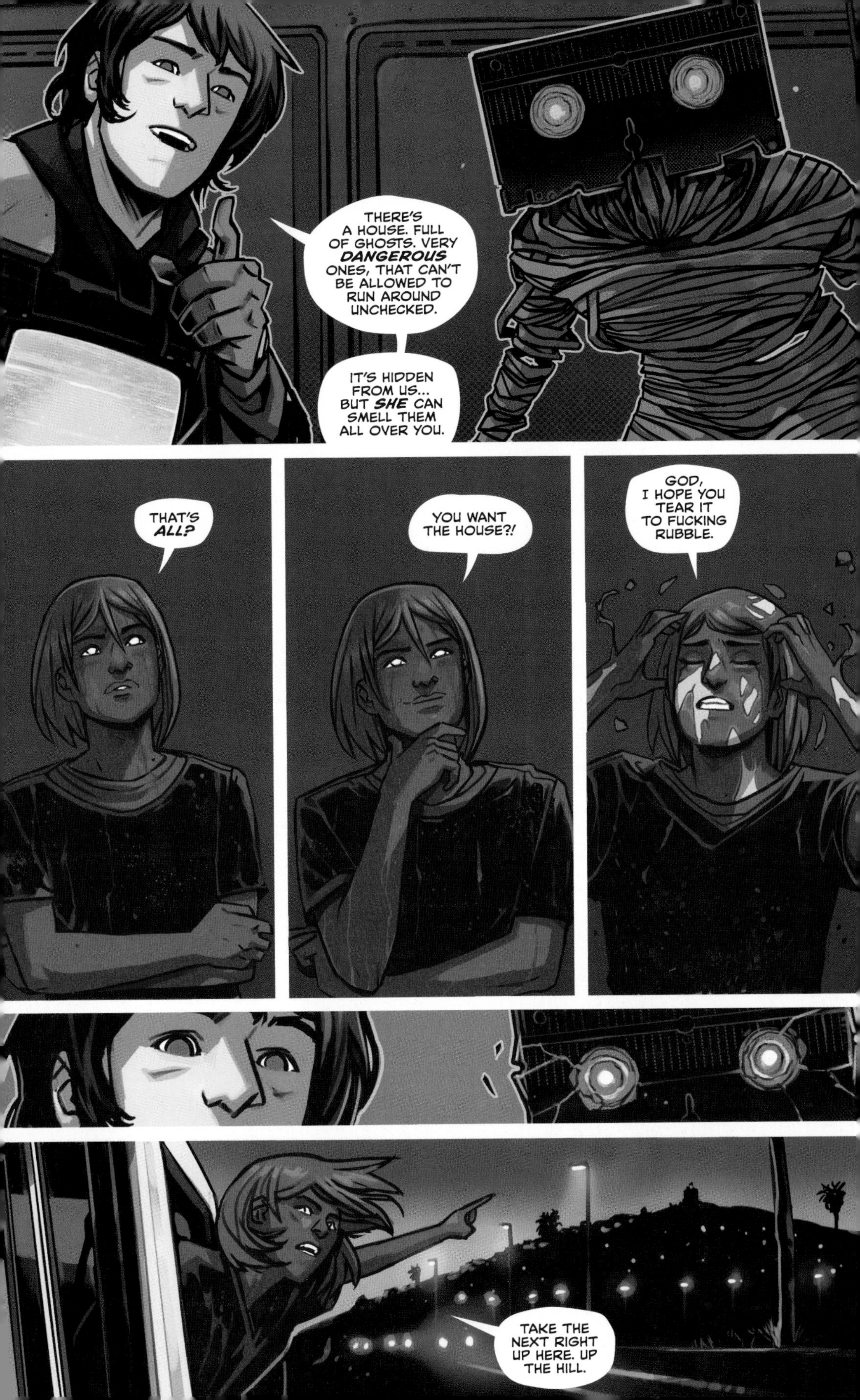
THERE'S A HOUSE. FULL OF GHOSTS. VERY DANGEROUS ONES, THAT CAN'T BE ALLOWED TO RUN AROUND UNCHECKED.
IT'S HIDDEN FROM US... BUT SHE CAN SMELL THEM ALL OVER YOU.
THAT'S ALL?
YOU WANT THE HOUSE?!
GOD, I HOPE YOU TEAR IT TO FUCKING RUBBLE.
TAKE THE NEXT RIGHT UP HERE. UP THE HILL.

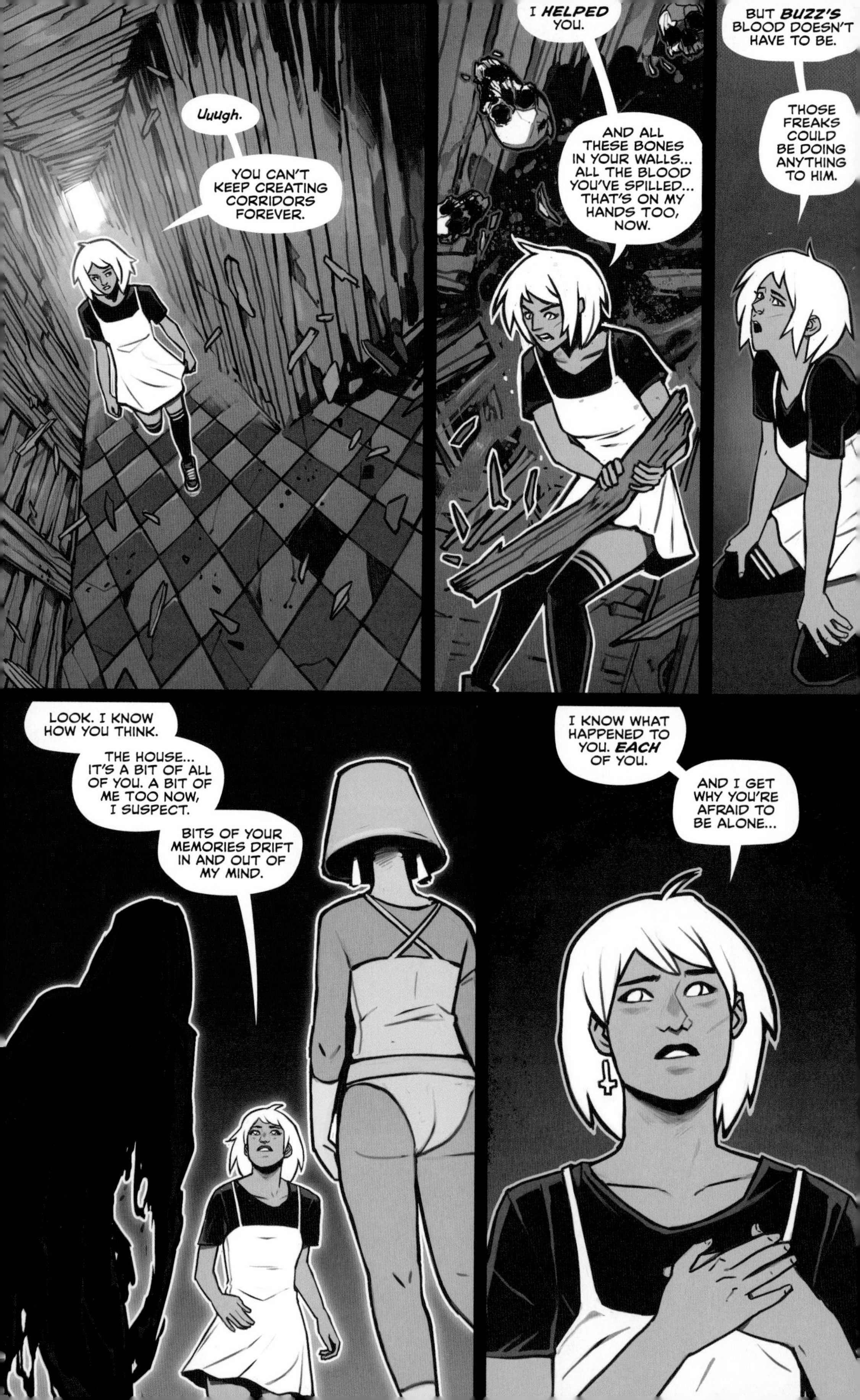
Uuugh.
YOU CAN'T KEEP CREATING CORRIDORS FOREVER.
I HELPED YOU.
AND ALL THESE BONES IN YOUR WALLS... ALL THE BLOOD YOU'VE SPILLED... THAT'S ON MY HANDS TOO, NOW.
BUT BUZZ'S BLOOD DOESN'T HAVE TO BE.
THOSE FREAKS COULD BE DOING ANYTHING TO HIM.
LOOK. I KNOW HOW YOU THINK.
THE HOUSE... IT'S A BIT OF ALL OF YOU. A BIT OF ME TOO NOW, I SUSPECT.
BITS OF YOUR MEMORIES DRIFT IN AND OUT OF MY MIND.
I KNOW WHAT HAPPENED TO YOU. EACH OF YOU.
AND I GET WHY YOU'RE AFRAID TO BE ALONE...

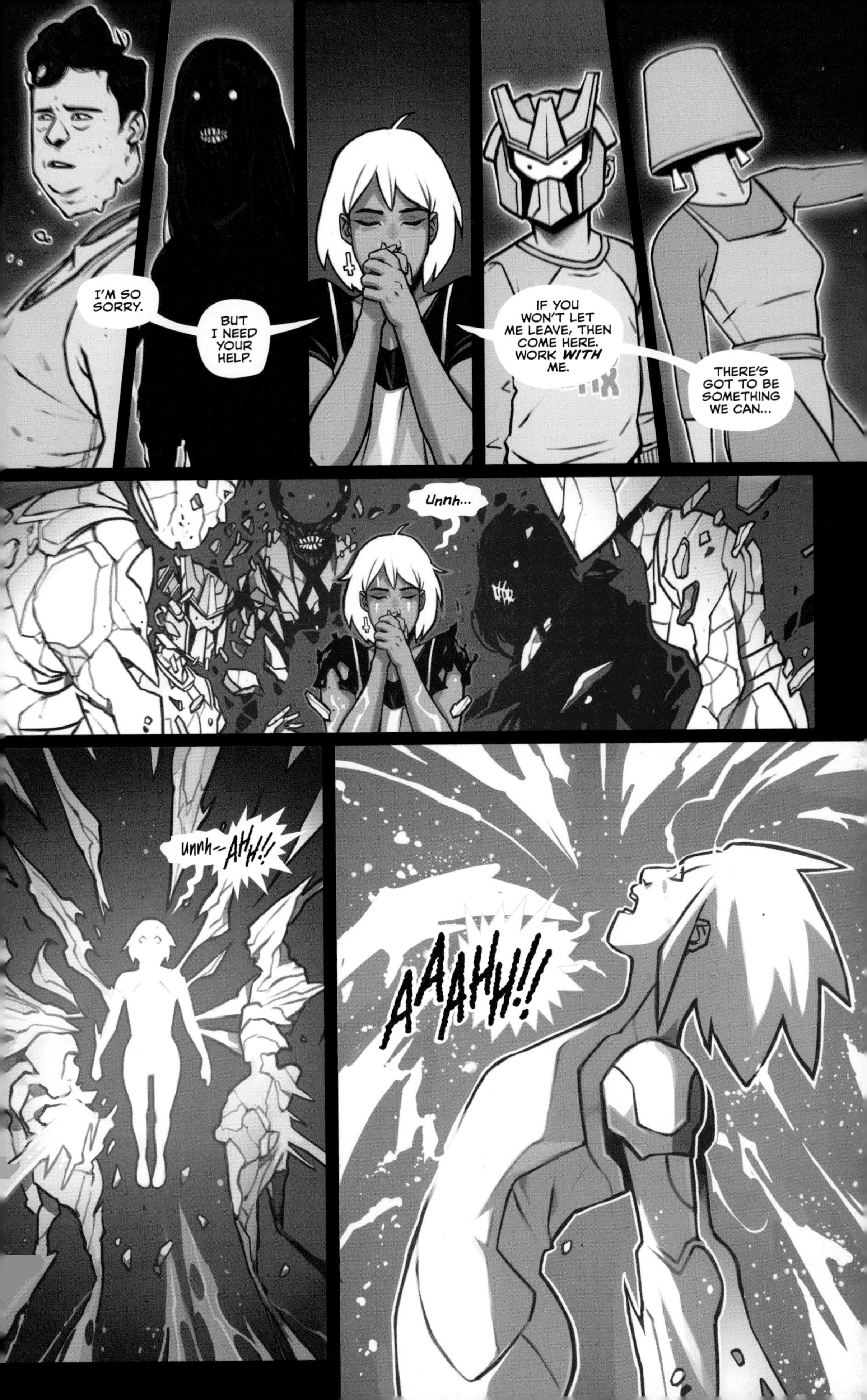

I'M SO SORRY.
BUT I NEED YOUR HELP.
IF YOU WON'T LET ME LEAVE, THEN COME HERE. WORK WITH ME.
THERE'S GOT TO BE SOMETHING WE CAN...
Unnh...
unnh--AHH!!
AAAHH!!

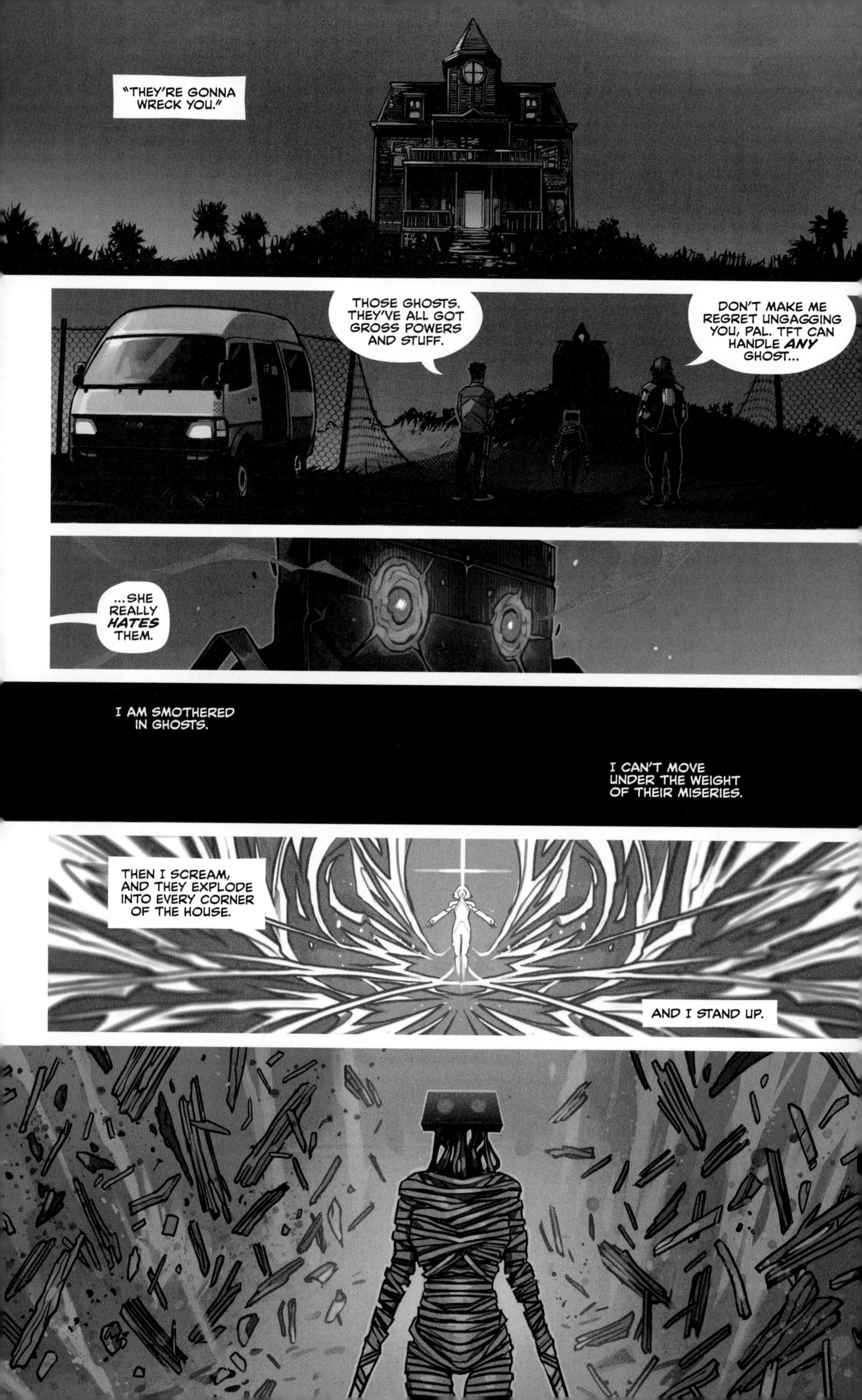
"THEY'RE GONNA WRECK YOU."
THOSE GHOSTS. THEY'VE ALL GOT GROSS POWERS AND STUFF.
DON'T MAKE ME REGRET UNGAGGING YOU, PAL. TFT CAN HANDLE *ANY* GHOST...
...SHE REALLY *HATES* THEM.
I AM SMOTHERED IN GHOSTS.
I CAN'T MOVE UNDER THE WEIGHT OF THEIR MISERIES.
THEN I SCREAM, AND THEY EXPLODE INTO EVERY CORNER OF THE HOUSE.
AND I STAND UP.

AND WE **ALL** STAND UP.

I BALANCE THE GHOSTS.

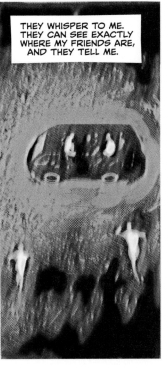

THEY WHISPER TO ME. THEY CAN SEE EXACTLY WHERE MY FRIENDS ARE, AND THEY TELL ME.

AND I TELL THEM HOW TO MOVE THE WALLS, SHIFTING CORRIDORS AND BEDROOMS INTO THE FORM OF LIMBS...

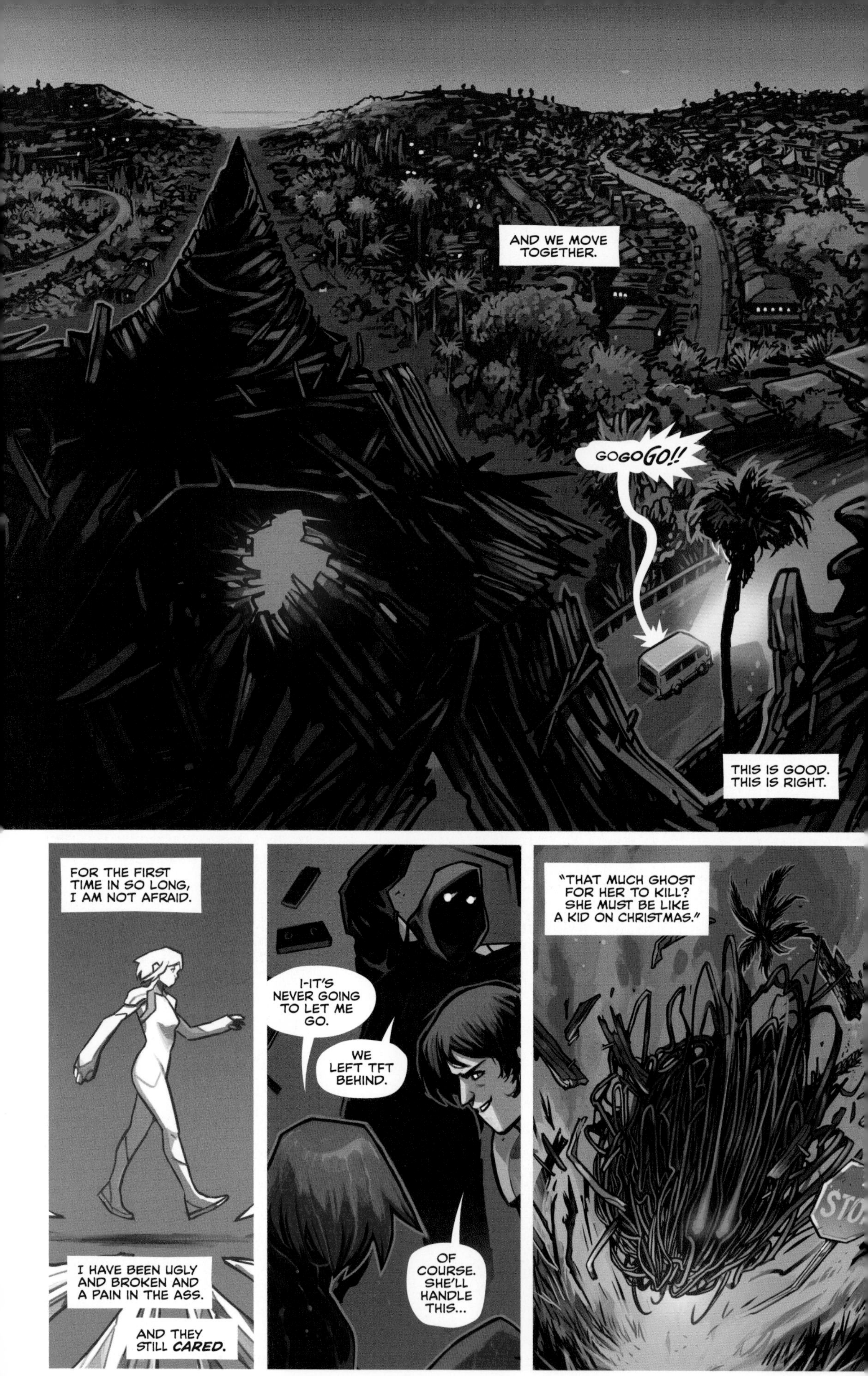
AND WE MOVE TOGETHER.
GOGOGO!!
THIS IS GOOD. THIS IS RIGHT.
FOR THE FIRST TIME IN SO LONG, I AM NOT AFRAID.
I HAVE BEEN UGLY AND BROKEN AND A PAIN IN THE ASS.
AND THEY STILL CARED.
I-IT'S NEVER GOING TO LET ME GO.
WE LEFT TFT BEHIND.
OF COURSE. SHE'LL HANDLE THIS...
"THAT MUCH GHOST FOR HER TO KILL? SHE MUST BE LIKE A KID ON CHRISTMAS."
STO

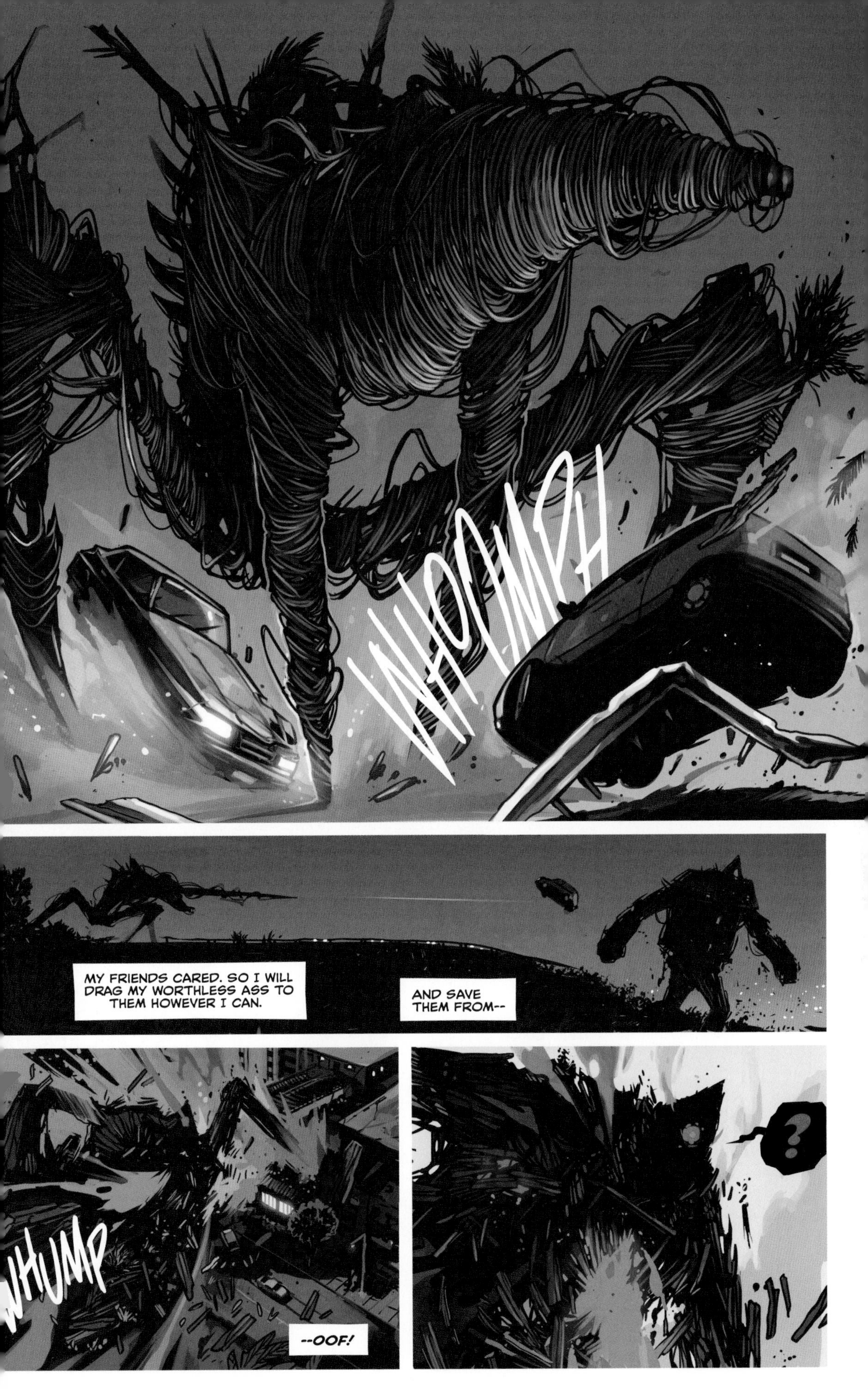
WHOOMPH
MY FRIENDS CARED. SO I WILL DRAG MY WORTHLESS ASS TO THEM HOWEVER I CAN.
AND SAVE THEM FROM--
WHUMP
--OOF!
?

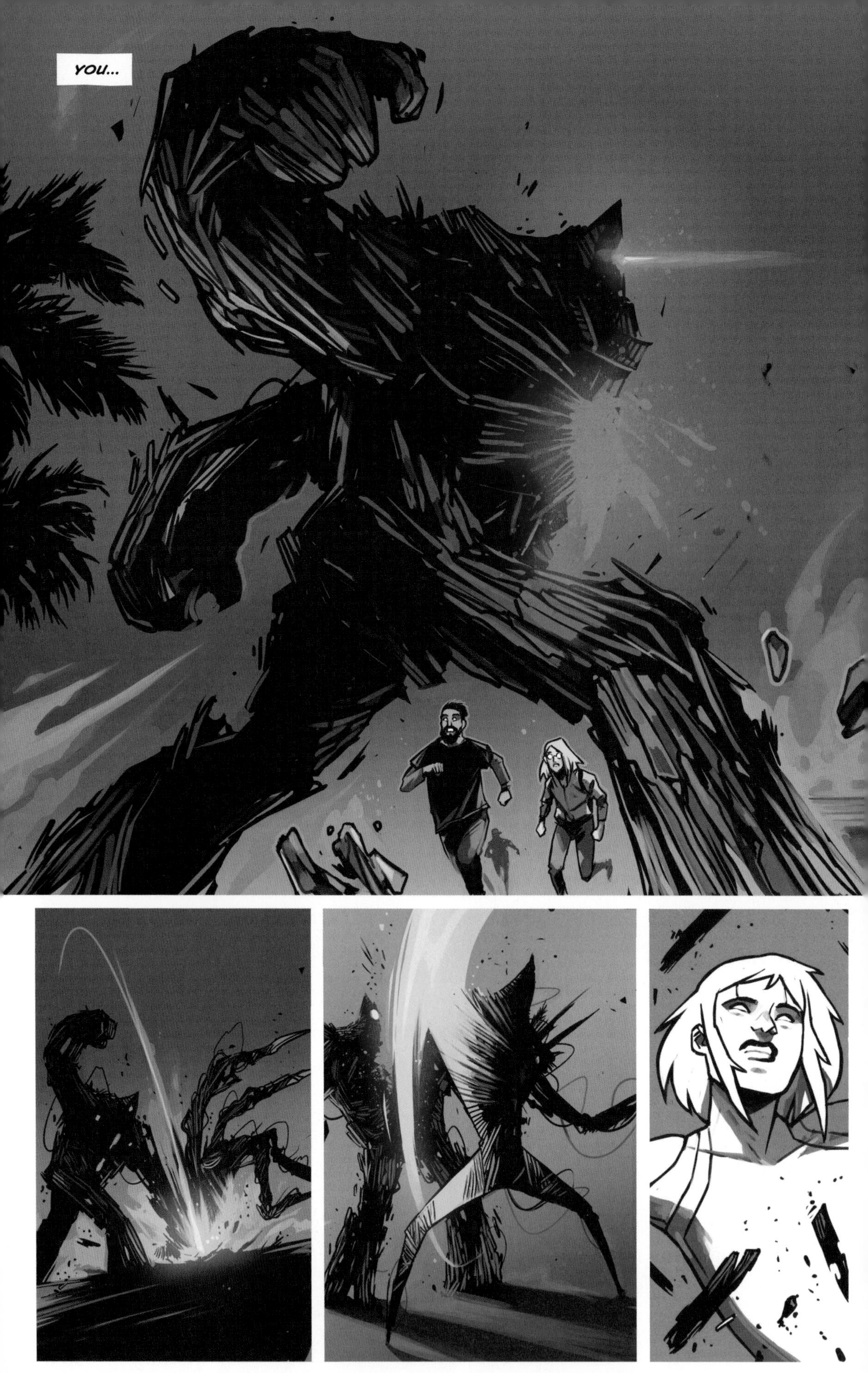
YOU...

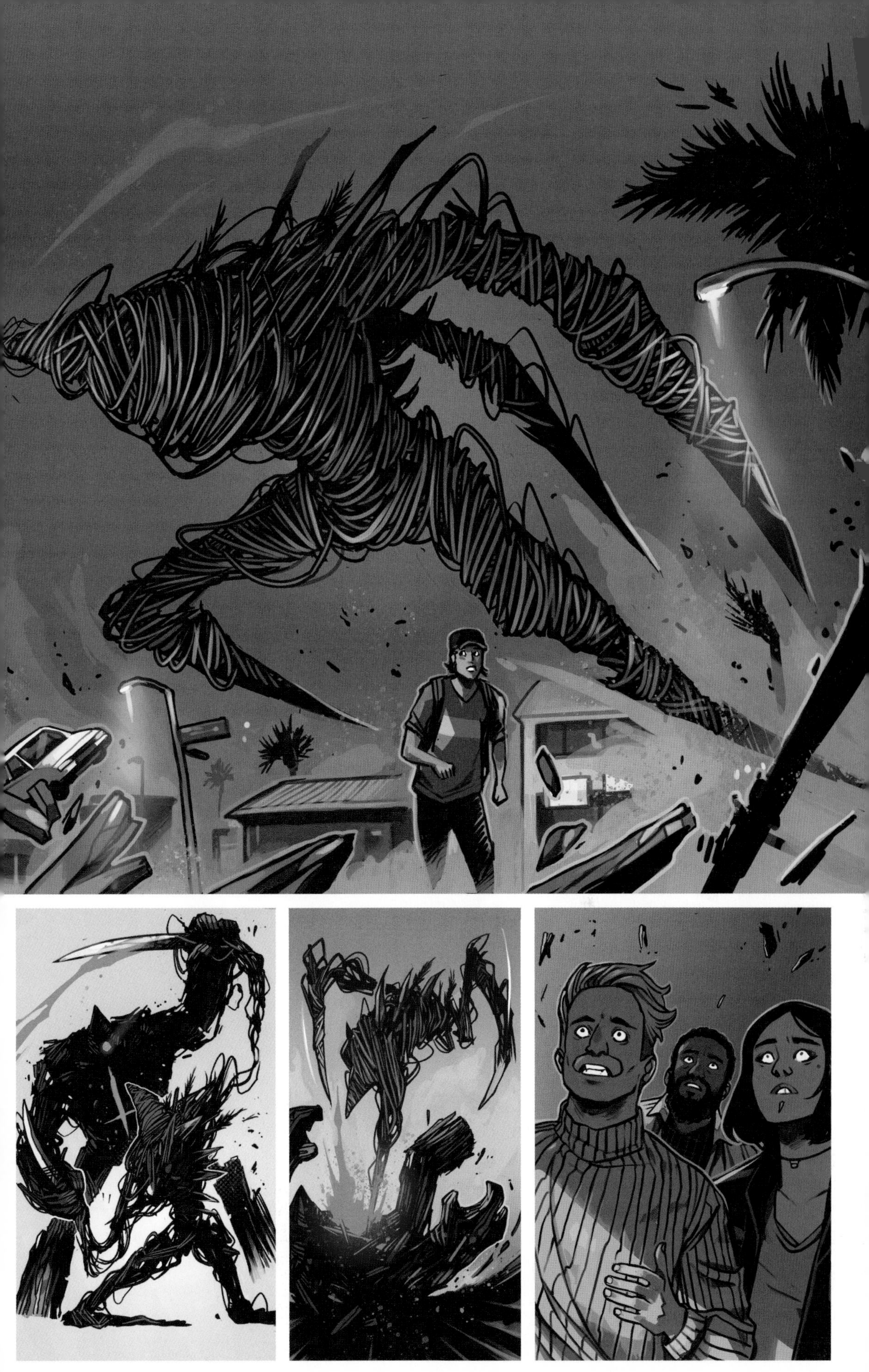

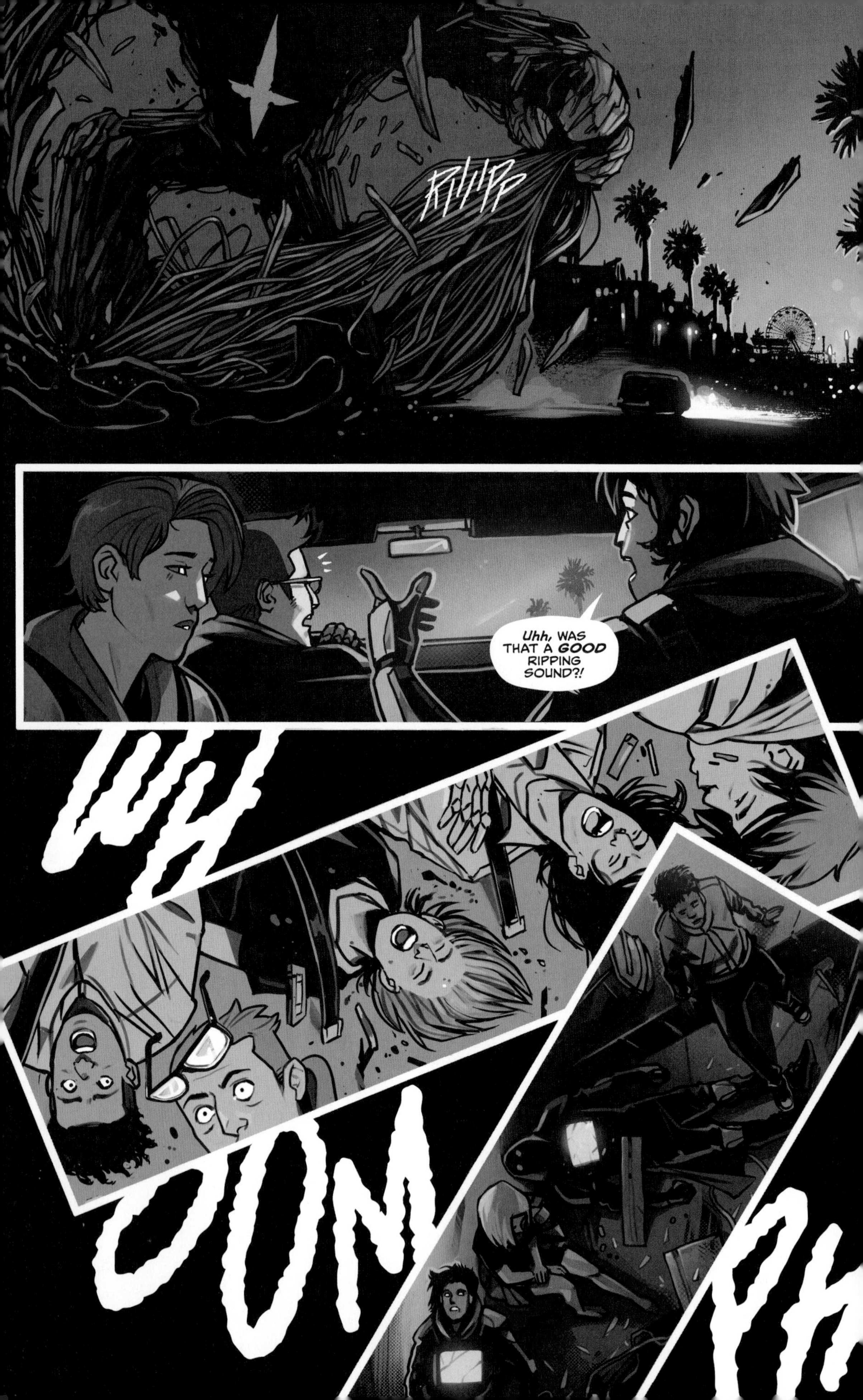
RIIIPP
Uhh, WAS THAT A ***GOOD*** RIPPING SOUND?!

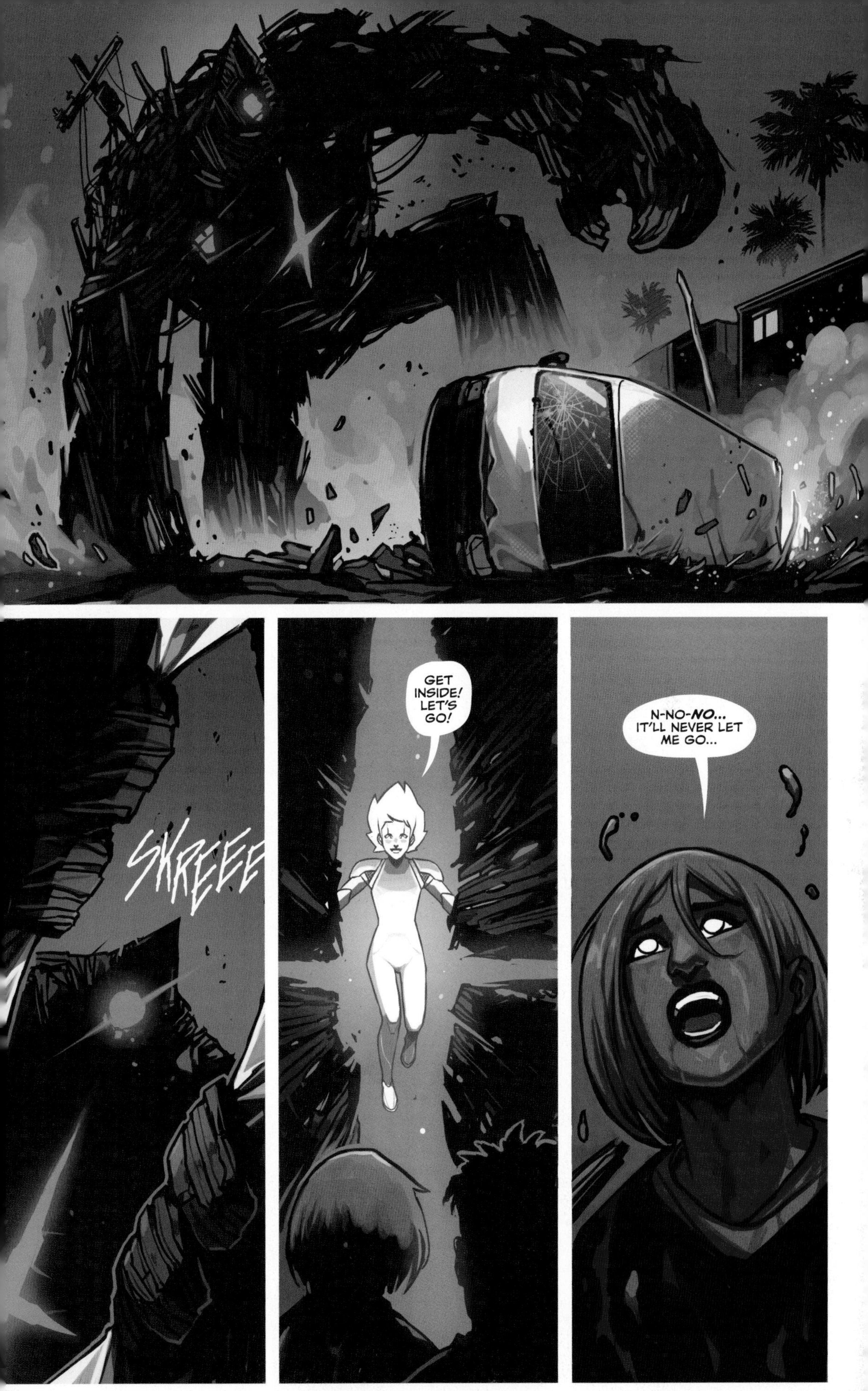
SKREEE
GET INSIDE! LET'S GO!
N-NO-NO... IT'LL NEVER LET ME GO...

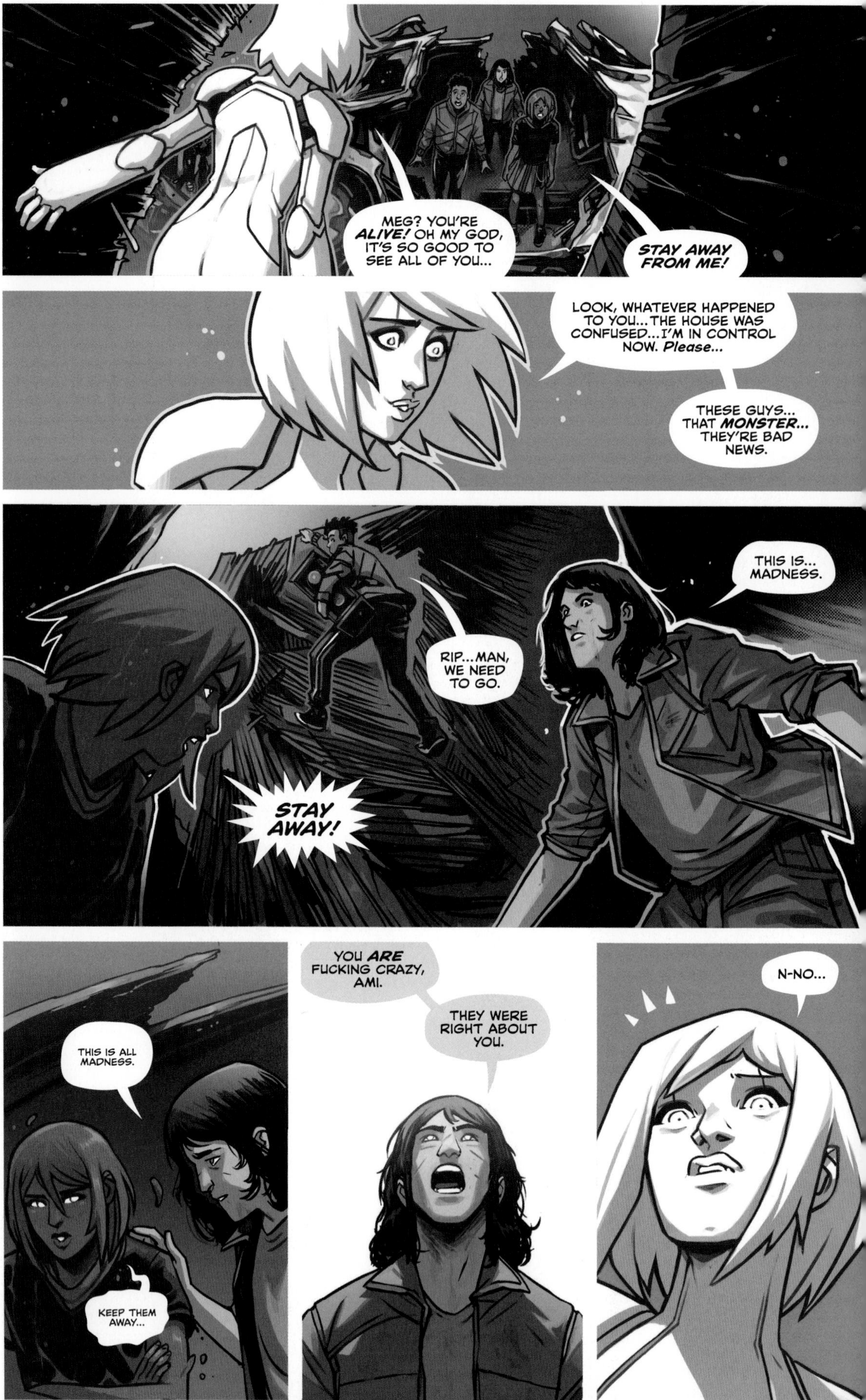
MEG? YOU'RE ALIVE! OH MY GOD, IT'S SO GOOD TO SEE ALL OF YOU...
STAY AWAY FROM ME!
LOOK, WHATEVER HAPPENED TO YOU... THE HOUSE WAS CONFUSED... I'M IN CONTROL NOW. Please...
THESE GUYS... THAT MONSTER... THEY'RE BAD NEWS.
THIS IS... MADNESS.
RIP... MAN, WE NEED TO GO.
STAY AWAY!
THIS IS ALL MADNESS.
KEEP THEM AWAY...
YOU ARE FUCKING CRAZY, AMI.
THEY WERE RIGHT ABOUT YOU.
N-NO...

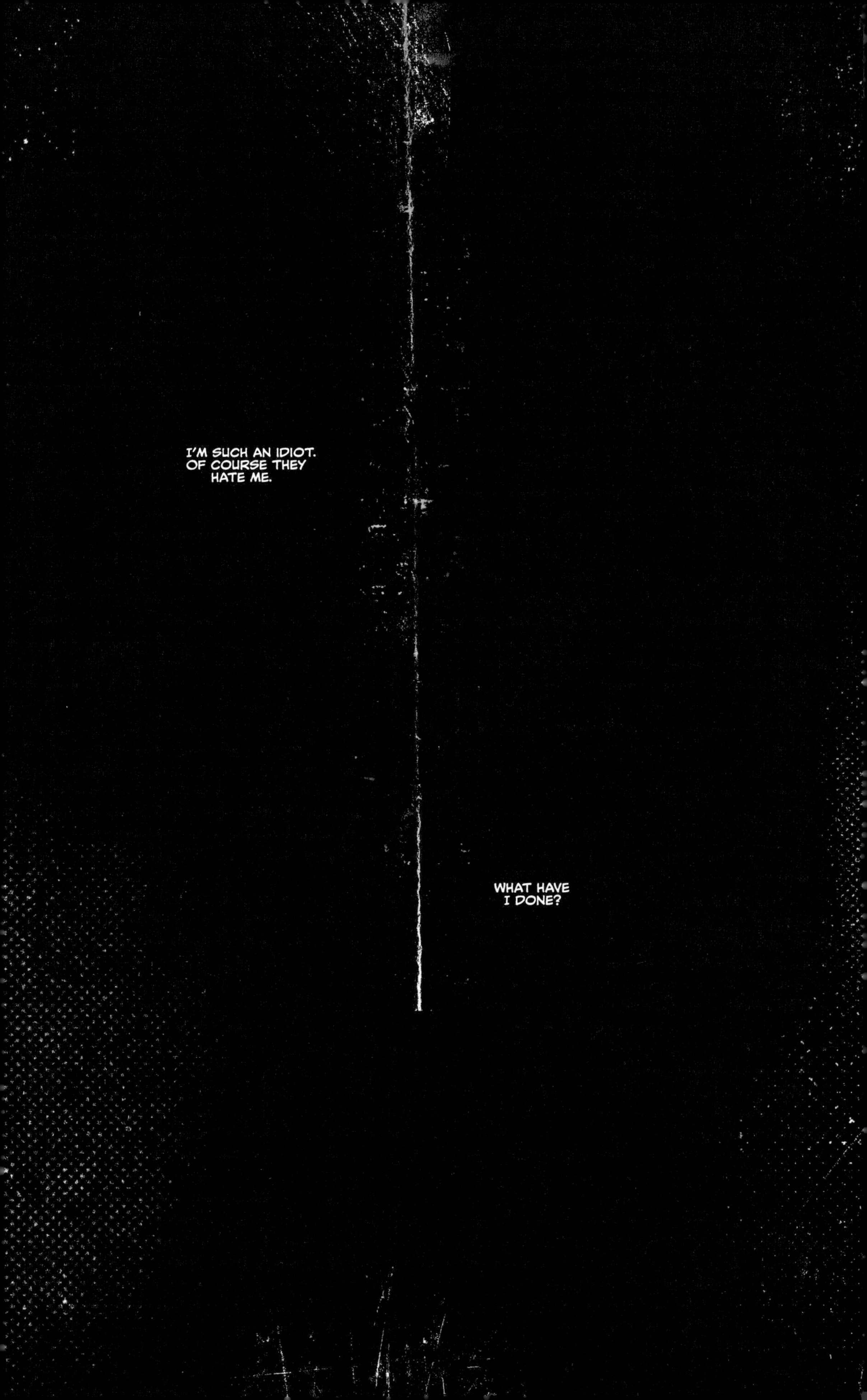
I'M SUCH AN IDIOT. OF COURSE THEY HATE ME.
WHAT HAVE I DONE?

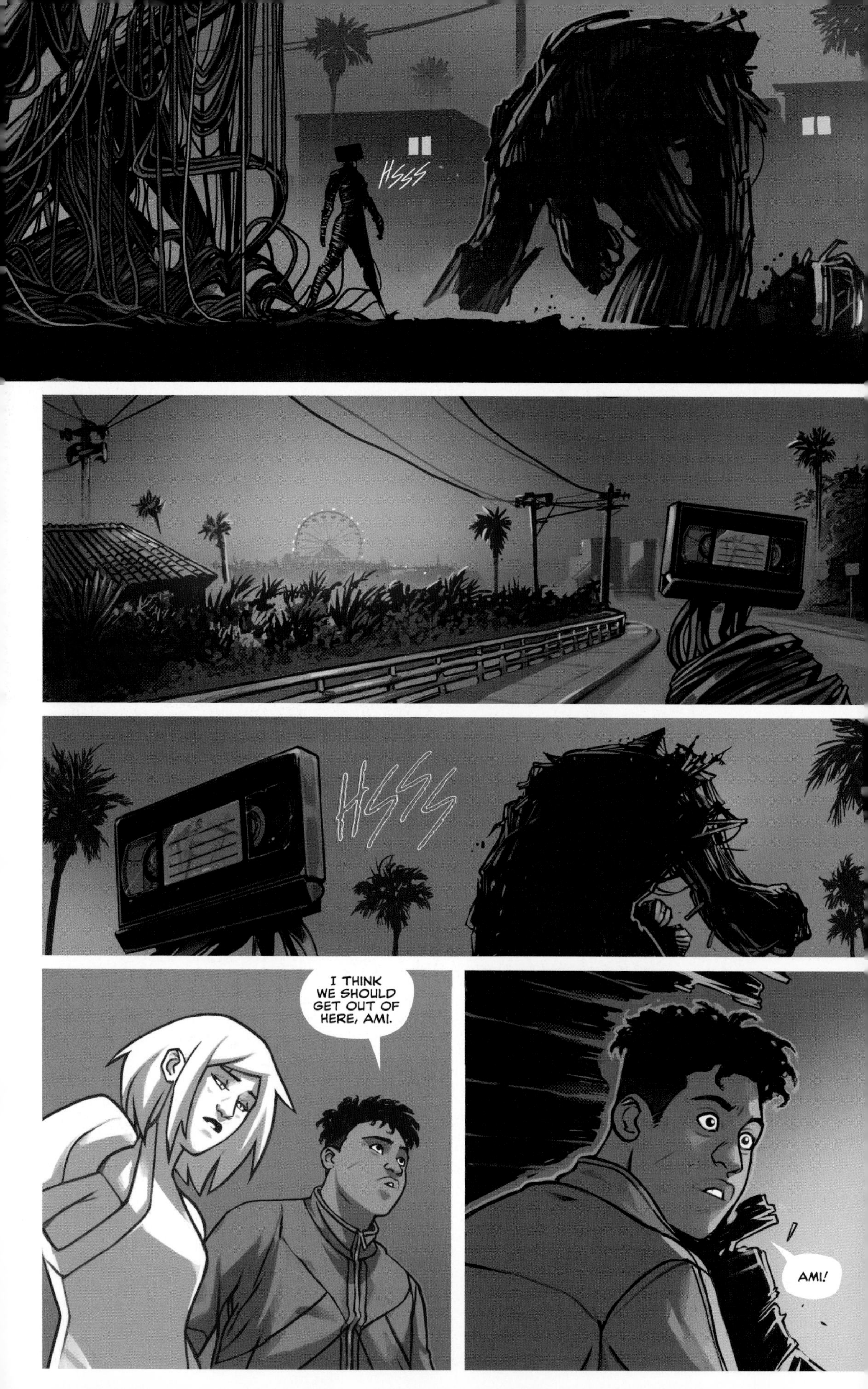
HSSS
HSSS
I THINK WE SHOULD GET OUT OF HERE, AMI.
AMI!

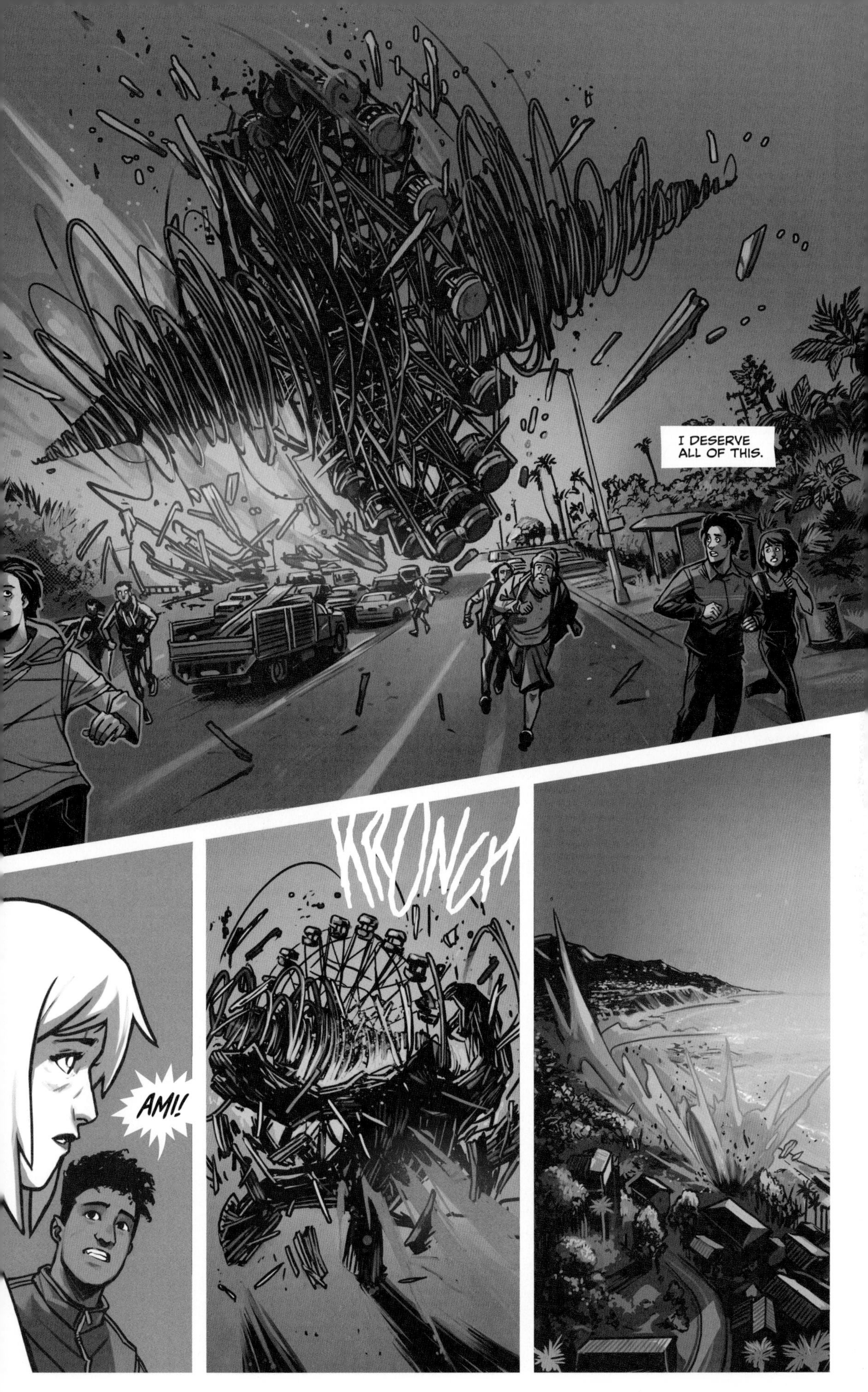
I DESERVE ALL OF THIS.
AMI!
KRONCH

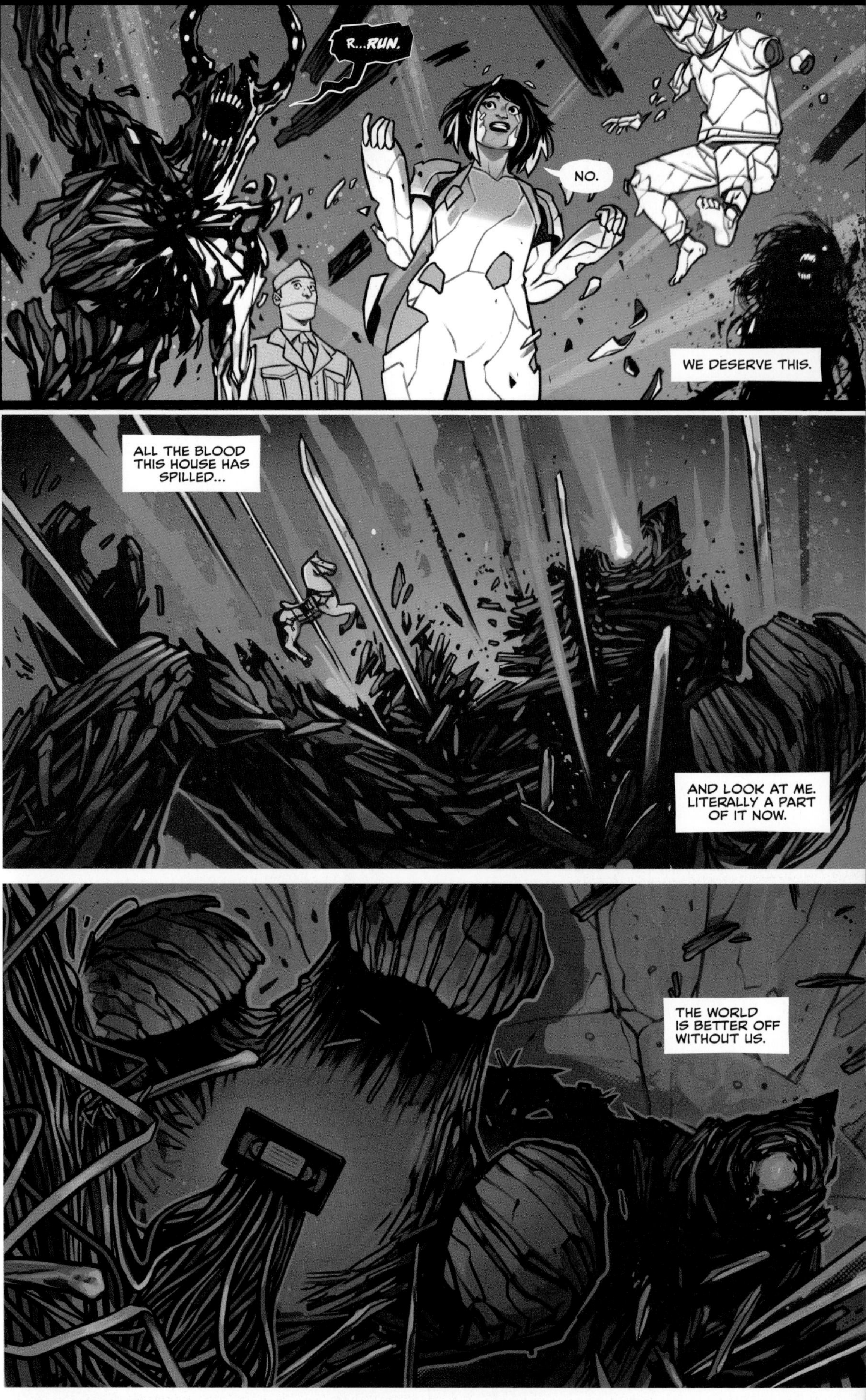
R...RUN.
NO.
WE DESERVE THIS.
ALL THE BLOOD THIS HOUSE HAS SPILLED...
AND LOOK AT ME. LITERALLY A PART OF IT NOW.
THE WORLD IS BETTER OFF WITHOUT US.

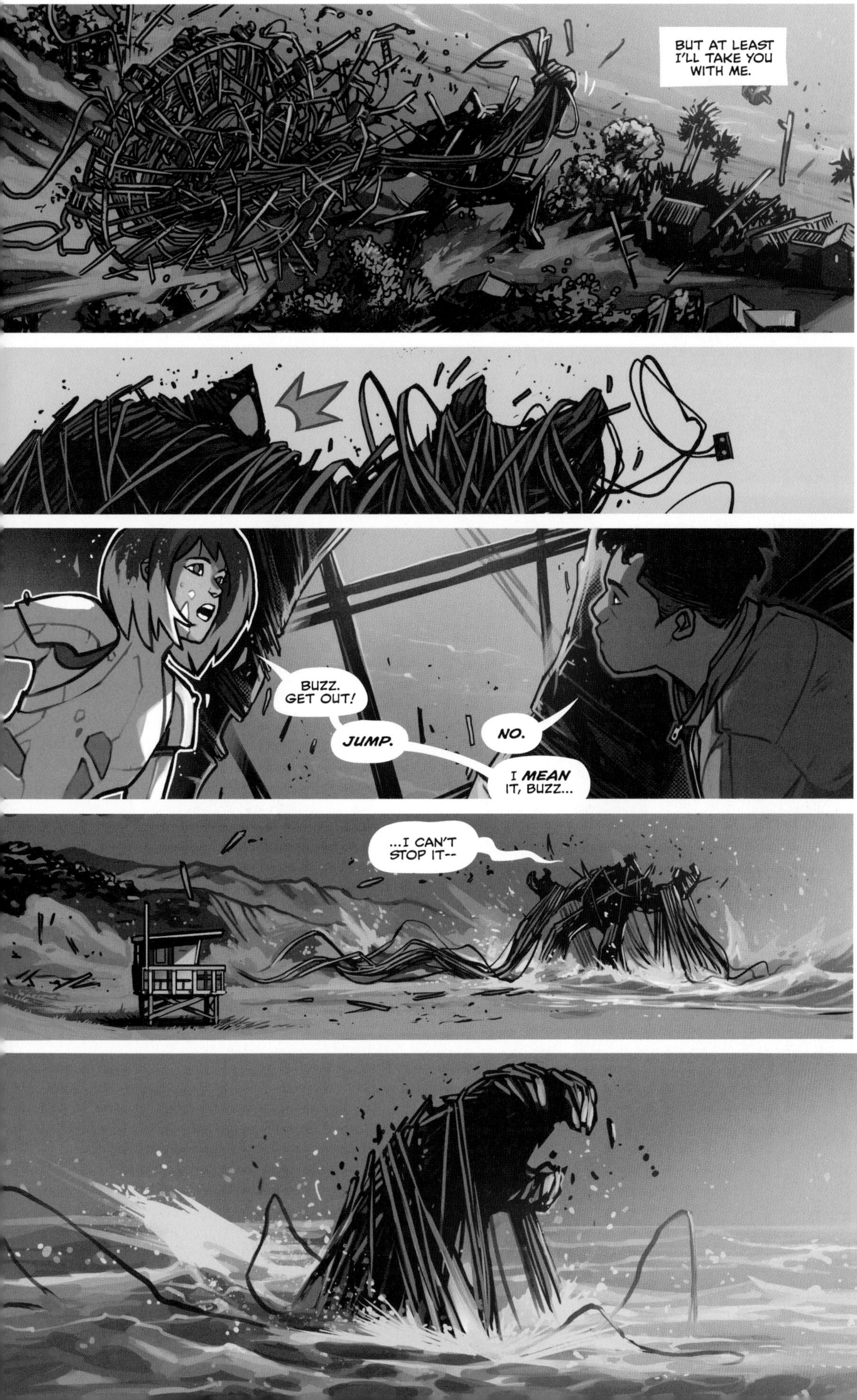
BUT AT LEAST I'LL TAKE YOU WITH ME.
BUZZ. GET OUT!
JUMP.
NO.
I MEAN IT, BUZZ...
...I CAN'T STOP IT--

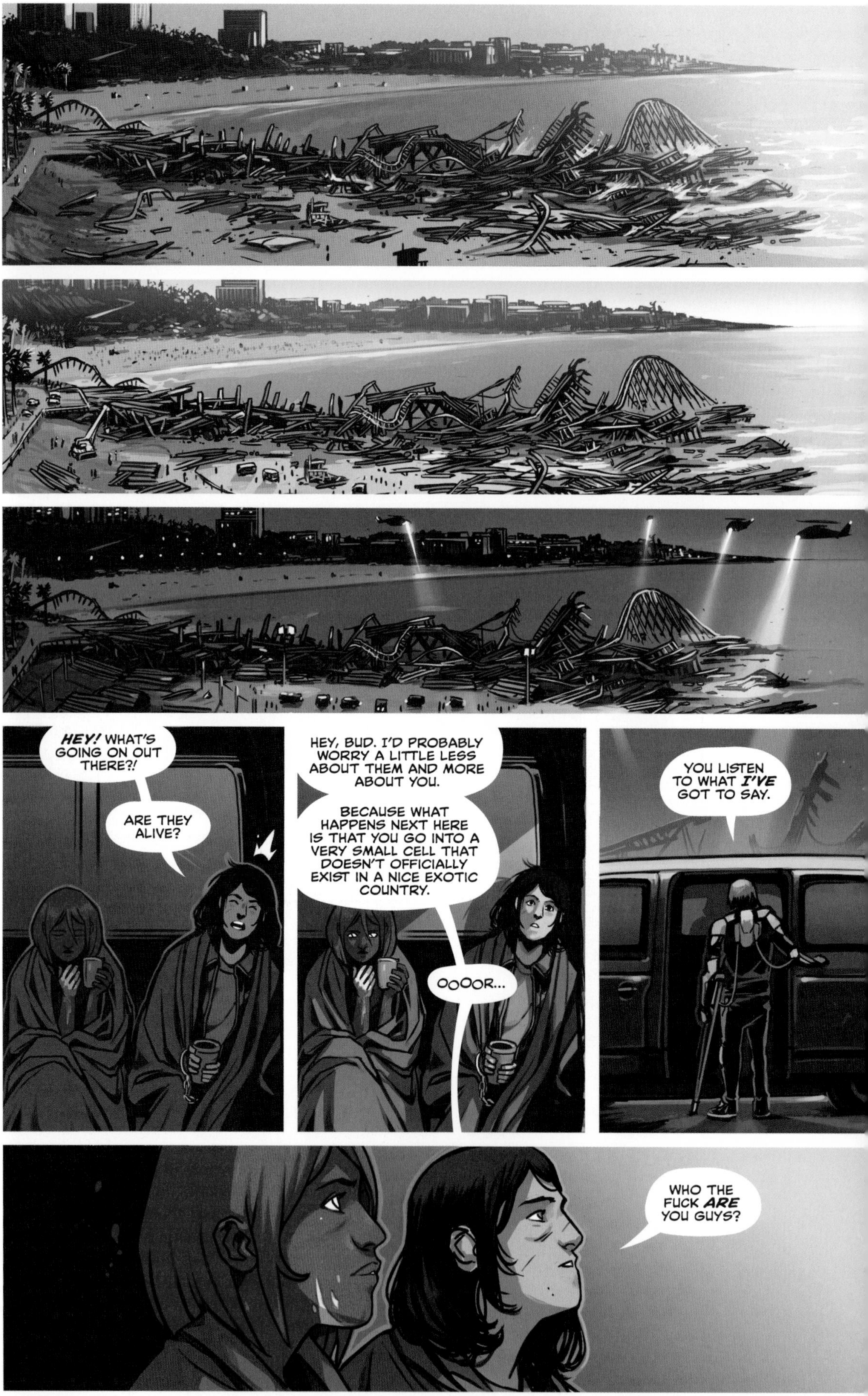
HEY! WHAT'S GOING ON OUT THERE?!
ARE THEY ALIVE?
HEY, BUD. I'D PROBABLY WORRY A LITTLE LESS ABOUT THEM AND MORE ABOUT YOU.
BECAUSE WHAT HAPPENS NEXT HERE IS THAT YOU GO INTO A VERY SMALL CELL THAT DOESN'T OFFICIALLY EXIST IN A NICE EXOTIC COUNTRY.
OOOOR...
YOU LISTEN TO WHAT I'VE GOT TO SAY.
WHO THE FUCK ARE YOU GUYS?

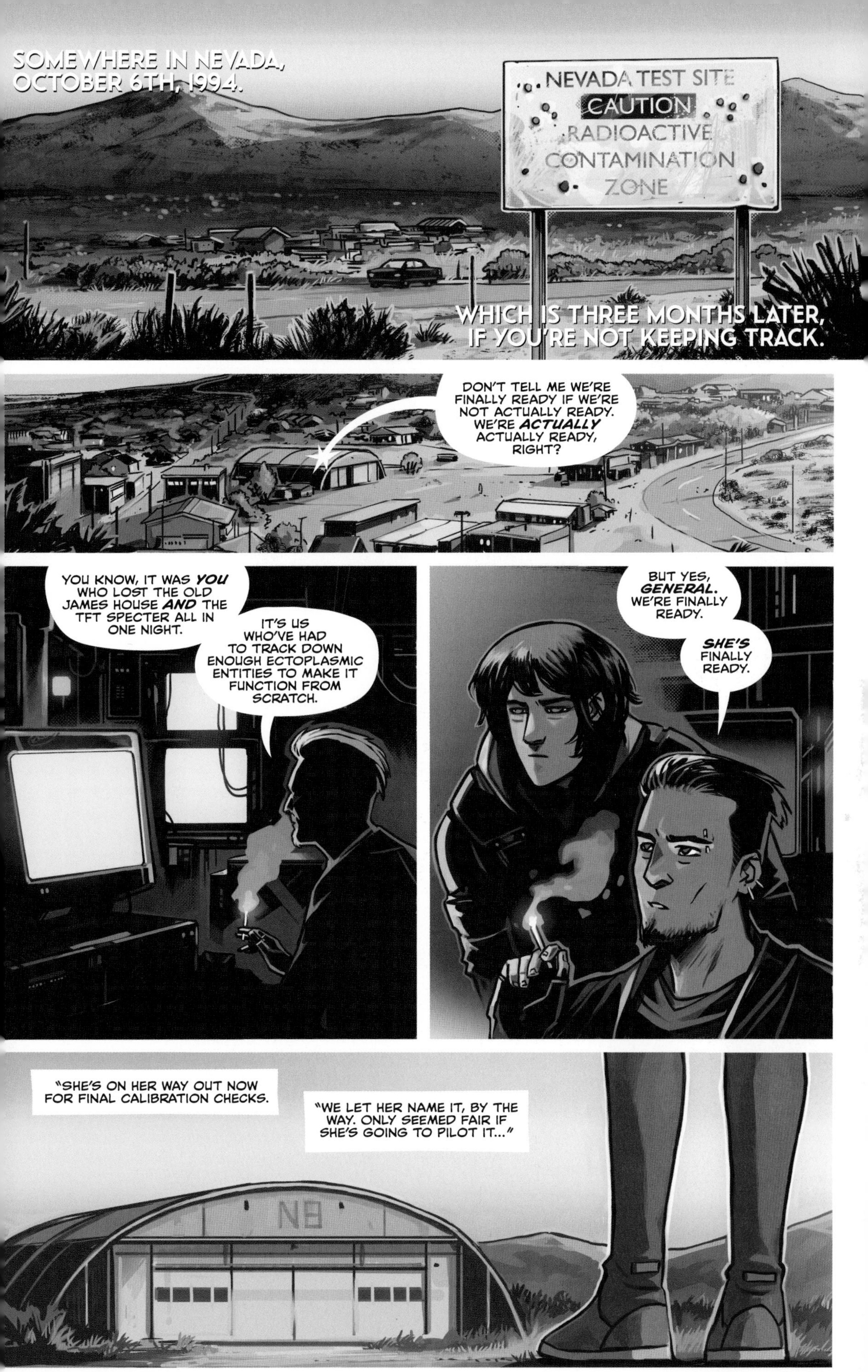
SOMEWHERE IN NEVADA, OCTOBER 6TH, 1994.
NEVADA TEST SITE
CAUTION
RADIOACTIVE CONTAMINATION ZONE
WHICH IS THREE MONTHS LATER, IF YOU'RE NOT KEEPING TRACK.
DON'T TELL ME WE'RE FINALLY READY IF WE'RE NOT ACTUALLY READY. WE'RE ACTUALLY ACTUALLY READY, RIGHT?
YOU KNOW, IT WAS YOU WHO LOST THE OLD JAMES HOUSE AND THE TFT SPECTER ALL IN ONE NIGHT.
IT'S US WHO'VE HAD TO TRACK DOWN ENOUGH ECTOPLASMIC ENTITIES TO MAKE IT FUNCTION FROM SCRATCH.
BUT YES, GENERAL. WE'RE FINALLY READY.
SHE'S FINALLY READY.
"SHE'S ON HER WAY OUT NOW FOR FINAL CALIBRATION CHECKS.
"WE LET HER NAME IT, BY THE WAY. ONLY SEEMED FAIR IF SHE'S GOING TO PILOT IT..."
N8

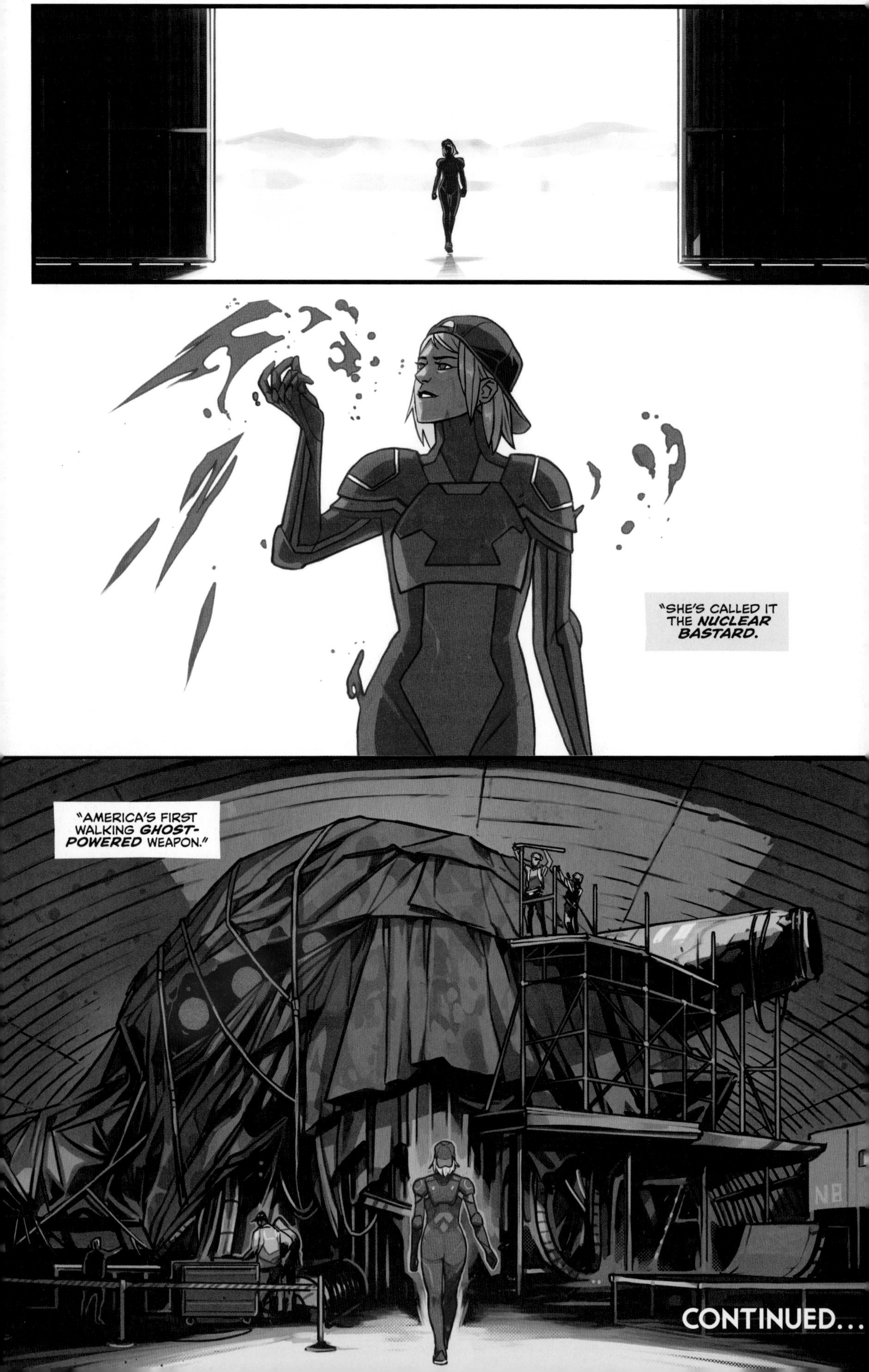
"SHE'S CALLED IT THE *NUCLEAR BASTARD.*
"AMERICA'S FIRST WALKING *GHOST-POWERED* WEAPON."
NB
CONTINUED...

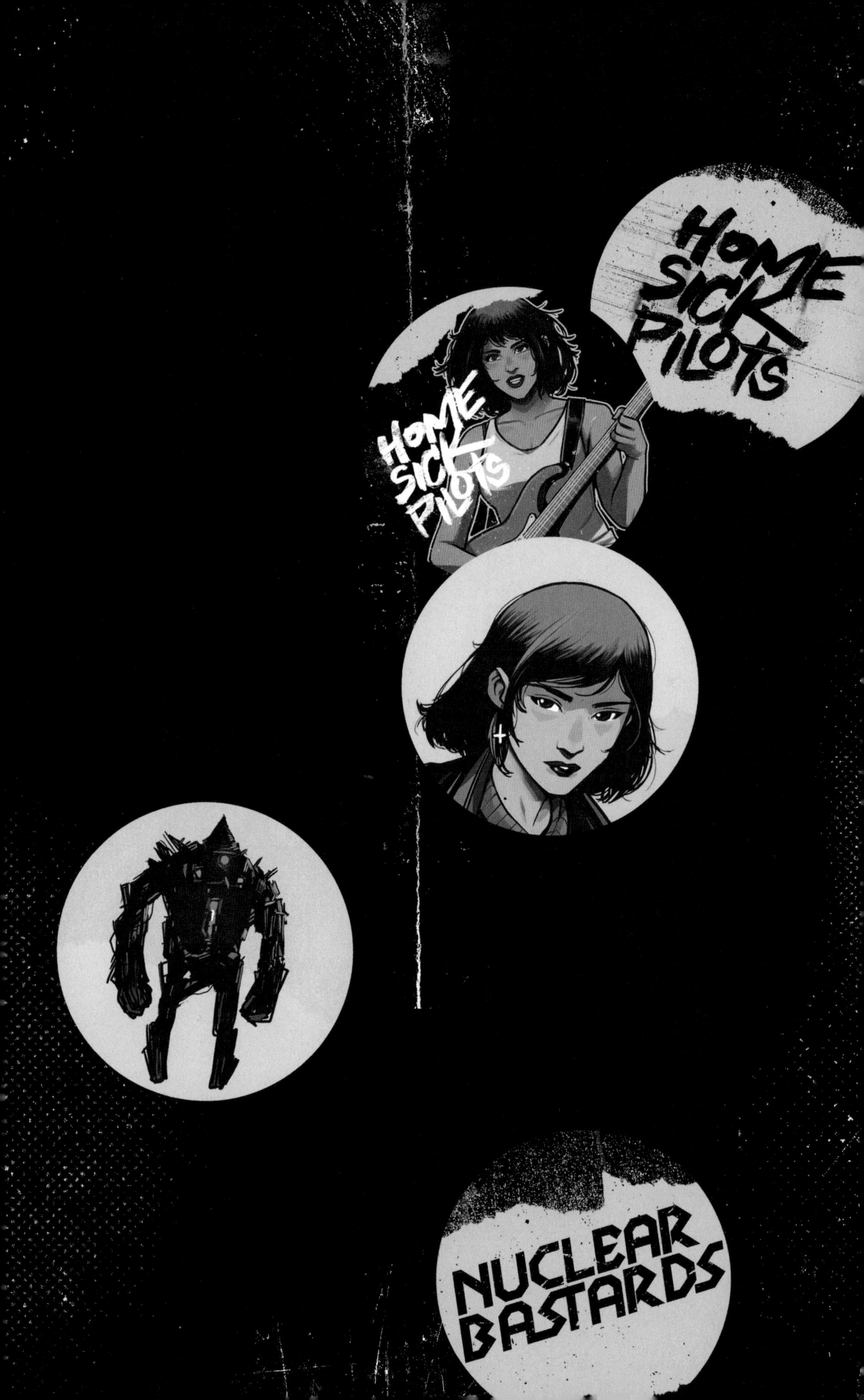
HOME SICK PILOTS
HOME SICK PILOTS
NUCLEAR BASTARDS

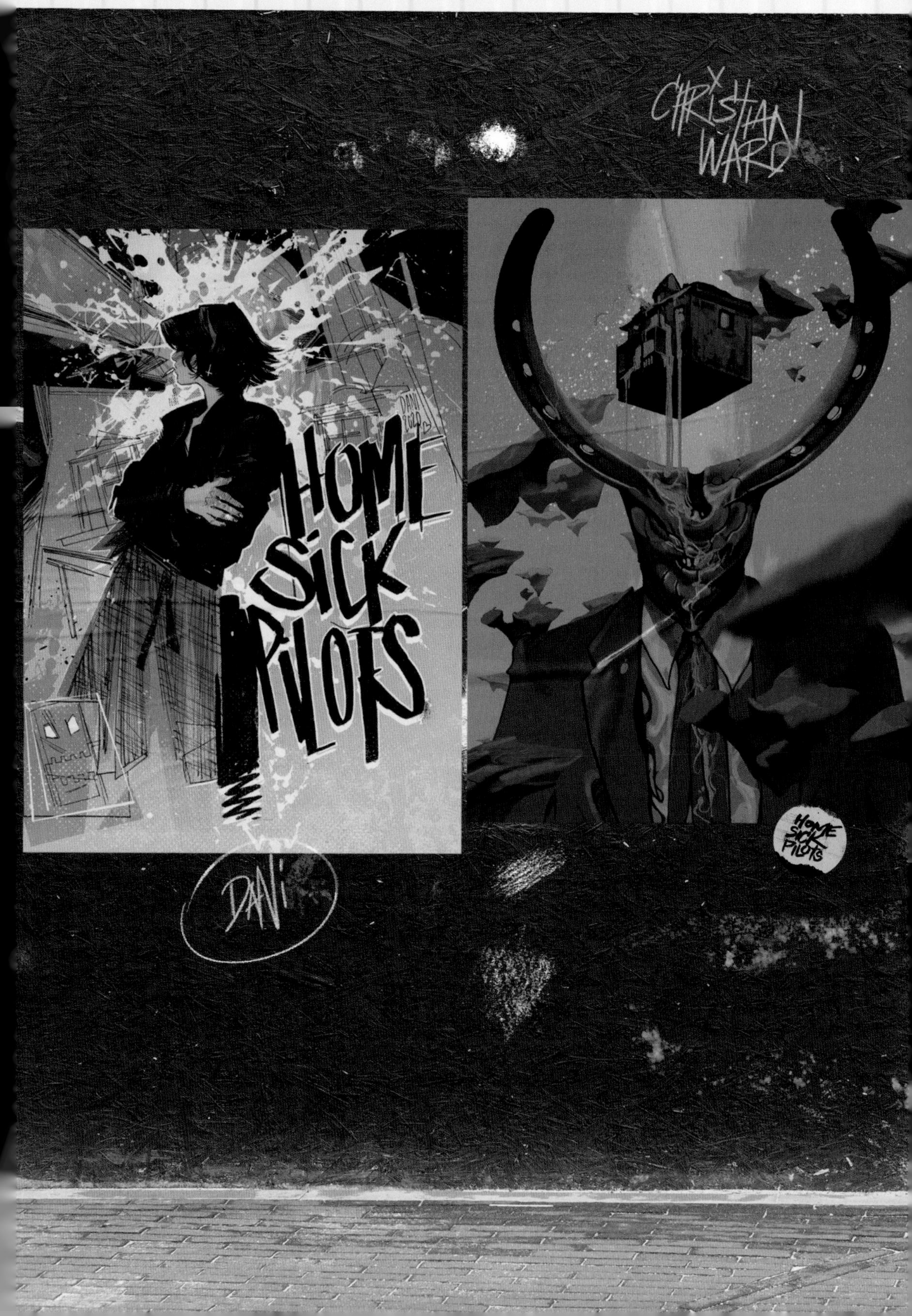
x CHRISTIAN WARD
DANI 2020
HOME SICK PILOTS
DANI
HOME SICK PILOTS

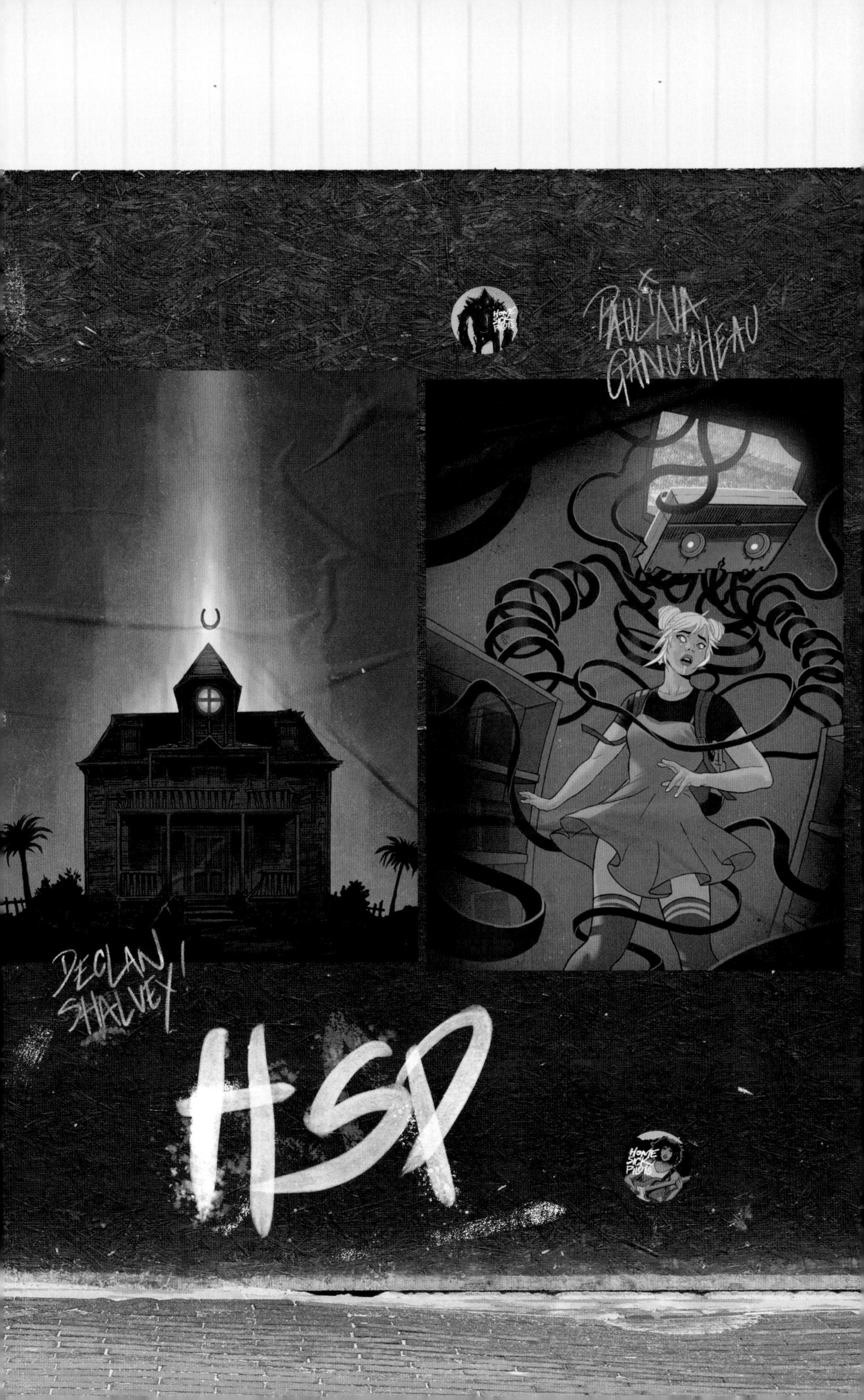
HOME SICK PILOTS
PAULINA GANUCHEAU
DECLAN SHALVEY!
HSP
HOME SICK PILOTS

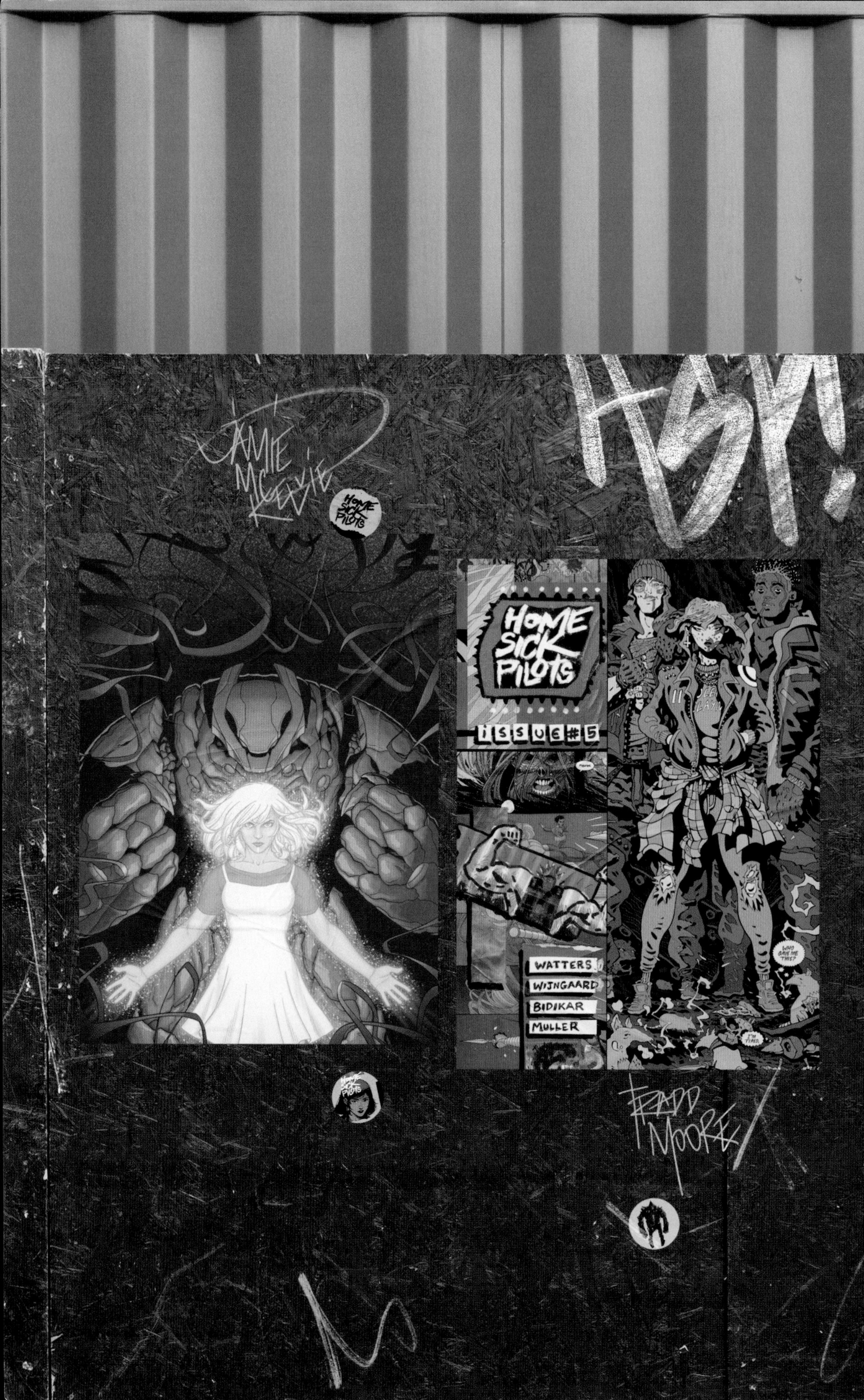
JAMIE MCKELVIE
HOME SICK PILOTS
HOME SICK PILOTS
ISSUE #5
WATTERS
WIJNGAARD
BIDIKAR
MULLER
WHO GAVE ME THIS?
TRADD MOORE

BIG WITCH FILES: DOC 1

[REDACTED] FILE: by **[REDACTED]**

The newspapers have taken to calling it the 'Big Witch Event'. The newspapers having wind of it at all is a colossal screw-up that is going to cost many costly hours of intense coverup work.

We have begun laying misinformation trails, hampered by the fact that we are still piecing together the events of July 1994 ourselves. We expect the body count to rise based on our findings.

The 'Big Witch' appears to be made of a single haunted entity. This would make the event the largest act of poltergeist activity ever measured, by a significant margin.

The key may be found in that there appears to have been an organic element to the manifestation; some among the **[REDACTED]** retrieval unit who were present at the event insist that this was a living person. They further insist that this person appeared to have a measure of control over the haunted entity. The unit were, of course, under immense stress at the time.

The concept, however, is not easily dismissed. What we have seen here may have been a party of poltergeists, no longer content with simply rearranging furniture or smashing plates, but working together to make an entire piece of architecture move as though it were a single body. It is conceivable a living mind could have pulled the phenomena together, giving them purpose- coordinating them.

For the want of a better word... a pilot.

SPECS:

Height:
75ft (estimate)
Materials:
hardwood, mortar, brick (ext)
copper, steel, (int. plumbing/ wiring)
Firepower:
unknown

Current Location:
unknown
Previously:
Los Manos suburbs

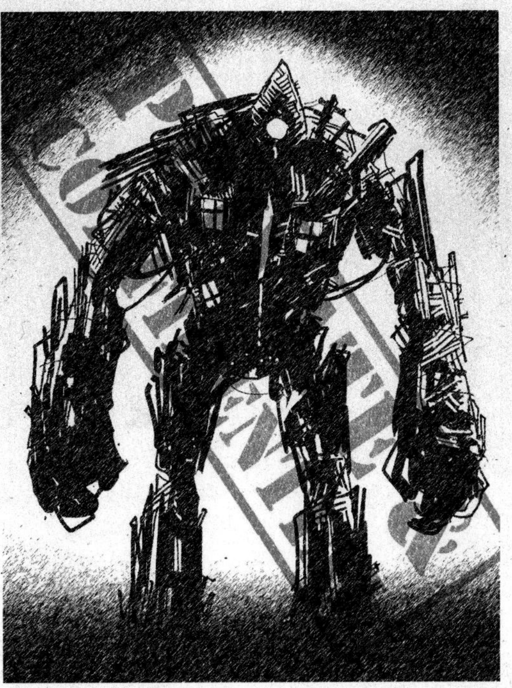

AGENT [REDACTED], GENERAL [REDACTED] WOULD LIKE YOU TO HAVE A DIG INTO THIS AND SEE IF THERE'S ANYTHING TO IT. I GUESS THAT'S WHAT YOU GET FOR NOT COMPLIMENTING HIS NEW DYE JOB, HAHA. ON HIS DESK BY TOMORROW MORNING, PLEASE.

LIGHT OF OUR LIVES... AND OUR DEATHS!

It seemed like an ordinary purchase at an ordinary garage sale... but for Rute Simpson, a sophomore at Trigger High and her friends, it turned into a nightmare. She had picked up what had seemed like a perfectly innocent lamp as a gift for her mother. After things got freaky, she tried to return the lamp... and found that the garage sale had vanished all together!

"She likes those kinds of things. Really old stuff. From like, ten years ago," she told this reporter over the phone. "Then my friends Becca and Angie were round for cheerleading practice, and it got kind of dark in the garage. So I realized I had just picked up the perfect thing. That's when things started to get strange." Strange indeed. According to the girls, the shadows that the lamp was casting on the garage walls were wrong.

"It took us a while to notice because we were super into our routine, but our shadows were totally not actually doing what we were doing? Instead they were being really freaky. Like Becca's shadow didn't look like it had a head... and it looked like there was a spray of something coming out of her neck like a fountain. And Angie's was all hunched and little... like an old lady's shadow. And then it just like, fell over. But Angie hadn't fallen over—she was standing right next to me. It was totally wild!" When asked about her own shadow, Rute goes quiet. "I'd rather keep that to myself," she says.

Though our readers who might wish to check out this freaky light for themselves may be disappointed. "It's gone," Rute tells us. "The lady in white came for it. She's taken it home." Rute ended the phone call there and hasn't returned any further requests for interviews.

NOTES!

Most hauntings attach themselves to items of significance for the deceased. Items that may or may not have played a role in the spirit's death.

Should be noted that this tends to be how garage sales function in general.

We've found little internal consistency as to how ghosts make themselves known, but they do seem to vary broadly. Ghosts manifest in ways that seem to display distinctive powers, which are possibly acts of supernatural wish fulfilment- the deceased acting in ways that might have saved them when they were alive.

OK... so I've done some digging, and a Rebecca Stevenson of New Vows High, California was decapitated in a freak chicken wire/cheerleading accident, days after this article originally ran. This could be the real deal.

If this lamp really is showing people their deaths before the fact, the militaristic opportunities such a device could afford would be unimaginable. A retrieval team should be detached immediately.

We have been theorizing for some time that many supernatural objects on the West Coast originated in a single location- one that is cloaked from us by paranormal means. However, the reference to a 'woman in white' might imply that the ghosts are being returned to the location, cloaked to our reach, probably by a more mobile spirit. Unless the ghosts have a human accomplice? How would that even be possible?

BIG WITCH FILES: DOC 3
PHOTOGRAPHIC ANALYSIS:
ON THE MALLEABILITY OF ECTOPLASM

An incident was reported prior to the Big Witch event. Since there was no tangible evidence left behind and the pool of witnesses were smaller, containment was more feasible, and in the aftermath of what followed the smaller even was largely forgotten. However, eyewitness accounts and a series of blurred photographs snapped at the time point us toward another unique supernatural manifestation, which might tell us more about the nature of what we're dealing with.

FIG 1: 20:07hrs destruction of a local squad car. Photo evidence seized from anonymous citizen. Eyewitnesses and police involved in the incident disagree as to whether the destruction of the car appeared intentional. The officers involved report that the being seemed fluid to an extent- almost like a liquid metal- leading us to a hypothesis of ectoplasm.

It was once believed that ectoplasm- physical matter left behind by ghosts- always consisted of a viscous slime. Since proper research into the field began, it has been found that ectoplasm may be formed of almost any material- but usually maintains a liquid malleability. The physicality with which the manifestation landed seems to suggest that it was formed of liquid metal, which implies the ghost in question has attached itself to a metal object- which could be anything from a kitchen knife to a Buick.

FIG 1

FIG 2

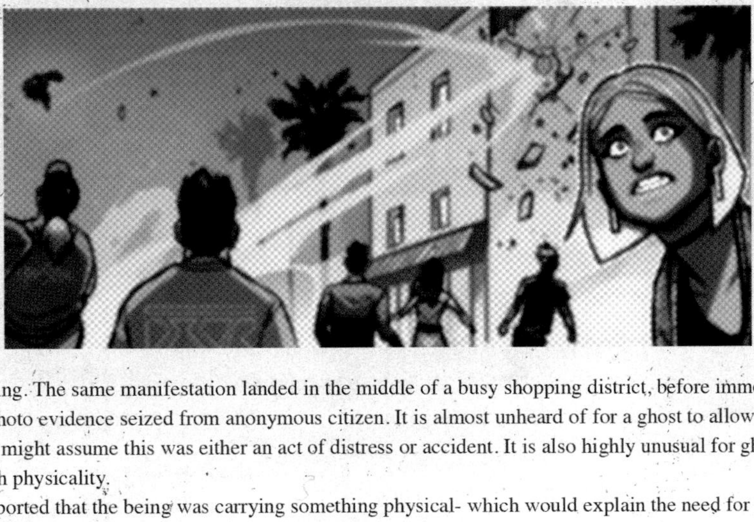

FIG 2: 20:23hrs sighting. The same manifestation landed in the middle of a busy shopping district, before immediately launching off again. Photo evidence seized from anonymous citizen. It is almost unheard of for a ghost to allow itself to be seen so openly. We might assume this was either an act of distress or accident. It is also highly unusual for ghosts to move around with such physicality.

Some eyewitnesses reported that the being was carrying something physical- which would explain the need for physical manifestation, but opens up many more questions. Even more concerning, some witnesses claimed the object was a limp figure- a human being. Combined with the Big Witch incident, we have no choice but to conclude that the world's ghosts are becoming emboldened and aggressive. We must be prepared to respond in kind, and double our efforts on Project [REDACTED].